gta edition 1

VITRUVIUS WITHOUT TEXT

THE BIOGRAPHY OF A BOOK

ANDRÉ TAVARES

PROLOGUE	07
THE BIOGRAPHY OF A BOOK	25
Setting Authority, 1486–1536	26
Crossing Regional Boundaries, 1526–1556	41
The Age of Orders, 1556–1649	55
Grounding Theory, 1673–1791	68
Diffuse Knowledge, 1796–1909	88
Author of the Twentieth Century, 1914–1964	107
Vitruvius Academicus, 1964–2016	124
THE TETRASTYLE HYPOTHESIS	141
Proportional Deadlock	144
The Tomar Enigma	157
Model and Theory	176
Shifting Type	195
Vitruvius by Accident	212
EPILOGUE	225
VITRUVIANA 1486–2016	231
ANNEX	257
Bibliography	258
Image Credits	272
Acknowledgments	274

PROLOGUE

The Volatile Word

This essay is not about Vitruvius, nor is it an attempt to reconstruct *De Architectura* in relation to the author's life and cultural context. Instead it aims to assess the rich and eventful printing history of Vitruvius's text.[1] Printing has shaped our idea of Vitruvius, turning it from a text into a haunting entity, a mirage embodied in a book whose status as a reference for architectural theory is confirmed by five centuries of printed iterations. A review of the editions of Vitruvius traces how architectural theory has, in the past, been presented. Vitruvianism and the architectural ideas associated with it took shape in these books: in physical objects comprising words, certainly, but also in visual elements such as printed forms and illustrations. In its material qualities, each book embodies a plethora of information that contributes as much to the content as the words do. Hence, the hypothesis here has been to assess Vitruvius by ignoring its text and discovering its content beyond the words. When the tradition of Vitruvian publishing is stripped of words, instead of a naked body we discover a nuanced vision of the history of ideas and architecture.

It is not hard to chart the over one hundred editions of Vitruvius, beginning with the *editio princeps* by Sulpizio da Veroli, printed in Rome between 1486 and 1487. Less than sixty years later, the text had been reprinted, illustrated, and commented on in Florence, Venice, Como, Lyon, Toledo, Lisbon, Perugia, Strasbourg, Paris, and Nuremberg. Each new edition varied in format, layout, paper, size and content. A timeline demonstrates that this frantic editorial pace continued in response to various demands, with every version of the book spreading and reconstructing Vitruvius's ideas. However, from the early Fra Giocondo pocket edition of 1513 to Luigi Marini's glorious and monumental 1836 folio edition in four volumes, the

---

1 All Vitruvius editions are referred to in the footnotes by simply their editor(s) and date(s). The complete bibliographic references are listed in full in the "Vitruviana" section.

form of each edition mangles the Roman architect's words: even in the most accurate philological reconstructions, the editor's work takes precedence over the source text. In the process of commenting on and reformatting it, even before the modern concept of the editor as we know it today was shaped, the editor—himself a publisher, a scholar, a translator, or any other professional—becomes an author. There is "Cesariano's Vitruvius," "Gros's Vitruvius," but no such thing as "just Vitruvius." This multitude of authors dealing with the same source provides us with a unique overview of five centuries of architectural publishing. If we abandon the text to concentrate instead on the forms by which the text has reached us, we obtain a telling account of the uses of architectural books, demonstrating how they were used to shape theory and how theory was shaped to be handled.

A pitfall in assessing architectural books is to get caught up in their form, forgetting about the architecture the books aim to convey. This can be avoided by anchoring the analysis to a precise architectural theme, allowing us to navigate the various editions by looking at different responses to the same problem. In the case of Vitruvian theory this has been dominated by attention to the rules of proportion and the principles of the architectural orders that have driven architectural theory and practice since the fifteenth century. Nevertheless, Vitruvius discussed and considered a wealth of other architectural topics. One of them, described in a rather humble sentence in the third chapter of Book VI, Chapter III, Paragraph 1, provides a key theme by which to survey how the book impacted the design of unique architectural projects: the tetrastyle *cavaedium*.[2] The sentence concerned places the *cavaedium* in the interior of the private house without

---

2 On the Vitruvian *cavaedium*, see Pierre Gros, "Les lectures vitruviennes du XVIe siècle et quelques-unes de leurs conséquences à l'âge classique: L'exemple de la domus," in *Architecture et théorie: L'héritage de la Renaissance* (Paris: Institut National d'Histoire de l'Art, 2012), 1–21, https://books.openedition.org/inha/3436; Pier Nicola Pagliara, "L'attività edilizia di Antonio da Sangallo il Giovane," *Controspazio*, no. 7 (July 1972): 19–47.

specifying whether it is meant for use in an atrium or a courtyard, and it offers several models to define its architecture: Tuscan, Corinthian, tetrastyle, displuviate, and testudinate. Vitruvius goes on to explain that "in the tetrastyle, the girders are supported at the angles by columns, an arrangement which relieves and strengthens the girders; for thus they have themselves no great span to support, and they are not loaded down by the crossbeams."[3] Unlike the orders, the tetrastyle room is quite marginal in the Vitruvius canon, but despite, or perhaps due to this apparent insignificance, an image of such a room appears in the first illustrated printed edition of Vitruvius.[4] As a result, the sentence was transformed from text into architecture—an architecture at once virtual in its challenge to future editors of Vitruvius and real in its influence on future buildings.[5] Other themes might have been as equally telling of the wanderings between Vitruvian theory and architectural practice. The fact is that the tetrastyle room, without being prominent or emphasized by any architect, is as pervasive as it is discrete, providing a backdoor entrance to design that avoids architects' common rhetorical pledges.

If there were any images in Vitruvius's original manuscript, they are long lost.[6] Nevertheless, there have been over ten different tetrastyle rooms illustrated in the numerous editions of the book. While they share an allegiance to the sentence quoted above, the spaces represented display significant dif-

---

3 Morgan 1914, VI, 3, 1, 176. "The tetrastyle courtyards have angle columns under the beams, which gain thereby in usefulness and strength, because they are not compelled to bear great pressure and are not loaded by the trimmers," Granger 1934, VI, 3, 1, 25. "Tetrastyle interiors, with columns under their corner beams, offer both the greatest soundness, as they are neither forced to sustain great stresses nor are they weighed down with joists," Rowland-Howe 1999, VI, 3, 1, 78.

4 Giocondo 1511, 61.

5 On architects reading Vitruvius as a source for domestic architectural design, see Linda Pellechia, "Architects Read Vitruvius: Renaissance Interpretations of the Atrium of the Ancient House," *Journal of the Society of Architectural Historians* 51, no. 4 (December 1992): 377–416, https://doi.org/10.2307/990736.

6 Pierre Gros, "Les illustrations du *De architectura* de Vitruve: Histoire d'un malentendu," in *Vitruve et la tradition des traités d'architecture: Fabrica et ratiocinatio*, 1st ed. 1996 (Rome: Publications de l'École française de Rome, 2006), 363–388, https://books.openedition.org/efr/2515.

ferences that are more telling of the architectural credos of each editor than of Vitruvius's intended meaning. Equally, these dissimilarties reflect the historical contexts of the editors' respective lives and eras. For example, the discovery and documentation of the archaeological remains of Pompeii and Herculaneum in the eighteenth century offered new evidence that had not been available to Renaissance writers, who instead relied exclusively on literary descriptions for their knowledge of the Roman house. New archaeological discoveries meant that Vitruvius interpreters could access first-hand descriptions and representations of *cavaedia,* and the resulting change in the representation of the tetrastyle room was abrupt. Prior to this, and lacking any such clues, in the Renaissance there had also been much more space for invention and speculation due to Vitruvius's interchangeable use of the words atrium and *cavaedium* and the ambiguity of their meanings. Such architectural freedom—running contrary to the eventual normative bias of Vitruvianism—echoes the editorial freedom enjoyed when printing the text. This liberty does not arise from the words or from the meaning of the architectural theory but from their materialization in the built forms of books and buildings.

Thus, this humble and simple sentence will act as a pointer to guide us to the same page of each edition of Vitruvius, and so allowing a comparison of the books and their architecture. Such an exercise ignores the commonly recognized aim of Vitruvius's treatise to establish an architectural canon. However, even when the text of a Latin manuscript is published word for word, the print version shapes the text into a book and in doing so transforms the canonic source, manipulating the words to tailor them into a specific print and architectural culture. The books, in that sense, are the material traces of this culture.

Vitruvius's treatise was well known as a manuscript long before it was first published in the late 1480s. In its original form, it must have consisted of ten handwritten rolls, the so-

1   Charles-François Mazois, *Les Ruines de Pompéi*, 1821–1824, House Championnet

called "Ten Books," but no copies in this format seem to have survived. Until the late fourteenth century, copies of Vitruvius were handmade and bound as codices. And once the scholars of the early Renaissance homed in on Vitruvius as the main reference for ancient Roman architecture, they produced their own hand-written and hand-copied manuscripts in dialogue with their ancient predecessor, beginning a long line of "Vitruvian" writing.[7] Vitruvianism thus has two aspects:[8] first, the use of the Roman model as a template from which to articulate original contemporary architectural theory; and second, the production of authoritative Vitruvius editions to feed this dialogue with the source. Moreover, printed books could provide the needed support for both.[9]

Despite Leon Battista Alberti (1404–1472) and Johannes Gutenberg (ca. 1400–1468) being contemporaneous, there is no direct technologically driven link between the spread of the printing press and Renaissance architecture.[10] The connection between architecture and print culture is more subtle

---

7 See Carol Herselle Krinsky, "Seventy-eight Vitruvius Manuscripts," Online edition, *Journal of the Warburg and Courtauld Institutes* 30 (1967): 36–70, https://doi.org/10.2307/750736.

8 See Georg Germann, *Vitruve et le vitruvianisme: Introduction à l'histoire de la théorie architecturale*, 1st ed. 1987, trans. Jacques Gubler (Lausanne: Presses Polytechniques et Universitaires Romandes, 2016).

9 A review of Vitruvian scholarship can be found in Ingrid D. Rowland, "Vitruvian Scholarship to Vitruvian Practice," *Memoirs of the American Academy in Rome* 50 (2005): 15–40, https://www.jstor.org/stable/4238827.

10 This counters Mario Carpo's argument that the rise of Renaissance architecture was intimately related to the technology of the printing press in his presentation of Sebastiano Serlio as a "typographical architect." See Mario Carpo, "The Making of the Typographical Architect," ed. Vaughan Hart and Peter Hicks, in *Paper Palaces: The Rise of the Renaissance Architectural Treatise* (New Haven, CT: Yale University Press, 1998), 158–169; Mario Carpo, *Architecture in the Age of Printing: Orality, Writing, Typography, and Printed Images in the History of Architectural Theory*, 1st Italian ed. 1998, trans. Sarah Benson (Cambridge, MA: MIT Press, 2001). Carpo's sophisticated and inspiring idea is discussed further in this prologue, but it is worth mentioning that Carpo himself, in the preface to the French translation of his book, acknowledged that in light of more recent literature on book history, the causal relationship may not have been as direct as he first implied. See Mario Carpo, "Préface à la traduction francaise," trans. Ginette Morel, in *L'architecture à l'âge de l'imprimerie: Culture orale, culture écrite, livre et reproduction mécanique de l'image dans l'histoire des théories architecturales* (Paris: La Villette, 2008), 5–9.

and relies on figures like Aldus Manutius, who bridged the gap between private intellectual research and collective printed discussion on humanist topics.[11] Alberti's treatise, written to overcome what he perceived as the limitations of Vitruvius's text, was handwritten, with the expectation that it would be copied and disseminated in manuscript, and the first printed edition only came out years after the text had been in circulation.[12] Two other key treatises of the Renaissance are those of Antonio Averlino Filarete (ca. 1400–1469),[13] neither of which was printed until centuries after it had been written. Their "low-tech" format was clearly no obstacle to circulation, as they were widely read by scholars and architects alike. Less well-known manuscripts—either incomplete or not intended for wide circulation—include those by Giovanni Battista da Sangallo and Raphael Sanzio,[14] and ultimately Leonardo da Vinci (1452–1519), to whom we owe the most famous Vitruvian man.[15] This wealth of writings commuted between manuscript and print, an indeterminacy that itself sheds light on the im-

---

11 See Guido Beltramini and Davide Gasparotto, eds., *Aldo Manuzio: Il rinascimento di Venezia* (Venice: Marsilio, 2016).

12 Several manuscript copies circulated between about 1450, when a version of the treatise was presented to the pope, and 1486, when it was first printed. See Joseph Rykwert, ""Introduction"," in *On the Art of Building in Ten Books*, by Leon Battista Alberti (Cambridge, MA: MIT Press, 1991), xviii–xix.

13 First published by Wolfgang von Oettingen in 1896 as Antonio Piero Averlino Filarete, *Tractat über die Baukunst: Nebst seinen Büchern von der Zeichenkunst und den Bauten der Medici* (Vienna: Graeser, 1896). In his English translation, John R. Spencer dismisses the first edition as "far from adequate" due to its inconsistencies. See his introduction to Antonio Piero Averlino Filarete, *Filarete's Treatise on Architecture*, trans. John R. Spencer (New Haven, CT: Yale University Press, 1965), xviii; and Francesco di Giorgio Martini's treatise, which was first published as Carlo Promis, *Trattato di architettura civile e militare di Francesco di Giorgio Martini* (Turin: Chirio & Mina, 1841). Martini also prepared a translation of Vitruvius, which was only later recognized as his and that was first published in 1967. There is a complex interrelation between Martini's theoretical work and his Vitruvian translation. See Massimo Mussini, *Francesco di Giorgio e Vitruvio: Le traduzioni del* De architectura *nei codici Zichy, Spencer 129 e Magliabechiano II.I.141*, 2 vols. ([Florence]: Leo S. Olschki, 2003); Marco Biffi, *La traduzione del* De architectura *di Vitruvio dal ms. II.I.141 della Biblioteca Nazionale Centrale di Firenze* (Pisa: Scuola Normale Superiore, 2002).

14 See Ingrid D. Rowland, "Introduction," in Sulpitius 2003, 1–64.

15 See Toby Lester, *Da Vinci's Ghost: The Untold Story of the World's Most Famous Drawing* (London: Profile Books, 2011).

portance of thinking and writing in relation to drawing and building. Despite the hope that the ultimate expression of their arguments would be the built work, such architects defined themselves in their capacity to articulate knowledge and thus made use of various devices by which to fix that experience.

This indeterminacy between manuscript and print demonstrated by the coexistence of both in Renaissance Vitruvianism might suggest that there is no substantial difference between the written and the printed word. Nonetheless, the technological shift of the printing press and the subsequent flood of books presented substantial challenges to architecture but also opened up new possibilities. Mario Carpo connects the era of printing to the normative quality of Renaissance architecture, presenting sixteenth-century Sebastiano Serlio's theory of the architectural orders, built on Vitruvian foundations, as the architectural counterpart of movable type, with buildings being assembled from the orders as sentences are assembled from letters.[16] If movable type inspired a normative architectural strategy, woodcuts were similarly able to stabilize architectural drawings. With woodcuts—unlike with manuscript drawings based on a textual description or imprecisely copied from other images—an illustration of a window frame became the same in every copy of a book, permitting a Parisian architect to use it as reference in the same way a Milanese architect would. Before the printing press, verbal architectural descriptions were privileged over images, based on the assumption that textual transcriptions bore a higher degree of similitude between original and the copy than images did. In fact, and perhaps surprisingly, text is much more volatile than images. While woodcuts and, later on, copper and steel engravings could be relied upon to produce exact copies of architectural images, text was constantly changing. As language evolves, concepts shift and new words are coined. Book editors are expected to keep up, and so even in cases where a book's visual references might be frozen in

16 Carpo, *Architecture in the Age of Printing*.

time by its illustrations, writing requires an ongoing effort to update bygone ideas to match contemporary concepts.

Vitruvius's use of ancient concepts, Greek sources, unknown examples, outdated Latin, and cumbersome syntax made his words more cryptic than explicit. More than a millennium after it was written, and despite its attractiveness as an authoritative reference, Vitruvius's content was anything but clear and accessible. Its intricacy was a constant challenge for readers, and new editions, while attempting to crack the textual enigmas, not only rescued the author's reputation from oblivion but expanded it over the centuries. Printing was a relatively cheap way to make hundreds of identical copies of a book, avoiding the inevitable inaccuracy of manuscript copies, making the work ubiquitous and the author and the message longlasting. Ultimately, the success of an author, Vitruvius included, relies on the capacity of its content to be reprinted. Hence the enduring Vitruvian performance was not due to the said eternal values of his message but rather from its vagueness and volability.

Each new edition responds to a specific editorial context: What budget is available, who is the audience, and when does the book have to be ready? Such questions, as relevant today as they were in Gutenberg's time, end up defining the qualities of the layout, the choice of paper, the provenance of the ink, and the material characteristics of each edition. And beyond the material qualities of the edition, the integrity of the book itself can be circumscribed: Which version of the text to use? Which illustrations? In what order? Every time the book is reprinted, these decisions have to be made all over again. For such a specialized author as Vitruvius, publishers have relied on editors to guide them throughout the process. Just as a reader shapes a text with their voice when reading aloud, an editor shapes a formless text into an object. And, just as with bound manuscripts, printed editions steer content and use the book form to fit the editors' own intellectual and social purposes. As a result, each reprint is also the reshaping of the text into a new form, whose reading and reception are equally determined by its cultural and social contexts.

Architecture is built on architecture. This—the idea that precedents matter and that every new building benefits from the accumulated knowledge of past constructions—is one of the major legacies of Vitruvianism. However, simply observing the buildings of the past is often not enough, as old stones are mute on many aspects of their lives. For the Renaissance thinkers who sought their model in ancient Rome, Vitruvius's text was a precious source that gave Roman ruins a voice—a companion to help decipher the revered ancient precedents. Following Vitruvius, the scholars and philologists of the Renaissance who laid out the precepts of architecture as a liberal practice envisioned the architect as an intellectual who could bridge the conceptual world of ideas and the physical realm of everyday life.

Vitruvius was a key author in articulating this new definition of the profession because of the comprehensive character of his theory and the Renaissance veneration of antique sources as guarantors of legitimate thought. According to Indra McEwen, citing Cicero (106–43 BCE), Vitruvius's purpose in his Ten Books was to unite the "body of architecture," to give architecture a coherence, and to "bind together" the parts of a "fragmentary knowledge, formerly 'diffuse and all in pieces.'"[17] The Roman numeral X had somewhat of a magical resonance, and the entire set of original rolls constituted a conceptual corpus. This unitary sense was reinforced when, long after Vitruvius's time, the ten Roman rolls were united in a codex, a single object that physically established a coherent relationship between the ten parts for the reader, instead of requiring the reader to make the connection mentally. Therefore, the codex made a physical unit of the book that was only implicit in its writing.

---

17 Indra Kagis McEwen, *Vitruvius: Writing the Body of Architecture* (Cambridge, MA: MIT Press, 2003), 58, citing Cicero, *De oratore*, 1.188.

Vitruvius was the sole survivor of a complete ancient corpus of knowledge, and this, combined with the unity of the Ten Books, granted Vitruvius an authoritative status. From the time of its *editio princeps*, Vitruvius's word was thought of as "divine."[18] However, this Renaissance reliance on both ancient texts and ancient remains to provide references for contemporary design, ultimately resulting in the construction of new buildings "*all'antica*," led to problems as a new architectural canon took shape. Often, the ancient ruins did not provide confirmation of what they were expected to confirm. Instead of supporting design, the extant references became an encumbrance. Furthermore, despite his quasi-sacred authority, architects and scholars also freely criticized Vitruvius's writing. Leon Battista Alberti went so far as to say in his own treatise *De re aedificatoria* that Vitruvius "wrote neither Latin nor Greek, so that as far as we are concerned he might just as well not have written at all, rather than writing something that we cannot understand."[19]

This weakness, however, was in fact Vitruvius's strength. His book presents a comprehensive corpus of theory about a subject area that had previously been described only partially and scattered across a range of sources, if it had been described at all. The absence of a written codification in architecture meant that he had to construct an appropriate vocabulary by drawing on various sources, ranging from practice to foreign references. The results of his eclectic endeavor endured for over a thousand years before it was picked up by Renaissance scholars as the principal reference in formulating the contours and specifics of a new discipline. Although the work had been read and used throughout Europe during the interim, this fifteenth-century interest in Vitruvius relates to its disciplinary coherence. Scholars of the time, fascinated by the role language plays in articulating

---

18 In the first sentence of his advice to the reader, Sulpizio writes "*Cum diuinú opus Victruuii.*" Sulpitius 1486, n.p.

19 Leon Battista Alberti, *On the Art of Building in Ten Books*, trans. Joseph Rykwert, Neil Leach, and Robert Tavernor (Cambridge, MA: MIT Press, 1988), 154.

various disciplines and fields within a comprehensive vision of knowledge, found in it a worthy example.[20] In this context, Alberti's critical words reveal the goal of his own treatise to raise the standard of architectural theory to its modern potential by superseding the ancient model. He emulated Vitruvius's structure and some of its main concepts to invent a new form, establishing a new unified architectural theory and eventually dismissing his predecessor as an oddity of time. But although Alberti succeeded in perpetuating Vitruvius's reputation as a dubious writer, he was unable to stymie widespread interest in the book. Indeed, the fluctuant character of Vitruvius's words invited subsequent editors to participate in a rich dialogue with both the vocabulary of the primary source and its overall structure. And this dialogue has been key to Vitruvius's enduring success.

In 1739 Giovanni Poleni (1683–1761) published *Exercitationes Vitruvianae*, an extensive annotated bibliography of the print history of Vitruvius's treatise.[21] The entries consist of comments on the background and major features of each edition, providing a historical context for readers to ponder while consulting whichever version of Vitruvius's book they might have in hand. Poleni's work proved influential: his bibliographic background would appear in the introductions of many subsequent editions of Vitruvius alongside biographical notes and other contextual remarks. Later, in 1826, Joseph Gwilt identified forty-two editions, arranging them chronologically by language—Latin, Spanish, French, German, English, and Italian.[22] Ten years later the compendium was updated by Luigi Marini, who presented separate lists for Latin versions

---

20 Other classical sources, such as Pliny the Elder, were also used as gateways to antiquity, but none surmounted Vitruvius's mythological status. Peter Fane-Saunders, *Pliny the Elder and the Emergence of Renaissance Architecture* (New York: Cambridge University Press, 2016).

21 Giovanni Poleni, *Exercitationes Vitruvianae Primae* (Padua: Ioannem Manfrè and Franciscum Pitteri, 1739).

22 Joseph Gwilt, "List of the Several Editions and Versions of Vitruvius," in Gwilt, 1826, xxi–xxxi.

and translations, organizing the sequence according to a mix of criteria that included editors, places of publication, and publishers.[23] From then on, most new editions of Vitruvius included an updated version of Marini's list, although it was frequently abbreviated to include just the most representative editions. A chronological update was published in 1918 by Bodo Ebhardt,[24] and in 1978 Luigi Vagnetti and Laura Marcucci published an ambitious record of 166 printed editions of Vitruvius, attempting to establish a sequence according to language; separating complete from abridged versions; and grouping editions, reprints, and facsimiles by the same editor together.[25] The result is particularly impressive when one considers that it predates the existence of digital catalogues, but it is also beset by the inevitable faults and ambivalences, suggesting why attempts at such comprehensive bibliography are rare. Supplementing this, some architectural libraries published catalogues in the late twentieth century that contain more accurate and thorough bibliographical descriptions,[26] covering such collections as the Royal Institute of British Architects Library's early printed books[27] or the Mark J. Millard Architectural Collection.[28] Part of the bourgeoning discipline of book history, these catalogues assemble detailed information and discuss the life, provenance, and use of each edition. Unfortunately, each of these only covers the holdings of a single library, so a comprehensive overview of

23 Luigi Marini, "De codicibus Vitruvianis" and "De Editionibus Vitruvianis," in Marini, 1836, XXIII-LXIX.

24 Ebhardt 1918.

25 Luigi Vagnetti and Laura Marcucci, *2000 anni di Vitruvio*, Serie Studi e documenti di architettura, vol. 8 (Florence: Edizione della Cattedra di Composizione Architettonica IA di Firenze, 1978).

26 Lawrence Hall Fowler and Elizabeth Baer, eds., *The Fowler Architectural Collection of the Johns Hopkins University* (Baltimore: Evergreen House Foundation, 1961).

27 Royal Institute of British Architects, *Early Printed Books, 1478–1840: Catalogue of the British Architectural Library Early Imprints Collection*, 4 vols. (London: Bowker-Saur, 1994–2003). On Vitruvius, see pages 2272 to 2317.

28 *The Mark J. Millard Architectural Collection*, 4 vols. (Washington, DC: National Gallery of Art, 1993–2003).

Vitruvius editions has remained elusive. Additionally, in the last few years digital catalogues and online facsimiles have permitted access to new formats of Vitruvian bibliographies. Among the many varied and rich sources of digital information, the Werner Oechslin Library offers the direct download of over fifty editions,[29] and the website directed by Frédérique Lemerle and Yves Pauwels makes accessible French titles dating from the sixteenth and seventeenth centuries, as well as the associated critical apparatuses.[30] The drawbacks of the digital world in compiling an exhaustive inventory is that search engines help reveal the variations and subtleties of each edition in such excruciating detail that entry descriptions with typographical errors or based on erroneous presumptions may lead the reader to hypothesize that editions exist which in fact do not. Lastly, it is likely that more Vitruvius editions than ever before have been published in the forty years since Vagnetti and Marcucci compiled their list. All of this makes it difficult to inventory the full extent of the Vitruvius in print, and despite our attempt to do so the task is not yet complete.

Regardless of this shortcoming, in order to assess how printing shaped our idea of Vitruvius one must consider how best to organize a Vitruviana, and for that purpose chronology is the most effective strategy. If we follow a timeline of editions laid out on a map of Europe, we can track them geographically and witness a complex web of relations taking shape. The openness of Vitruvius's text led to the constant rearticulation of its content by means of editing, translating, annotating, illustrating, and formatting the book. Some editors drew on previous content to build up their own Vitruvian edition, recombining different sources in sometimes unexpected

---

[29] *Vitruviana: Online Access to Books Containing or Regarding Vitruvius's "10 Books on Architecture,"* Einsiedeln, Werner Oechslin Library Foundation, https://www.bibliothek-oechslin.ch.

[30] Frédérique Lemerle and Yves Pauwels, eds., *Architectura: Architecture, textes et images (XVIe–XVIIe siècles)*, online ed. (Tours: Centre d'Études Supérieures de la Renaissance, Université François-Rabelais, 2013), http://architectura.cesr.univ-tours.fr/Traite/index.asp?param=en.

ways. Daniele Barbaro, for instance, relied on Giocondo's edition to structure his sequence of original illustrations but also borrowed ideas and a good deal of hypothesis from Diego de Sagredo in Spain to support his arguments. Later, Joannes de Laet's Amsterdam edition picked up Barbaro's comments; and the Spanish epitome traveled to Amsterdam indirectly through Venice. In essence, the Vitruvian conundrums begin where these different editorial threads meet.

From an editorial perspective, chronology is helpful in determining a sequence but does not help in assessing the physical differences between objects that embody equivalent content. Indeed, there is tremendous variation between the shapes of Vitruvian editions, and if organizing them following a sequential logic—such as first and second editions—helps to understand certain shifts, it does not work when synchronous publications exhibit very disparate forms. Consider the two 1836 editions, one published in Leipzig and the other in Rome. The Leipzig book is a modest octavo, with 250 pages of dense text laid out with tight margins and no images. The Roman edition consists of four large folio volumes with wide white margins, one dedicated entirely to refined illustrations. The former weighs 300 grams, the latter 30 kilos. That both are the same book, published in the same year, signals an actively shifting formal appropriation of the book's content. But by adding geography to the mix, new dynamics can be seen to be at work. Leaving aside form, other motivations and connections start to emerge, with the geographical shifts alluding to the politics of editing and their agency in architectural theory. But it also happens that editorial threads in some areas move faster, or slower, than others, so geography can upset the chronological sequence. And when it comes to reading and comparing the editorial strategies of books derived from different lineages, order and sequence become irrelevant. Since the ambition of this study is not to establish a Vitruvian catalogue, I will use this progressive chronological and geographical layering as a means to present the various editions, accepting the risk of repetition when it comes to key publications and of losing sight of some other editions in relation to the overall picture.

Identifying tetrastyle spaces to discuss proved even more elusive than establishing a conclusive Vitruviana. Domestic spaces defined by the formal placement of four columns are not all that common, and those that do exist often deviate from the welcoming function Vitruvius attributes to the tetrastyle form, or simply pop up with no apparent connection to the printed treatise. Is the first paragraph of Book VI, Chapter III as relevant to architecture culture as one might imagine? Probably not. Considering such a specific passage of text as a clue to the architectural relationship between books and buildings means that there are few examples to analyze. Nonetheless, while somewhat scarce, the tetrastyle rooms discussed suggest countless hypotheses on topics ranging from the archetypal organization of rooms to the erudite quotation of architectural treatises. In most of the examples I discuss, direct and indirect references to Vitruvius are overshadowed by the practicalities of architectural practice. This ultimately leads to the ambivalent conclusion that architectural theory is a construct used to legitimize architects' activities rather than being something applied knowingly to practice as a result of active reading.

I am afraid there is no solution to the tetrastyle enigma. If there is a key, it lies in the interconnected trajectories of print culture—in particular book culture—and building culture. By relating tetrastyle rooms to Vitruvian pages, we negotiate the sensitive gap where ideas leap from author to reader, from book to building, and vice-versa. By considering these transfers, my aim is to assess the constant manipulation of elements of architectural culture. These manipulations are as often equivocal or accidental as they are deliberate, and result from compromise as frequently as from the imposed weight of authority. Vitruvius is just one of many windows into the passages that run between theory and practice. To analyze the use and abuse of Vitruvius is to better understand how architectural knowledge circulates—an understanding that is key to maintaining a critical stance and one that we need so as to keep building books and inventing buildings.

THE BIOGRAPHY
OF A BOOK

SETTING AUTHORITY, 1486-1536

In the first trio of Vitruvian editions, published between 1486 and 1497,[31] the place of publication moves from Rome to Florence and then to Venice. All are straightforward quarto Latin editions, and their major achievement was to reestablish the text, bringing the manuscript tradition into print. Appropriately for a Roman author, the *editio princeps* was printed in Rome between 1486 and 1487 and edited by Joannes Sulpitius, known as Sulpizio da Veroli.[32] The book does not have a colophon, and the debate on when and by whom it was printed is telling of its editorial context.

This debate is laid out in the detailed assessment of Sulpizio's Vitruvius in the Royal Institute of British Architects (RIBA) library catalogue.[33] Internal textual evidence—mentions of the achievements of Innocent VIII and the wars between the Papal States and the Kingdom of Naples—imply that the text could not have been printed before August 11, 1486. It also could not have been printed after August 16, 1487, as a copy held by an Oxford library presents evidence of having been purchased in Rome on that date.[34] Thus both the book's content and markings on the physical object help to narrow down

---

31 Sulpitius 1486; Cattaneo 1496; Bevilaqua 1497.

32 See Ingrid D. Rowland, "Introduction," in Sulpitius 2003, 1–64.

33 Royal Institute of British Architects, *Early Printed Books*, no. 3489, 2272–2274.

34 Dennis E. Rhodes, *A Catalogue of Incunabula in All the Libraries of Oxford University outside the Bodleian* (Oxford: Clarendon Press, 1982), 151, 355, referring to

2 Sulpitius 1486, inaugural printed Vitruvius edition

the time of its production. The printing attribution is disputed. Both Georg Herolt and Eucharius Silber (d. 1509/10) used a very similar type to the *editio princeps* of Vitruvius, although there are formal differences in the type used by each printer. "Silbner uses three characters (the hyphen, paragraph, and 'bus' or 'us' contraction) which Herolt does not,"[35] and Herolt's books are distinctive in their wider range of capital Qs, with different tails and ligatures. Such evidence is insufficient to make a conclusive attribution, particularly as variations between different copies of the same edition make the case even more convoluted, and possibly unsolvable.[36] Nonetheless, the RIBA catalogue tentatively attributes the printing to Silbner based on some additional clues. First, the formal layout of other pages printed by Silbner matches those of the *editio princeps*, with their "variety in the arrangement of headlines, drop-head titles, preliminary matter, registers and indices." Second, and even more revealing, is the circumstantial evidence of Sulpizio's involvement in the production of "at least four books printed by Silbner," as well as "the connections between Silbner and the writings of Frontinus" (ca. 40–103 CE).[37] To understand this last assertion, it is worth noting that from this edition onwards, Frontinus's treatise on the aqueducts of Rome was a regular companion to Vitruvius—possibly because both authors were Roman and both *editio princeps* were edited by Sulpizio—the two being frequently published side by side within the same volume.[38] This makes sense because of

a copy held by Corpus Christi College, inscribed "Bought by John Shirwood at Rome on 16 August 1487."

35 Royal Institute of British Architects, *Early Printed Books*, no. 3489, 2273.

36 According to the RIBA catalogue, copies in the British Architectural Library, the British Library, the Bodleian Library, and the Canadian Centre for Architecture differ in the text setting from the copy in the Stadtsbibliothek, Leipzig.

37 Royal Institute of British Architects, *Early Printed Books*, no. 3489, 2273.

38 It is not uncommon to find Vitruvius's treatise bound together with other books. The sum of pages that constitute each separate book within a shared binding is defined at the beginning by a frontispiece and at the end by the printer's colophon. This contextual apparatus defines the book beyond its content, beginning with the often-architecturally-framed frontispiece, where a long title describes the edition's multiple characteristics (including the author, title, content, publishers, date, and other short references). The frontispiece is often followed by a dedication, a table of contents, and

their related subject matter, but the motivation for binding the two treatises together in the first place, thus establishing a persistent pairing pattern, might well have been the connection between Sulpizio and Silbner.[39]

Sulpizio's edition was used as reference by an unnamed editor—eventually identified as Francesco Cattaneo Ravannale—to undertake the 1496 Florentine edition.[40] The colophon is ambiguous, locating the production of the book, which was most likely printed in Venice by Christophorus de Pensis, in two places: Florence in 1496 and Venice in 1495. The RIBA catalogue suggests two explanations for the ambiguity of a Venetian edition with a Florentine colophon. One would be the competition for printing rights, a license having been granted to another Venetian printer a few days after the Florence publication date; the other, that Poliziano might have owned a bookshop in Florence. Whatever the reason, most catalogues identify the edition as "Florence, 1496." As Lucia Ciapponi has demonstrated,[41] Cattaneo's text is a complex update of Sulpizio's version, involving the collating of sources from different manuscripts and the interpolation of the editor's own conjectures.[42] This Florentine edition was then closely

---

introductory remarks before the text begins. The end of the book is usually signaled by a remissive index and the colophon. The book itself comprises all of these elements, and these parts, from the binding to the endpapers, providing hints as to its historical meaning: how the book operated in its social context, where it was printed, and how it was used. Such editorial choices help scholars attribute the books to printers. Hence, the study of the physical evidence present in books—such as type and the context of their production, such as who printed them—can involve consideration of more implicit relationships, for instance the affiliation of Frontinus and Vitruvius. Nonetheless, Vitruvius's "body of architecture" only refers to the ten books themselves as they traveled from the manuscript tradition to Sulpizio's *editio princeps* of 1486.

39 The RIBA catalogue signals that the two books have different registers, were printed separately, and were often sold independently. Nonetheless, it confirms that "many subsequent editions ... cemented what was at first an informal alliance by combining the two texts in a single work." Royal Institute of British Architects, *Early Printed Books*, no. 3590, 2274.

40 Royal Institute of British Architects, *Early Printed Books*, no. 3590, 2274–2275.

41 Lucia Ciapponi, "Fra Giocondo da Verona and His Edition of Vitruvius," *Journal of the Warburg and Courtauld Institutes* 47 (1984): 72–90, https://doi.org/10.2307/751439.

42 Ciapponi, "Fra Giocondo da Verona and His Edition of Vitruvius," 73.

followed in 1497 by a Venetian edition, "virtually a reprint,"[43] published by Simone Bevilacqua.[44] Together, these three editions made a significant number of copies available,[45] forming a bedrock for the reading of the treatise that propelled further study of the cryptic text and, in turn, further editions.

The movement of the Vitruvian publishing enterprise toward Venice reflected the city's growing importance as a center of the book industry. The second group of editions was authored by Giovanni Giocondo (1433–1515), an architect and philologist whose Vitruvius of 1511 was a defining factor in elevating the former to a paramount position in humanist culture.[46] Since its publication, scholars have unanimously credited Giocondo for making Vitruvius's text "intelligible"[47] by means of three editorial strategies: first, working the Latin into a coherent form lacking in older manuscripts; second, designing over a hundred illustrations to help the reader interpret the text; and third, complementing the edition with a summary, synthetic annotations, and a thorough remissive index. Bringing coherence to the text included the restoration of Greek words, the use of Greek characters, and the printing of epigrams found in various manuscripts but missing from the first three print editions.[48] Giocondo shared this attention to Greek culture and knowledge of its references with his friend Aldus Manutius (ca. 1449–1515),[49] who was involved in notable

---

43 *The Mark J. Millard Architectural Collection*, vol. IV, cat. 155, 481.

44 In these two editions, some of the Book IX spaces Sulpizio left blank for readers' annotations were used for woodcut diagrams.

45 The total combined print run for these three editions is unknown, although it is likely that as many as 300 copies were printed of each.

46 For a detailed assessment of its characteristics and publication history, see Pier Nicola Pagliara, "Fra Giocondo e l'edizione del *De architectura* del 1511," ed. Pierre Gros and Pier Nicola Pagliara, in *Giovanni Giocondo, umanista, architetto e antiquario* (Venice: Marsilio, 2014), 21–52.

47 Ingrid D. Rowland, "Translator's Preface" in Rowland-Howe 1999, xiii–xiv, quoted by Pierre Gros, "Giocondo: Lectures de Vitruve," ed. Pierre Gros and Pier Nicola Pagliara, in *Giovanni Giocondo, umanista, architetto e antiquario* (Venice: Marsilio, 2014), 11–19, here 11.

48 Ciapponi, "Fra Giocondo da Verona and His Edition of Vitruvius," 82.

49 See Guido Beltramini, "La nuova lingua dell'architettura nei decenni di Aldo," in *Aldo Manuzio: Il renascimento di Venezia* (Venice: Marsilio, 2016), 29–41.

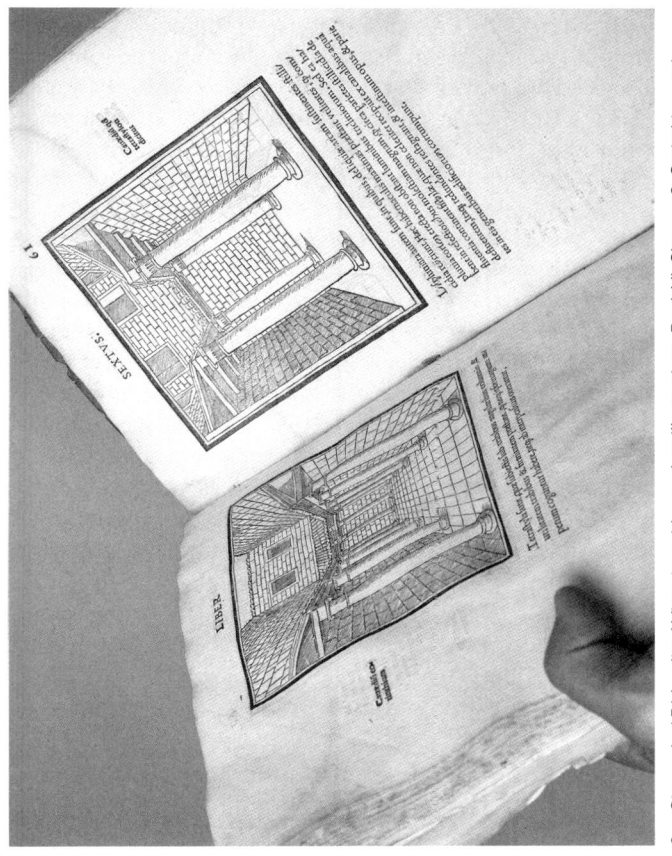

3 Giocondo 1511, edited Vitruvius with woodcut illustrations, Book VI, Chapter 3, Corinthian and tetrastyle *cavaedia*

editorship in his famous printing house.[50] Although Giocondo collaborated with Manutius on several other editorial projects, his Vitruvius was published by Giovanni da Tridino, or Tacuino (ca. 1482–1541),[51] during a period from 1509 to 1513 when Manutius was "inactive."[52] As Nicola Pagliara pointed out,[53] the 1511 quarto edition is quite different from the way Tacuino published other classical authors: in content in the synthetic character of Giocondo's annotations, and in form in the provision of wide margins that left space for readers to comment on and interpret the book in their own terms without the undue influence of the editor's position.[54] The austere delineation of the woodcut illustrations is matched by the elegant initial letters, devoid of decoration and similar to those in many of Manutius's books.[55]

The success of Giocondo's Vitruvius is confirmed by a new edition issued a mere two years later.[56] The new book was not a reprint but an octavo pocket edition, its type set in cursive italics. The woodcut illustrations follow the origi-

---

50 "The fame of Aldus Manutius comes not only from his work as a printer, but also from the profound effect of his scholarship upon the learning of the world." Paul J. Angerhofer, Mary Ann Addy Maxwell, and Robert L. Maxwell, *In aedibus Aldi: The Legacy of Aldus Manutius and His Press* (Provo, UT: Friends of the Harold B. Lee Library-Brigham Young University, 1995), 99. On Manutius's printing business, see also Martin Lowry, *The World of Aldus Manutius: Business and Scholarship in Renaissance Venice* (Oxford: Blackwell, 1979); G. Scott Clemons and H. George Fletcher, *Aldus Manutius: A Legacy More Lasting than Bronze* (New York: Grolier Club, 2015).

51 On the proximity between Manutius and Tacuino, see Francesca Salatin, "Giovanni Giocondo," in Beltramini and Gasparotto, *Aldo Manuzio: Il rinascimento di Venezia*. 270.

52 Pagliara, "Fra Giocondo," 28.

53 Pagliara, "Fra Giocondo," 37. See also Lowry, *The World of Aldus Manutius: Business and Scholarship in Renaissance Venice*, 47 and n. 106.

54 On the use of marginalia in Renaissance culture, see William H. Sherman, *Used Books: Marking Readers in Renaissance England* (Philadelphia: University of Pennsylvania Press, 2008).

55 Giocondo repeated the use of undecorated woodcut initials in Manutius, *Libri de re rustica* (Venice: Aldo Manuzio; Andrea Torresano, 1514). New York's Pierpont Morgan Library holds a copy of the book printed on blue paper with red initial woodcuts, creating a unique contrast and effective visual impact by employing simple printing means. See Beltramini and Gasparotto, *Aldo Manuzio: Il rinascimento di Venezia*, 289, cat. 66.

56 Giocondo 1513.

4 Giocondo 1513, pocket size edition with complete Latin text and woodcuts, Book VI, Chapter 3, Tuscan and Corinthian *cavaedia*

nal but are carefully scaled and condensed to maintain the characteristics of the first edition in the smaller book.[57] Such pocket editions of classical authors were a "revolution,"[58] first introduced to the publishing industry by Manutius in 1501[59] when he obtained the permission to cast a new cursive typeface designed by Francesco Griffo (1450–1518). Once again, however, it was not Manutius who printed his friend's new edition,[60] nor was it Giocondo's first publisher, Tacuino, but instead the Florentine Filippo di Giunta (1450–1517). Leaving aside the complex web of relationships between authors and publishers concerning printing rights, one of the most significant effects of the 1513 pocket edition was that it inaugurated a different way to use Vitruvius: its portability took Vitruvius out of the library, away from the study table, and into the luggage of traveling architects.[61] Was the format change prompted by Giocondo's ambition to have the book read and pondered more widely, a cultural strategy he must have shared with Manutius? Or was it a commercial strategy to lure repeat customers from among the buyers of his first edition? Whatever the case, the octavo version would set the paradigm for a "light" Vitruvius that culminated in Claude Perrault's abridged version of 1674 and was crucial for the continued success of Vitruvius's treatise.

It is significant that reprints of Giocondo's Vitruvius were made from the 1513 edition and not the original quarto. The

---

57 Additionally, some of the reversed printed images in the first edition were corrected.

58 Beltramini and Gasparotto, *Aldo Manuzio: Il rinascimento di Venezia*, 84.

59 Beltramini and Gasparotto, *Aldo Manuzio: Il rinascimento di Venezia*, cat. 10. Other authors in Manutius's octavo series were Virgilio, Orazio, and Petrarch.

60 In 1514 Manutius published another book organized by Giocondo, entitled *Libri de re rustica*, where he used similar undecorated initial letters to those he used in the 1511 edition of Tacuino. Manutius, *Libri de re rustica*; see Beltramini and Gasparotto, *Aldo Manuzio: Il rinascimento di Venezia*, cat. 66.

61 On the use of the different Vitruvian editions by Antonio da Sangallo the Younger, see Francesco Benelli, "Secondo Fra Giocondo: Antonio da Sangallo il Giovane e l'edizione di Fra Giocondo del 1513 del Metropolitan Museum of Art di New York," in *Giovanni Giocondo, umanista, architetto e antiquario* (Venice: Marsilio, 2014), 53–68.

first one appeared in 1522, under the imprint of the same Florentine publisher.[62] The second, published the following year in Lyon,[63] is likely an unauthorized edition, reflecting the rise of piracy in the publishing industry beginning in the early sixteenth century.[64] The pocket reprint of 1522 has only minor differences from its predecessor, but the 1523 pirate reprint significantly expanded the illustrations by adding thirty-three woodcuts copied from Cesare Cesariano's Italian edition of 1521. This heralded a tendency to mix illustrations from various printed editions, visually reinforcing the preexisting pattern of textual miscegenation. In line with trends seen in the many plagairisms of Manutius's books, the rise of Vitruvian piracy is a measure of the recognition value of the author and editor and the burgeoning interest in the content. Moreover, what is most striking, considering the permanence of Giocondo in Vitruvian scholarship, is that there were no further editions or reprints of his book after 1523.[65]

In Como in 1521, the year before the reprint of Giocondo's pocket edition, Cesare Cesariano (ca. 1475–1543) published a large and lavishly illustrated folio edition that translated the text into Italian with extensive annotations and new evocative illustrations.[66] The edition attests to "the complicated relation between contemporary and ancient architecture,"[67]

62 Giocondo 1522.
63 Giocondo 1523.
64 The notion of copyright in the book trade dates from the eighteenth century, when the concept of authorship was first used legally to distinguish intellectual property from material property. It addressed the long-standing issue of piracy that had nurtured conflicts between authors and their publishers, and between publishers in different territories. See Adrian Johns, *Piracy: The Intellectual Property Wars from Gutenberg to Gates* (Chicago: University of Chicago Press, 2009). For a compelling eighteenth-century narrative on book piracy, see Roger Chartier *The Business of Enlightenment: A Publishing History of the Encyclopédie 1775–1800* (Cambridge, MA: Belknap Press of Harvard University Press, 1979), chapter IV, "Piracy and Trade War," 131–176. See also Roger Chartier, *La main de l'auteur et l'esprit de l'imprimeur XVIe–XVIIIe siècle* (Paris: Gallimard, 2015).

65 In 2014 Pierre Gros announced a forthcoming facsimile of the 1511 edition to be published by the Centro Internazionale di Studi di Architettura Andrea Palladio in Vicenza. See Gros, "Giocondo: Lectures de Vitruve." 12.

66 Cesariano 1521.
67 Martha D. Pollak, *Italian & Spanish Books: Fifteenth through Nineteenth*

5 Cesariano 1521, Vitruvius, Book VI, Chapter 3, Tuscan, Corinthian and tetrastyle *cavaedia*, translation and commentary

since the illustrations tend to represent antique concepts by means of contemporary examples. The book's size required a significant financial outlay, leading to disputes between Cesariano and his sponsors, Luigi Pirovano and Agostino Gallo, and with the printer, Gottardo da Ponte (d. 1552). These and other squabbles provoked Cesariano to abandon the venture by absconding with the printing plates, which landed him in prison, so that, forced to return the plates, the book was published without his name on the colophon. Cesariano successfully sued the sponsors upon his release, but it was not until 1528 that he was legally acknowledged as an author and "awarded one third of the value of the 1,312 copies that had been printed."[68] Although his illustrations have been abundantly reproduced in other editions, Cesariano's full book had to wait another 500 years for its first reprint, produced in facsimile editions in the United States in 1968, in Munich in 1969, and finally, back in Lombardy, in Milan in 1981.[69]

Cesariano's effort to articulate his knowledge and find answers to some of the persistent Vitruvian riddles elevated the complex relationship between the multiple layers of content to a new level, and, as a result, his edition became a key reference within the Vitruvian tradition equal to Giocondo's. Such recognition was quick to come, first via the appropriation of the thirty-three illustrations in the pirated Lyon edition of 1523, again in 1524 with a Venetian edition by Francesco Durantino,[70] and in 1536 with Giovanni Caporali's (ca. 1476–1560) edition from Perugia.[71] Durantino presented his book as a new Italian translation from the Latin, comple-

---

Centuries, 4 vols., The Mark J. Millard Architectural Collection, vol. 4 (Washington, DC: National Gallery of Art, 2000), https://www.nga.gov/content/dam/ngaweb/research/publications/pdfs/mark-j-millard-vol-iv.pdf, 494. Cesariano, like many readers, "relied on the legacy of the Middle Ages to supplement their knowledge of ancient art." Carol Herselle Krinsky, "Introduction" in Cesariano 1969, 5–28.

68 Pollak, *Italian & Spanish Books*, 496. See further Manfredo Tafuri, "Cesare Cesariano e gli scritti vitruviani del quattrocento," ec. Arnaldo Bruschi, in *Scritti rinascimentali di architettura* (Milan: Polifilo, 1978), 389–437.

69 Cesariano 1968; Cesariano 1969; Cesariano 1981.

70 Durantino 1524.

71 Caporali 1536.

mented by a glossary that expanded the 1511 index and used Giocondo's woodcuts as illustrattions. As Vagnetti and Marcucci noted, Durantino lied in the book title, since his ersatz translation is really an unacknowledged reproduction—with minor adjustments—of Cesariano's text.[72] If Durantino's edition blends Giocondo and Cesariano, Caporali's incomplete edition follows Cesariano's translation of Books I though V very closely. Despite criticizing Cesariano's version, he made few amendments to the text and reproduced many of the 1521 illustrations.

The burgeoning Vitruviana of the early sixteenth century consolidated the text's position as an authority. Vitruvius advanced to be the main reference to complement the study of the physical remains of ancient architecture, which had become a fundamental learning exercise for architects seeking to achieve the integrity of the ancient models. Some, like Flavio Biondo (1388–1463) and Pirro Ligorio (1510–1583), specialized as architect-antiquarians, conducting surveys of ruins while also poring over the literary sources. Of these, Pliny the Elder (d. 79 CE)—whose descriptions do not always coincide with Vitruvius's—was another key reference in the emergence of Renaissance architecture.[73] But Pliny failed to triumph Vitruvius's fame. How then did Vitruvius come to be the paramount source to quote to legitimize contemporary architectural design? Beyond its useful presentation of the orders, the success of the Ten Books can be ascribed to its coherence as a presentation of a complete body of knowledge, and, paradoxically, to the flexibility afforded by the incoherence of its content.[74]

As Pier Nicola Pagliara has shown,[75] a growing interest in Vitruvius existed long before print culture was introduced to

---

72 Vagnetti and Marcucci, *2000 anni di Vitruvio*, 42–43.
73 See Fane-Saunders, *Pliny the Elder*.
74 The way Vitruvius operated as a "body of knowledge" within the Renaissance context has been traced by McEwen, *Vitruvius: Writing the Body of Architecture*.
75 Pier Nicola Pagliara, "Vitruvio da testo a cânone," ed. Salvatore Settis, in *Memoria dell'antico nell'arte italiana: Dalla tradizione all'archeologia*, 3 vols. (Turin: Giulio Enaudi, 1986), 5–85.

Europe. Extant manuscript comments on scattered images and passages, especially on the correspondence between the measure of the human body and the measure of architecture, date back as far as the ninth century. Interest expanded in the fourteenth century as intellectuals like Petrarch (1304–1374) and Giovanni Boccaccio (1313–1375) read Vitruvius,[76] preceding the move forward into architectural theory propelled by Alberti. From then on, Vitruvius was quoted as an authority on a wide range of topics, including the orders, machinery, military architecture, the construction of walls, the origins of architecture, and much more besides. The appropriate use of the orders with respect to their hierarchy and correct proportions, which were aspects treated by Vitruvius, became key aspects of Renaissance architecture, and in the first half of the sixteenth century his authority was invoked to legitimize architectural criticism. Thus his text, combined with the multiple ways to read it, fueled the connection between practice and theory.[77] The need to edit—if not to translate—the book's content, as well the range of possible ways the arguments could be illustrated, allowed Vitruvius to operate as an open work, its indeterminacy key to its success as a normative authority.

This first set of Vitruvian editions printed between 1486 and 1536 and covering a geographical distance stretching from Rome to Lyon, with its center in Venice, shows a complex blend of materials and forms, ranging from the variants of the hard-to-establish Latin original, the editor's notes and comments, the illustrations, the visual characteristics of headers and title-letters, as well as the various book sizes, from folio to quarto or octavo. They render visible the dynamics of appropriation—mixing chronology and geography with varying

---

76 Pagliara, "Vitruvio da testo a cânone," 16

77 Both Antonio da Sangallo the Younger (1484–1546) and his brother Giovanni Battista da Sangallo (1496–1548), who after Donato Bramante (1444–1514) and Raphael Sanzio (1483–1520) attempted to edit their own version of the book, played a crucial role in reinstating the Vitruvian authority within the Rome architecture circle. Pagliara, "Vitruvio da testo a cânone," 46–55. See also Sulpitius 2003 and the introductory essay by Ingrid Rowland.

respect for legal status and licenses—that would continue to shape future editions and the physical form of architectural theory.

CROSSING REGIONAL BOUNDARIES, 1526–1556

Before Sebastiano Serlio's (1475–1554) *Regole generali d'architetura*—a 1537 book that disseminated the Vitruvian canon by means of a treatise on the orders—Diego de Sagredo (ca. 1490–1528) published his *Medidas del Romano* in Toledo, a 1526 Castilian compendium that relates Vitruvianism to contemporary Iberian practice.[78] Despite Vagnetti and Marcucci's inclusion of Sagredo's treatise in the Vitruvian bibliography,[79] the book is in fact not an edition of Vitruvius. Nevertheless, it popularized the Roman author within various circles, and after being translated into French in 1536 it was consistently reprinted in Paris, Madrid, Toledo, and Lisbon.[80] Sagredo's book diverges from Vitruvius in both content and form, as the text is a dialogue and the theory of classical architecture is epitomized in just seventy-four pages by means of effective illustrations.[81] However, as Nigel Llewellyn has emphasized,

---

78 Diego de Sagredo, *Medidas del Romano: Necessarias alos oficiales que quieren seguir las formaciones delas Basas, Coluncs, Capiteles, y otras pieças delos edificios antíguos* (Toledo: Remó de Petras, 1526).

79 "Epitome Sagredina o Compendio Spagnolo Primo" in Vagnetti and Marcucci, *2000 anni di Vitruvio*, 43.

80 Paris: Simon de Colines, 1537, 1539, and 1542; Lisbon: Luis Rodriguez, 1541 and 1542 (two print runs); Madrid: Luis Rodriguez, 1542; Toledo: no publisher, 1549; Paris: Regnau et Claude Chaudiere, 1550; Toledo: Juan de Ayala, 1564; Paris: D. Cavellat, 1608; and various facsimile and reprints since the 1946 edition by the Associación de Libreros y Amigos del Libro.

81 See Fernando Marías, "Medidas del Romano," ed. Frédérique Lemerle and Yves Pauwels, in *Architectura: Architecture, textes et images (XVIe–XVIIe siècles)*, online ed. (Tours: Centre d'Études Supérieures de la Renaissance, Université François-

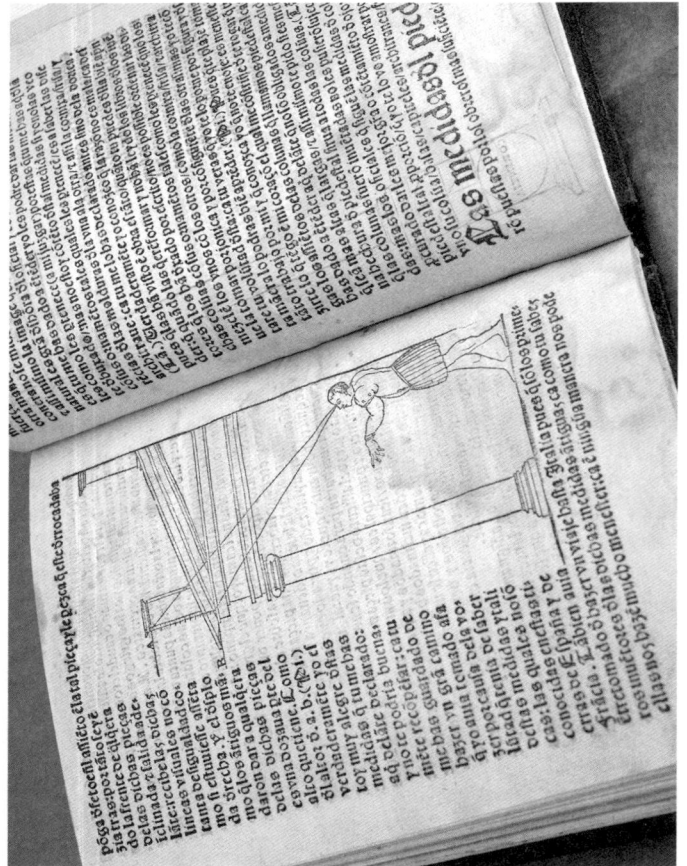

Sagredo's thought corresponds to Vitruvian principles on "the character and training of the architect, on anthropomorphism and human proportion, and on the qualities of the architectural Orders."[82]

Sagredo's book was based on three printed Vitruviuses: those by Veroli, Giocondo, and Cesariano.[83] The difference between Sagredo's relatively modest and straightforward edition and the refined printing of its predecessors is striking. Most of Sagredo's precise and detailed woodcuts are set into the margins of the text—only one occupies a full page—and this interweaving of text and image would have been an effective cost-cutting measure. The type is rotunda blackletter, which draws its form from manuscript culture and whose main characteristic is that "the darkness of the characters overpowers the whiteness of the page."[84] This gives it a completely different appearance than the extant Vitruvius editions that were set in the standard roman type developed by fifteenth-century printers. Sagredo's humanist readers might have missed the elegant combination of Carolingian lowercases and classical uppercases of roman type, along with the smooth contrast of the text block it creates against the background of the page. Nonetheless, despite these differences the page layout of Sagredo's book matches the classical canon of the content discussed, with each thirty-four-line text block following a perfect 2:3 ratio. Sagredo's 1536 edition, printed in Paris, reveals a different print culture, and not only uses roman type but

---

Rabelais, 2012), http://architectura.cesr.univ-tours.fr/Traite/Notice/Sagredo1526.asp?param=en; Fernando Marías and Felipe Pereda, eds., *Medidas del romano, Diego de Sagredo: Toledo 1526*, 2 vols. (Toledo: Pareja, 2000).

82 Nigel Llewellyn, "'Hungry and Desperate for Knowledge': Diego de Sagredo's Spanish Point of View," ed. Vaughan Hart and Peter Hicks, in *Paper Palaces: The Rise of the Renaissance Architectural Treatise* (New Haven, CT: Yale University Press, 1998), 122–139.

83 See Llewellyn, "'Hungry and Desperate for Knowledge'," 125; Marías, "Medidas del Romano."

84 Paul Shaw and Peter Bain, "Blackletter vs. Roman: Type as Ideological Surrogate," in *Blackletter: Type and National Identity* (New York: Princeton Architectural Press, 1998), 10–15, here 10.

mixes it with cursive italics and enlists a wider array of graphic solutions to emphasize the book's structure and content.

Sagredo's significance to the argument presented here relies on how his book disseminated the classical canon to a wider audience and promoted Vitruvius and his treatise as a key source for the development of regional appropriations in dialogue with Roman principles. Contemporary to the 1541 Lisbon reprint of Sagredo's treatise was an unpublished translation of Vitruvius into Portuguese by the eminent scholar Pedro Nunes, a manuscript that was taken to Madrid in the late sixteenth century and has not been seen since.[85] According to Rafael Moreira, these Vitruvian efforts propelled the writing of an original Portuguese architectural treatise between 1576 and 1579,[86] of which the manuscript still exists today.[87] The Portuguese-Spanish political disputes of the sixteenth century may have relegated these treatises to the fate of forgotten manuscripts, but they nonetheless did not prevent the development of a discrete but relevant local Renaissance architecture in Portugal.[88] Indeed, it is within this intellectual dynamic, stimulated by the printed books of Vitruvius and Sagredo, that the tetrastyle room inside Tomar's Convent of Christ, designed in 1543 by João de Castilho, Miguel de Arruda, and maybe António Rodrigues, will be later discussed.[89]

---

85 See M. Justino Maciel, "Principais manuscritos, edições e traduções em Português," in Maciel 2006, 21. Later Portuguese editions were published by Helena Rua in 1998 (after Perrault's French translation) and by M. Justino Maciel in 2006 (a complete translation from the Harleianus 2767 manuscript). Maciel's translation was preceded by partial publications in 1995 and 1996. A Brazilian translation was published by Marco Aurélio Lagonegro in 1999. On Portuguese editions, see the following bibliographical survey, which despite several lacunae and flaws is still worth consulting: Formosinho Sanchez, *O De Arquitettura de Vitrúvio, numa recolha bibliográfica manuscrita e impressa existente em Portugal* (Lisbon, 1991).

86 Rafael Moreira, "Um tratado português de arquitectura do século XVI (1576-1579)," ed. Helder Carita and Renata Araújo, in *Universo Urbanístico Português: 1455-1822* (Lisbon: Comissão Nacional para as Comemorações dos Descobrimentos Portugueses, 1998), 353-398.

87 [Rodrigues, António], "Tratado de arquitectura" (Ms. [1575/1576] in Biblioteca Nacional de Portugal, cod. 3675; ms. 1579 in Biblioteca Municipal do Porto).

88 See Domingos Tavares, *António Rodrigues: Renascimento em Portugal* (Porto: Dafne Editora, 2007).

89 See the section "The Tomar Enigma" below.

The Paris editions of *Medidas del Romano* dated 1536 and 1537 were followed by the Vitruvius published in Strasbourg in 1543 by Walther Hermann Ryff (1500–1548) and the commentary on Vitruvius by Guillaume Philandrier (1505–1565), first published in Rome in 1544 and reprinted the following year in Paris.[90] Philandrier was a French humanist who took part in diplomatic missions to Venice and Rome between 1536 and 1545. In Rome, he was a member of the Accademia della Virtù, where he conducted philological studies of antique texts, a task that led him to write his Vitruvius commentary. The work follows the chapter structure of Vitruvius's Ten Books, but in lieu of reproducing the entire text it consists only of Philandrier's comments in relation to specific passages quoted from the source, both in Latin. It is an octavo volume, with the quotations set in roman capitals and the extensive commentary in lowercase italics.

The following year, Philandrier returned to Paris, where the book was reprinted. The layout was retouched, with the all-capital lettering of the quotations replaced by roman lowercase one point larger than the comments to distinguish the hierarchy of the two. The book was again published in Venice in 1557, with a layout closer to the original Roman edition. Philandrier's commentary was highly appreciated and his comments quoted and discussed by many of the subsequent editors of Vitruvius, including Daniele Barbaro and Claude Perrault. More significantly, they were added to a revised 1550 edition of the complete text of Vitruvius edited by Ryff, printed by Georg Messerschmidt in Strasbourg. Here, Philandrier's comments were set in relation to the full text of Vitruvius, but in a version that he did not edit.[91] This was also the case for a

---

90 See Frédérique Lemerle, "Philandrier et le texte de Vitruve," *Mélanges de l'école française de Rome* 106, no. 2 (1994): 517–529; Guillaume Philandrier, *Les annotations sur l'architecture de Vitruve: Livres I à I'/*, Frédérique Lemerle ed. (Paris: Classiques Garnier, 2000); Guillaume Philandrier, *Les annotations sur l'architecture de Vitruve: Livres V à VII*, Frédérique Lemerle ed. (Paris: Classiques Garnier, 2011). See also Dora Wiebenson, "Guilaume Philander's Annotations to Vitruvius," in *Les traités d'architecture de la Renaissance* (Paris: J. Guillaume, 1988).

91 There are references to Philandrier's original version of the Vitruvian text that

7 Philandrier 1545, comments and annotations, Book VI, Chapter 3

Vitruvius published in Lyon by Jean I de Tournes (1504–1564) in 1552, for which Philandrier revised his comments into a definitive version but again was not credited as the Latin editor of the text. In 1586 this edition was reprinted in Geneva, newly set by Jean II de Tournes (1539–1615), the previous publisher's son, while the move from Lyon to Geneva reflected political conditions that affected the publishing business in the late sixteenth century.[92] These numerous editions of Philandrier's commentary signal a step forward in the international spread of Vitruvian scholarship. Written in Rome, they entered the French publishing scene via Paris, Strasbourg, and Lyon, while also circulating in Venice and, later, in Amsterdam.[93] The extent of this geographical dissemination might explain Philandrier's overwhelming presence in subsequent Vitruviana—to the extent, according to Dora Wiebenson, that his "notes would be cited almost without exception by every Vitruvius commentator and translator, from the date of its first appearance until the nineteenth century."[94]

In Strasbourg the year before Philandrier's Roman commentary came out, a Latin Vitruvius edited by Ryff was published. Within seven years, Ryff had published three Vitruviuses: first, the Latin version in 1543, his own German translation in 1548, and the aforementioned revised Latin edition accompanied by Philandrier's comments in 1550.[95] Ryff

---

was lost and therefore never printed. See Frédérique Lemerle, "Vitruve: De Tournes's editions, 1552," ed. Frédérique Lemerle and Yves Pauwels, in *Architectura: Architecture, textes et images (XVIe–XVIIe siècles)*, online ed. (Tours: Centre d'Études Supérieures de la Renaissance, Université François-Rabelais, 2013), http://architectura.cesr.univ-tours.fr/Traite/Notice/Phil1552.asp?param=en.

92 Being a Protestant, Jean II de Tournes left Lyon in 1585.

93 Philandrier's annotations from the 1552 Lyon edition were later included in a 1649 compilation of treatises on architectural theory organized around Vitruvius. See Dora Wiebenson, *French Books: Sixteenth through Nineteenth Centuries*, 4 vols., The Mark J. Millard Architectural Collection, vol. 1 (Washington, DC: National Gallery of Art, 1993), https://www.nga.gov/content/dam/ngaweb/research/publications/pdfs/mark-j-millard-french-books.pdf, cat. 165, 471–474.

94 Wiebenson, *French Books: Sixteenth through Nineteenth Centuries*, 474.

95 See Harry Francis Mallgrave, "Introduction," in *Northern European Books: Sixteenth to Early Nineteenth Centuries*, 4 vols., The Mark J. Millard Architectural Collection, vol. 3 (Washington, DC: National Gallery of Art, 1998), 1–61, https://www.

gathered his text and many illustrations from the Giocondo and Cesariano editions, and his main contribution was to introduce new concepts and ideas to a "readership scarcely familiar even with such terms as 'architect' and 'architecture,'" to use the words of Hanno-Walter Kruft.[96] The compact octavo volume of 1543, published by Messerschmidt, was similar to the successful pocket-sized Giocondo edition in its size and its use of italic type. The compact format would have been a prudent choice for reducing the economic risks of an edition that was, as stated in the frontispiece, "*nunc primum in Germania.*"[97] The edition must have been a commercial success,[98] because seven years later the same Messerschmidt printed a new version, amended and significantly revised by Ryff and with the addition of the comments by Philandrier, in a larger quarto volume. Vitruvius's text was set in roman, and italics were used for Philandrier's comments, which follow each chapter, and sometimes even each paragraph, so that every spread presents the reader with the text and the annotations in different types.

Between the publications of his two Latin versions, Ryff's German translation *Vitruvius Teutsch* came out in 1548 under the imprint of Johann Petreius (1497–1550) of Nuremberg, who used a fraktur blackletter type.[99] If in early fifteenth-century Spain the rotunda blackletter would have been a natural choice due to the limited types available to the printer, this would probably not have been the case for the Nuremberg edition. Variations of blackletter, such as fraktur, schwabacher,

nga.gov/content/dam/ngaweb/research/publications/pdfs/mark-j-millard-northern-european-books.pdf.

96 Hanno-Walter Kruft, *A History of Architectural Theory from Vitruvius to the Present*, 1st German ed. 1985 (New York: Princeton Architectural Press, 1994), 71.

97 Ryff 1543, frontispiece.

98 In 1918, Bodo Eberhardt condemned it for being "too close" to its sources, Cesariano and Giocondo–a comment that may be too harsh considering the effort necessary to present a classical text in a different cultural context. Mallgrave, "Introduction," 8; Kruft, *A History of Architectural Theory from Vitruvius to the Present*, 71. See also Erik Forssman's commentaries in the Ryff 1973 reprint.

99 The book followed the publication of his own treatise in 1547, also printed by Johan Petreius in Nuremberg.

and rotunda, had been used in Germany since Gutenberg used textura in his famous 42-line bible of 1455.[100] With Martin Luther's German translation of the Bible, published in Wittenberg in 1534, type became a locus of religious and political dispute. Many editions of Vitruvius used roman type, and its classical tone was easily identified with Rome and its Church. Petreius had had a choice: he had access to both fraktur and roman type, and thus it is significant that he chose to reject the usual classical typography in his Vitruvius in favor of a more up-to-date and politically charged type. The immediate and continued success of *Vitruvius Teutsch* is attested to by its being thrice reprinted in Basel in 1575, 1582, and 1614, with each edition bearing the same characteristics as the Nuremberg edition.

In 1547, the year before Ryff's German translation and two years after the Parisian edition of Philandrier's comments, Jean Martin (ca. 1507–1553) published the first French translation of Vitruvius in Paris. Martin translated a number of key architectural texts before tackling Vitruvius, including Books I and II of Serlio in 1545[101] and the *Hypnerotomachia poliphili* in 1546,[102] and continued afterwards with Alberti's *De re aedificatoria*,[103] posthumously published in 1553. Like Ryff, he based his Vitruvius translation on Giocondo's and Cesariano's editions, and besides the exercise of adapting the text and its vocabulary to French, the edition was renewed by a set of independent illustrations by Jean Goujon (ca. 1510 – ca. 1566), who signed the book's postface. As Frédérique Lemerle has pointed out, Goujon's contribution, commissioned for this edition, is not an illustration of the text but rather a "graphic poem,"

---

100 For an example of an early printed book on architecture set in blackletter, see Matthäus Roriczer, *Geometria Deutsch* ([Nuremberg]: [Peter Wagner], 1489).

101 Sebastiano Serlio, *Il primo e secondo libro d'architettura di Sebastiano Serlio*, trans. Jean Martin (Paris, 1545).

102 Jean Martin, trans., *Hypnerotomachie, ou, discours du songe de Poliphile: Deduisant comme amour le combat à l'occasion de Polia* (Paris: Jaques Kerver, 1546).

103 Leon Battista Alberti, *L'architecture et art de bien bastir* (Paris: Jaques Kerver, 1553).

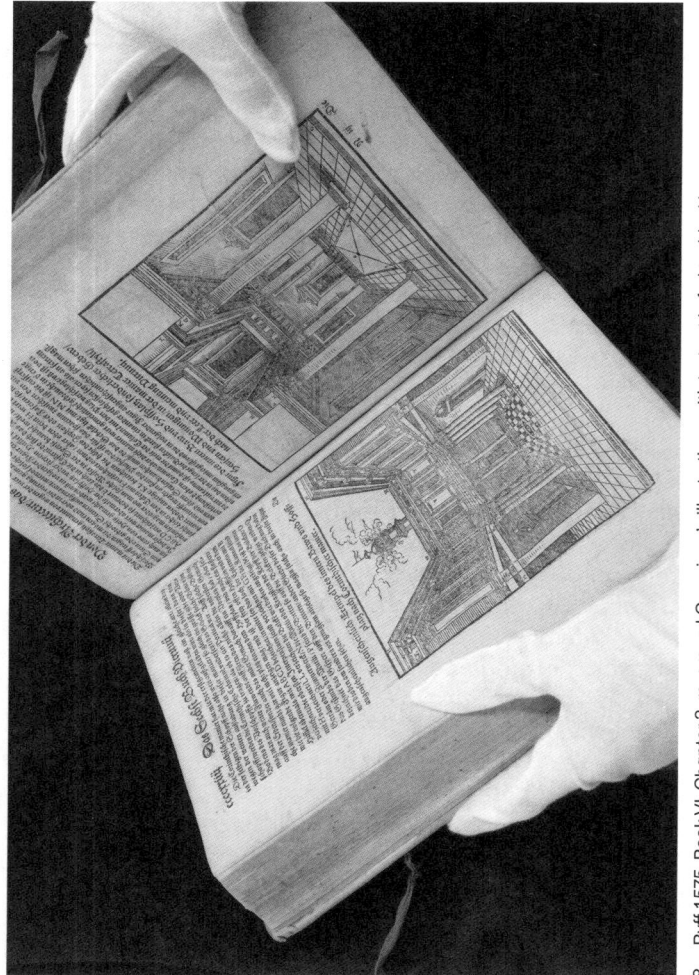

8 Ryff 1575, Book VI, Chapter 3, revamped Cesariano's illustrations with text set in fraktur blackletter type

or a "digression in images."[104] This original French touch, when mixed in among images drawn from Giocondo and Cesariano—and three taken from Serlio's second book—renders the book's visual apparatus rather heteroclite, a sign of the ongoing blending of the Roman source into contemporary regional practices. The book was printed in a large folio format, an ambitious editorial choice that might explain the commission to Goujon that in the end counters the straightforward layout of Martin's translation.

More modest in size is the second French translation, the printing of which was completed in Toulouse in 1559 (as is stated on the last page) after being initiated in 1556 (as is stated on the title page). Translated by Jean Gardet and illustrated by Dominique Bertin (d. 1578), it is a straightforward octavo, with comments on Books I, II, and III set in italics on separate pages that follow the complete translation. As Daniel Millette has pointed out, the text and illustrations are based on Giocondo's edition and react to the previous translation by Martin and Goujon, reflecting the "need to reconcile personal classical architectural imaginations (derived at least partly from the panorama of ruins in southern France) to Vitruvius's set of classical precepts."[105] This reconciliation is evident in the annotations, where the authors recall their travels through the French Midi and the remnants of antiquity they saw there. Their method is characteristic of the tendency throughout

---

104 Frédérique Lemerle, "Vitruve Editions Martin: Traduction de Vitruve 1547," ed. Frédérique Lemerle and Yves Pauwels, in *Architectura: Architecture, textes et images (XVIe–XVIIe siècles)*, online ed. (Tours: Centre d'Études Supérieures de la Renaissance, Université François-Rabelais, 2013), http://architectura.cesr.univ-tours.fr/Traite/Notice/ENSBA_LES1785.asp?param=.

105 Daniel Millette, "Vitruvius and the French Landscape of Ruins: On Jean Gardet and Dominique Bertin's 1559 Annotations of *De Architectura*," McGill-Queens University Press, ed. Alberto Pérez-Gómez and Stephen Parcell, *CHORA: Intervals in the Philosophy of Architecture* 5 (2007): 259–284, here 262. See also Daniel Millette, "Vitruve: Editions Gardet/Bertin, 1556/1559," ed. Frédérique Lemerle and Yves Pauwels, in *Architectura: Architecture, textes et images (XVIe–XVIIe siècles)*, online ed. (Tours: Centre d'Études Supérieures de la Renaissance, Université François-Rabelais, 2012), http://architectura.cesr.univ-tours.fr/traite/Notice/GardetBertin1559.asp?param=en.

9 Gardet 1556–1559, abridged edition, Book VI, Chapter 3, French translation summarizing Vitruvius's arguments

Europe to juxtapose Vitruvius's text with an examination and progressive appropriation of regional realities.

The publication history of Gardet and Bertin's book is quite convoluted. After their publisher Guyon Boudeville (d. 1562), a Protestant, was sentenced to death and executed in 1562, the remaining copies were brought to Paris where a new publisher, Gabriel Buon (d. 1595?), reprinted and replaced the colophon and title page to reissue the book in 1565, 1567, and 1568. The copies left in 1595, when Buon died, were given a new title page, dedication and colophon in 1597, along with the new title *Abrege des dix livres d'architecture*, and sold by Antoine Du Breuil. During these years, both Martin's translation and Philandrier's comments were reprinted in Paris and Lyon, suggesting that Gardet's translation occupied a relatively marginal position within the French context.[106]

In short, the second quarter of the sixteenth century marked the spread of Vitruvius's text into Spanish-, Portuguese-, French-, and German-speaking regions, with the consistency of editorial voices challenged by a mix of illustrations imported from previous editions and a more complex articulation of the relationship between the original text and the annotations. From an architectural perspective, these editorial moves were accompanied by attempts to foster the establishment of theories grounded in regional realities, as demonstrated by Ryff's contemporary treatise, Goujon's illustrations, and Gardet and Bertin's reading of the Midi's antiquities. From an editorial point of view, the books reflect a certain homogeneity across regional print cultures, with variations between blackletter and roman type being the characteristic that most distinguishes one from another. In any case, the geographical circuit highlights the

---

106 Another French Vitruvian publication of the time worth noting is Jean Borrel, *Logistica, quae, arithmetica vulgo dicitur, in libros quinque digesta*, 1559, where he discusses, on pages 387 and 396, "excerpts of difficult passages" from Vitruvius. Being just an excerpt, it is hard to include it in the Vitruviana. See Vagnetti and Marcucci, *2000 anni di Vitruvio*, 64.

dominant influence of Giocondo and Cesariano's editions as reference sources for the various Vitruvian iterations, with the Venice—Como axis operating as a hinge between the regional systems that were developing. Moreover, mapping the movement of Vitruvius between 1523 and 1556, from Giocondo's Lyon edition to Barbaro's Venetian one, demonstrates the complex network of knowledge transfer operating at the apogee of the treatise's era.

THE AGE OF ORDERS, 1556–1649

While throughout Europe Vitruvius's text was finding its way into new languages and editions, in Venice the nobility were using it to establish a theoretical framework for classical architecture. As Manuela Morresi has pointed out, the Venetian architectural scene was polarized between practitioners who incorporated *all'antica* precepts with a free hand and erudite authors eager to renovate the Serenissima's landscape according to specific classical models, among them Fra Giocondo.[107] The latter's 1514 proposal for the renovation of the Rialto market, rejected by the city's Senate, which took issue with how "an out-of-place *all'antica* language was being superimposed upon a site regulated by age-old laws governing settlement in the lagoon,"[108] epitomizes the confrontation between the two camps that represented both cultural and political factions. Vitruvius was a key reference in this conflict between local conventions and the *all'antica* canon, as Daniele Barbaro's edition of 1556, illustrated by Andrea Palladio, would demonstrate.

The ambiguities of this dispute were also visible through the pages of editions of Vitruvius. In 1554 the notice of the imminent publication of Barbaro's Vitruvius might have con-

---

[107] Manuela Morresi, "Treatises and the Architecture of Venice in the Fifteenth and Sixteenth Centuries," ed. Vaughan Hart and Peter Hicks, in *Paper Palaces: The Rise of the Renaissance Architectural Treatise* (New Haven, CT: Yale University Press, 1998), 262–280.

[108] Morresi, "Treatises and the Architecture of Venice," here 270.

tributed to the decision of the publisher Giolito de' Ferrari (ca. 1508–1578) to cancel the printing of an illustrated Italian translation of the treatise that Giovan Antonio Rusconi (ca. 1520–1587) had completed in 1552.[109] After a long delay, it finally appeared in print in 1590 but in a much-diminished form: only 160 of the original 300 plates were included, the translation was omitted (and later lost), and the text is reduced to some "equivocal"[110] remarks by an anonymous editor. Rusconi was not an erudite scholar, nor were his Vitruvian illustrations informed by firsthand knowledge of Roman antiquities, but his illustrations nevertheless remain faithful to *all'antica* principles. The way buildings are represented, as well as the clothes of the characters who inhabit his illustrations, point to an antiquarian reconstitution of Vitruvius's passages. But the instruments and techniques used by the "ancient" workers in the "ancient" buildings shown are those in use in sixteententh-century Venice, betraying Rusconi's loyalty to Vitruvius in the representation of contemporary local construction practices.[111]

This tension between the *all'antica* and contemporary practice underlies the multitude of books on the orders that sprang up in the sixteenth century. It is relevant that Vitruvius never referred himself to architectural "orders," instead making a few references to the building's "*genera*" to clarify the difference between the Doric, Tuscan, Ionic, and Corinthian columns that were used alone or in combination in various building types.[112] During the sixteenth century, *genera* was

---

109 Anna Bedon, "Giovan Antonio Rusconi: Illustratore di Vitruvio, artista, ingegnere, architetto," in *Della architettura di Gio: Antonio Rusconi* (Vicenza: Centro Internazionale di Architettura Andrea Palladio, 1996), x.

110 Bedon, "Giovan Antonio Rusconi," xii.

111 "Its most precious illustrations are the ones that, betraying his mainly techno-scientific interests while being faithful illustrations of Vitruvian procedures, are a rich and accurate documentation of techniques and instruments used in sixteenth-century Venetian construction." Pagliara, "Vitruvio da testo a cânone," 82–83, quoted by Bedon, "Giovan Antonio Rusconi," xviii. See specially Book VII, plate III, representing wall decoration, reproduced here in image 11. See also Morresi, "Treatises and the Architecture of Venice," 279.

112 Germann, *Vitruve et le vitruvianisme*, 29. See also Louis Callebat and

THE AGE OF ORDERS, 1556–1649

10 Barbaro 1567, Latin edition, Andrea Palladio's illustration for Vitruvius, Book VI, Chapter 3, tetrastyle *cavaedium*

translated as "order" and codified as a standard comprising column base, shaft, capital, and entablature. After Sagredo's 1526 *Medidas del Romano*, Serlio's *Regole generali d'architetura,* published in 1537, established the paradigm of the orders as the basic Vitruvian vocabulary. Like Alberti before him, Serlio based the structure of his original treatise on Vitruvius's series of independent and numbered books, although the troubled history of their publication prevented him from completing the intended seven volumes.[113] Serlio refers to Vitruvius as "The Great Architect,"[114] and his *Regole*'s subtitle "with examples from antiquity, that agree, for the most part, with the doctrine of Vitruvius"[115] is explicit in referring to his source. This, however, does not imply reverence—Serlio had no trouble deviating from the Vitruvian model. Instead, his aim was to decipher Vitruvius's difficult precepts and translate them into a practical contemporary grammar, teaching the reader to build *all'antica* without the need to have been in contact with Roman antiquity. Unable to secure appropriate and stable patronage, the editorial enterprise met a bitter success: by 1539 Book IV had been pirated in Antwerp by Pieter Coecke (1502–1550) in an unauthorized Flemish translation.[116] Book III, the volume on antiquities, came out in 1540,[117] followed by reprints of Book IV. In 1545 Serlio published Books I and II, in

Philippe Fleury, eds., *Dictionnaire des termes techniques du* De architectura *de Vitruve* (Hildesheim: Olms-Weidmann, 1995).

113 For a detailed account of the complex publishing history of Serlio's books, see Magali Vène, *Bibliographia Serliana: Catalogue des éditions imprimées des livres du traité d'architecture de Sebastiano Serlio (1537–1681)* (Paris: Picard, 2007).

114 Sebastiano Serlio, *Regole generali di architetvra sopra le cinqve maniere de gliedifici: Cioe, thoscano, dorico, ionico, corinthio, et composito; Con gliessempi dell'antiqvita, che per la magior parte concordano con la dottrina di Vitrvvio* (Venice: F. Marcolini da Forli, 1537), CXXXI/112r.

115 Serlio, *Regole generali di architetvra*. Title translation in Alice Jarrard, "Review: Metodo ed ordini nella teoria architettonica del primi moderni; Alberti, Raffaello, Serlio e Camillo by Mario Carpo. La maschera e il modello: Teoria architettonica ed evangelismo nell'extraordinario libro di Sebastiano Serlio by Mario Carpo," *Journal of the Society of Architectural Historians* 55, no. 1 (March 1996): 103–105.

116 Pollak, *Italian & Spanish Books*, 398.

117 Sebastiano Serlio, *Il terzo libro di Sebastiano Serlio bolognese: Nel qual si figurano, e descrivono le antiquita di Roma, e le altre che sono in Italia, e fuori d'Italia* (Venice: Francesco Marcolino da Forli, 1540).

which a pragmatic focus on geometry and perspective distances the work from Vitruvius's theoretical approach.[118] For the rest of his life Serlio struggled in vain to complete the publication of his treatise. The sequence was later reshuffled with the publication of Books V, VII, and the complementary *Livre extraordinaire*. Book VI, dedicated to houses, matched the Vitruvian numbering but remained in manuscript until the twentieth century.

Serlio's practical books and their translations were not the only books on the orders. In Zurich in 1550, Hans Blum (ca. 1520–ca. 1560) published his own version of how to draw the Vitruvian orders.[119] His book, addressing a German-speaking audience, complemented the recent publication of Ryff's treatise and the German-language Vitruvius. But the paramount book on the orders, the *Regola delli cinque ordini* of Giacomo Barozzi da Vignola (1507–1573), was first printed in 1562.[120] From an editorial perspective, Vignola's book is distinguished from those of his predecessors in its use of copper engravings, a printing technique that granted an astonishing accuracy to the details of his drawings. Its visual effectiveness would eventually earn it the title of most-reprinted architectural book, with more than five hundred editions between 1562 and 1974.[121]

At this point it is worth noting that the precise quality of copper plate engravings made them ideal for practical books

---

118 An authorized French translation was published that same year. Serlio, *Il primo e secondo libro*.

119 Joannem Bluom, *Quinque columnarum exacta descriptio atque deliniatio, cum symmetrica earum distributione* (Zurich: C. Froschouerum, 1550).

120 Iacomo Barozzio da Vignola, *Regola delli cinqve ordini d'architettvra* (Rome, [1562]). See Richard J. Tuttle, "On Vignola's Rule of the Five Orders of Architecture," ed. Vaughan Hart and Peter Hicks, in *Paper Palaces: The Rise of the Renaissance Architectural Treatise* (New Haven, CT: Yale University Press, 1998), 199–218, 204.

121 See Maria Walcher Casotti, "Giacomo Barozzi da Vignola: Regola delli cinque ordini d'architettura," ed. Elena Bassi, Sandro Benedetti, Renato Bonelli, Licisco Magagnato, Paola Marini, Tommaso Scalesse, Camillo Semenzato, and Maria Walcher Casotti, in *Trattati: Pietro Cataneo, Giacomo Barozzi da Vignola; Con l'aggiunta degli scritti di architettura di Alvise Cornaro, Francesco Giorgi, Claudio Tolomei, Giangiorgio Trissino, Giorgio Vasari* (Milan: Polifilo, 1985), 499–577, 539–577.

that relied on detailed and instructive images. Nonetheless, because the technical challenges of printing such plates led to the separation of images within the book, many text-based books continued to be illustrated with woodcuts, a process that allowed for an easier blending of words and images. In fact, and underlining the distance between Vitruvius and practical books like Vignola's, it is telling that engraved illustrations were not used in an edition of Vitruvius until more than a century later when Claude Perrault used the technique to strengthen and support his argument in 1673.

It is against this backdrop of a growing faith in the architectural orders, and the Venetian rejection of innovations in *all'antica* style, that Daniele Barbaro (1514–1570) undertook the ambitious task of bridging Vitruvian precepts and the analysis of Roman antiquities with contemporary architectural practice to constitute a unified corpus of knowledge around Vitruvius's text. Barbaro's 1556 Italian translation and commentaries are a landmark of Vitruvian scholarship for his accurate reading of the complex Latin passages, his thorough discussion of the readings and hypotheses of previous commentators,[122] and the fundamental contribution of Andrea Palladio (1508–1580) in illustrating the book that made it highly valuable within a contemporary architectural framework.[123] Barbaro invested great time and resources in this enterprise, including scholarly missions to Rome with Palladio to study ancient monuments and to compare Vitruvius's ideas with the built sources. It is also significant that his book transported quotations from Sagredo, Philandrier, and Ryff (besides Giocondo, Cesariano, and other Italian sources) to Venice,[124] marking the back-and-forth circulation of ideas

---

122 See Manfredo Tafuri, "La norma e il programma: Il Vitruvio di Daniele Barbaro," in Barbaro 1987, XI—XL, XLI—LVIII.

123 On the images of the Barbaro edition by Palladio, see Louis Cellauro, "Palladio e le illustrazioni delle edizioni del 1556 e del 1567 di Vitruvio," *Saggi e memorie di storia dell'arte*, no. 22 (1998): 55–128.

124 See Louis Cellauro, "Notice on Daniele Barbaro," ed. Frédérique Lemerle and Yves Pauwels, in *Architectura: Architecture, textes et images (XVIe–XVIIe siècles)*, online (Tours: Centre d'Études Supérieures de la Renaissance, Université François-

among sixteenth-century Vitruvian scholars across Europe. The ambition of his edition is evident in its folio size, high-quality print, and diligent layout. Seemingly, Barbaro was using Vitruvius to impose the potential of ancient Rome as a normative influence in the Venetian context, making use of his power and political influence to produce an authoritative source for contemporary practice and the shaping of the city.

Such a readable and useful Vitruvius was expected to provide a common ground from which to overcome the atavism of local builders. But, as Morresi states, the edition's "luxury" quality suggests it "was aimed at readers who were cultured and erudite," and that "the main public to whom a work on architectural theory was destined was not one of artisans."[125] Not by chance, the publisher of Barbaro's 1556 edition was Francesco Marcolini (ca. 1500–1559), who was not only "among the most outstanding figures in Venetian artistic and cultural circles"[126] but had also previously published Serlio's Book III on the architectural orders.[127] In fact, Serlio was much more successful in bringing classical concepts into mainstream architectural practice. In 1567 two new Vitruviuses were issued with corrections and amendments by Barbaro: a large quarto Latin edition, which collated his comments and illustrations with a text following the 1552 Lyon edition, and a small quarto with the amended Italian translation and comments. Both were published by Francesco de' Franceschi (ca. 1530–1599), and the same illustrations were recut by Giovanni Chriegher with the addition of some new drawings, also by Palladio, including variations of the *cavaedia* discussed in Book VI, Chapter III, Paragraph 1. The layout of both editions is similar. Morresi sees in this double second

---

Rabelais, 2010), http://architectura.cesr.univ-tours.fr/Traite/Notice/Barbaro1556.asp?param=en.

125 Morresi, "Treatises and the Architecture of Venice," 275.
126 Morresi, "Treatises and the Architecture of Venice," 275.
127 On Francesco Marcolini, Serlio, and the Lyon connection, see Sylvie Deswarte-Rosa, ed., *Sebastiano Serlio a Lyon: Architecture et Imprimerie, Volume 1; Le traité d'architecture de Sebastiano Serlio. Une grande entreprise éditoriale au XVIe siècle* (Lyon: Mémoire Active, 2004).

11 Rusconi 1590, illustration to Book VII, plate III, "ancient" workers using fifteenth-century Venice instruments and techniques for "ancient" buildings

edition the "start of a 'second phase' in Barbaro's project, a phase in which he seems to address himself to readers more interested in architectural practice."[128] The comprehensive quality of Barbaro's work granted his books a wide circulation, especially the smaller Italian quarto reissued by Franceschi in 1584, with additional reprints in 1629 and 1641.[129]

We have seen the impact of Sagredo's *Medidas del Romano* within the Iberian context, and Spanish scholars are recorded among the members of the Accademia della Virtù alongside Philandrier in 1538.[130] But it was only in 1582 that the first Spanish translation was printed, by Juan Gracián (d. 1587) in Alcalá de Henares—not by accident in the same year that the Real Academia de Matemáticas started to offer architectural education in Madrid under the direction of Juan de Herrera (1530–1597), underpinning the classical orientation of Iberian architecture.[131] The translation was authored by Miguel de Urrea (ca. 1520–1565/68), who had died around seventeen years prior to its publication.[132] The manuscript was kept by his widow, who received royal permission to print it in 1569, and Agustín Bustamante and Fernando Marías managed to identify a still-existing manuscript in Lisbon as the source of the printed version.[133] The manuscript is octavo, pre-

---

128 Morresi, "Treatises and the Architecture of Venice," 275.

129 These reprints of Barbaro's 1567 Italian edition were both published in Venice, by Alessandro de'Vecchi in 1629 and by Turrini in 1641. In 1938 the reprints were translated to Russian by Zubov and Gabrichevsky. A facsimile was published in Milan in 1987 by Il Polifilo, with critical essays by Francesco Tafuri and Manuela Morresi. It was translated into English: Kim Williams, trans., *Daniele Barbaro's Vitruvius of 1567* ([Basel]: Birkhäuser, 2019).

130 Such as "the pontifical protomedico Luis de Lucena (1491–1552) and the engineer Jerónimo de Bustamante de Herrera (ca. 1502–1557)." Fernando Marías, "Notice on Miguel de Urrea," in Lemerle and Pauwels, *Architectura: Architecture, textes et images (XVIe–XVIIe siècles)*, n.p.

131 See Fernando Marías, "Trattatistica teorica e Vitruvianesimo nella architettura spagnola del cinquecento," ed. A. Chastel and J. Guillaume, in *Les traités d'architecture de la Renaissance* (Paris: Picard, 1988), 279, 307–315.

132 Marías suggests the translation is based on either the Messerschmidt or the Jean I de Tournes edition of 1550 or 1552.

133 Miguel Urrea, "Marco Vitrubio *De architectura* dividido en X libros traduzido de latin en lengua castellana" (Biblioteca Nacional de Portugal, cod. 5179, 1582), https://purl.pt/24885.

pared to guide the publication with blank spaces indicating image placement and headers referring to the content of the chapters. It also suggests corrections that were then made to the printed version. The book was printed in quarto, and its most distinctive characteristic is the fact that the illustrations are drawn from multiple sources, with woodcuts copying illustrations from Cesariano, Giocondo, Philandrier, Barbaro, and Ryff, often mixing different, if not opposite, representations of the same topic. Scholars agree that the translation has many weaknesses, and the fact it was not to be found in the libraries of the most active contemporary architects suggests it was far from being an editorial success,[134] an idea underlined by Ortiz y Sanz's undertaking of a new Spanish translation in the eighteenth century.[135]

Except for Urrea's Spanish translation and Rusconi's delayed and partial illustrations, there were no other new Vitruvius editions until a complex compendium of architectural literature was published in Amsterdam in 1649 under Elzivier's imprint and edited by Joannes de Laet (1581–1649). It is a massive volume of 565 pages with eclectic content orbiting around its key text: Vitruvius's *De architectura*. It opens with de Laet's Latin translation of *The Elements of Architecture*, a theoretical book by Henry Wotton (1568–1639) published in London in 1624,[136] in the guise of a preface. The Vitruvian text, following the 1552 Lyon edition, forms the core of the book and is extensively annotated with comments from Philandrier and Barbaro, as well as with new references and commentary by various scholars in de Laet's circle. Vitruvius's book is fol-

---

134 Marías, *Notice on Miguel*, in Lemerle and Pauwels, *Architectura*, (online ed.), 2012.

135 Another almost published Spanish translation was authored by Lázaro de Velasco between 1573 and 1583. Marías, *Notice on Miguel*, in Lemerle and Pauwels, *Architectura: Architecture, textes et images (XVIe–XVIIe siècles)*. The manuscript was retained in Cáceres, Spain. Despite its accurate quality and various illustrations, it was not printed until 1999, when part of it was presented in facsimile. F. Pizarro Gómez and P. Mogollón Cano-Cortés, eds., *Los diez libros de arquitectura de Marco Vitruvio Polión según la traducción castellana de Lázaro de Velasco* (Cáceres: Ciclón, 1999).

136 Eileen Harris and Nicholas Savage, *British Architectural Books and Writers 1556–1785* (Cambridge: Cambridge University Press, 1990), 499.

12 De Laet 1649, Book VI, Chapter 3, a massive scholarly edition with eclectic content gravitating around Vitruvius

lowed by Claude Saumaise's (1588–1653) notes on Vitruvius, Nicolaus Goldmann's (1611–1665) essay on the Ionic capitals, and a detailed index. After this follows Bernardino Baldi's (1553–1617) glossary and a discussion of obscure passages in Vitruvius, extracts from Alberti's *De pictura* and Pomponius Gauricus's (ca. 1482–1528/30) *De sculptura*, and finally further comments by Saumaise. It is an erudite compilation of diverse materials, articulating a comprehensive survey of the subject in a single volume. The variety of content constitutes a theoretical compendium, while the editor remains silent. Its scholarly ambition is revealed by the fact it is all in Latin, a language shared by the learned classes but inaccessible to most contractors and builders. Judging on the singularity of this edition in comparison to the epoch's editorial frenzy targeting an architectural clientele, one can presume architects would have preferred to learn their trade via the practical vernacular books that were by then easily available.

In that sense, the erudite tone of de Laet's 1649 Vitruvius contrasts with the growing interest of architectural publishers in producing practical books, such as books on the orders and books of models. An early example of the latter is Jacques Androuet du Cerceau's (1510–1584) *Livre d'architecture*, published in Paris in 1559 and based in part on Serlio's unfinished survey of domestic architecture.[137] Du Cerceau's model-book is distinct from the treatise tradition in that it focuses on providing plans, sections, and perspective views of existing buildings useful to builders, a type that would later become the pattern book. It is within these pragmatic lines that Hans Vredeman de Vries (1527–ca. 1604) also addressed how to build Vitruvian buildings using Vitruvian orders, and in 1577 published the illustrated textbook *Architectvra, oder, Bauung der Antiquen auss dem Vitruuius*. At the time, he was just embarking on a

---

137 Jacques Androuet Cerceau, *Livre d'architectvre contenant les plans & dessaings de cinquante bastimens tous differens* (Paris: Benoît Prévost, 1559); Jacques Androuet Cerceau, *Second livre d'architectvre contenant plusieurs et diverses ordonnances de cheminees, lucarnes, portes, fonteines* (Paris: André Wechel, 1561). On Serlio's book, see the section "Model and Theory" below.

prolific career as a publisher of engravings featuring architectural models,[138] producing an extensive oeuvre within which the 1601 *Architecturae Formae* is an outstanding example.[139] Following Giovanni Antonio Dosio's (1533–1609) 1569 depictions of Roman antiquities,[140] de Vries' architectural forms are printed in landscape format, stressing their difference from the portrait format used for the text-based Vitruvian books. They also show de Vries' preference, like Vignola's, for detailed engravings—a clear and elegant alternative to the blunt appearance of earlier woodcuts. The success of these practical books by du Cerceau and de Vries, alongside those of Serlio and Vignola, was accompanied by the progressive disappearance of Vitruvius from the architectural publishing panorama.

After Barbaro's *ne plus ultra* Vitruvius, the editions by Urrea and de Laet were exceptions—and Rusconi's an oddity. Many of the illustrations in Barbaro made their way to Palladio's own treatise, *I quattro libri*,[141] whose appearance in 1570—three years after the second edition of Barbaro was published—was a novelty in architectural culture. Palladio's built work is coherent and complete to such an extent that in his book, which combines his architectural accomplishments and his theoretical reflections on theory, practice, and reference to the Roman canon and its contemporary application can be understood as a unified corpus. In the last resort, the allegiance between Barbaro's authoritative *De architectura* and Palladio's *I quattro libri* overcame the gap between the two streams of Vitruvian readership—scholarly and professional—and the frenzy of Vitruvian editorial activity in the first half of the sixteenth century faded away.

138 Mallgrave, "Introduction," here 19–21.
139 Hans Vredeman de Vries, *Variae architectvrae formae: A Ionne Vredemanni Vriesio magno artis hvivs stvdiosorvm commodo, inventae* (Antwerp: Theodorus Galleaeus, 1601).
140 Giovanni Antonio Dosio, *Vrbis Romæ ædificiorvm illustrivm qvæ svpersvnt reliqviæ* ([Rome], 1569).
141 Andrea Palladio, *I quattro libri dell'architettura di Andrea Palladio* (Venice: Dominico de' Franceschi, 1570). On Palladio, see the sections "Proportional Deadlock" and "Model and Theory" below.

GROUNDING THEORY, 1673–1791

When Claude Perrault (1613–1688) published his annotated French translation in 1673, new editions of Vitruvius were out of fashion. Barbaro's Vitruvius, the most authoritative edition thus far, was over a hundred years old, and in the interim, notwithstanding the less successful enterprises of Miguel de Urrea and Giovanni Rusconi, Vitruvian publishing had been dominated by reprints. Although these came out regularly and prolonged the lifespan of older editions—especially those of Martin, Ryff, Philandrier, and Barbaro—none contributed any substantial innovation or renewed the Roman author's position within the architectural field. De Laet's choice of scholarly Latin for his 1649 compendium underlines this progressive marginalization of Vitruvius within architectural theory. Perrault's work turned things around, bringing Vitruvius back into the spotlight and stimulating a renewed exchange that prompted a flurry of translations and reprints in the following century from Madrid to Moscow.[142]

Perrault's book is as large as Barbaro's luxurious edition of 1556, with exquisite copper engravings entwined with the text in a complex layout.[143] The massive tome was read aloud to the Académie des Sciences from June 1674 onwards,[144]

---

[142] See Antoine Picon, "Érudition et polémique, le Vitruve de Claude Perrault," in Perrault 1995.

[143] There were also sixty-five detailed copper plate engravings inserted within the letterpress.

[144] On September 20, 1673, Perrault presented the Académie with a copy of

13 Perrault 1673, Book VI, Chapter 3, plate LII, illustration of a tetrastyle *cavaedium*

and from the rooms of the Académie, as Indra McEwen put it, Perrault "made Vitruvius speak French," thereby diffusing "the splendour of the Sun King's reign throughout the royal courts of Europe and the emerging republic of letters."[145] That the edition was commissioned in 1667 by Jean-Baptiste Colbert (1619–1683), the *éminence grise* of Louis XIV and his superintendent of buildings, to provide the future Académie Royale d'Architecture with appropriate means to regulate the kingdom's architecture is telling, both of the ambitious nature of the publication and of its impact in renewing Vitruvius's authority.

Unlike previous editions, in which text and commentary were part of a unified reading apparatus, Perrault's structure articulates its components separately: a clear and faithful translation of the Latin text—that like many of his predecessors he deemed jumbled and confused—and, unfolding as "a treatise within the treatise,"[146] the philological and critical notes aimed at illuminating the obscure passages. The costly engravings (which amounted to 9,400 livres),[147] produced by Sébastien Leclerc (1637–1714) and others from 1668 to 1673, required an investment equal to the ambitious nature of the venture. Leclerc had previously collaborated with Perrault on the *Mémoires pour servir à l'histoire naturelle des animaux*, a highly successful two-volume presentation of anatomical research on European and exotic animals conducted by members of the Académie des Sciences and published sequentially in 1671 and 1676.[148] In the former enterprise, Leclerc's exquisite engravings effectively synthesize the written description and display the anatomical discoveries using a twofold

---

his book. Antoine Picon, *Claude Perrault, 1613–1688 ou la curiosité d'un classique* (Paris: Picard, 1988), 138, n. 47.

145 Indra Kagis McEwen, "On Claude Perrault: Modernising Vitruvius," ed. Vaughan Hart and Peter Hicks, in *Paper Palaces: The Rise of the Renaissance Architectural Treatise* (New Haven, CT: Yale University Press, 1998), 320–337, here 321.

146 Picon, *Claude Perrault*, 120.

147 Picon, *Claude Perrault*, 119.

148 Claude Perrault, *Mémoires pour servir à l'histoire naturelle des animaux* (Paris: Imprimerie Royale, 1671).

visual strategy: each plate shows a perspective view of the living animal in its native environment, and, seemingly pinned over this view, covering the sky, is an illusionistically presented leaf of paper that bears a series of analytic dissection drawings of the same animal's organs and other body parts.[149] In his monograph on the multiple activities of Perrault, Antoine Picon shows that a parallel strategy was used in the Vitruvius depictions, such that a view of an entire building is placed in relation to details showing its internal structure and various elements, usually presented as if on separate pieces of paper pinned over the general view.[150] This represents a conceptual breakthrough in connecting the visual languages used to present natural phenomena and biology with those used in the arts of architecture and construction. The significance of these costly plates goes beyond luxury: they stand for the complex ambitions of Perrault's translation to cement architecture and Vitruvius within the foundations of the French Enlightenment.

The preparation of Perrault's Vitruvius coincided with the institution of the Académie Royale d'Architecture in 1671. The Académie was responsible for securing the guidelines for the education of new architects but also provided technical oversight and ultimately represented the architectural profession. Although Perrault was neither an architect by training nor a founding member of the Académie, he followed its activities closely from its inception.[151] This must have been facilitated by the fact that his brother Charles was Colbert's deputy on matters related to the Académie des Sciences, of which the Académie d'Architecture was a branch. The

---

149 This double strategy is similar to the later visual descriptions of the *Éncyclopédie* by Diderot and d'Alembert, published in 1751. On the double representation, see Roland Barthes, "Les planches de l'encyclopédie," in *Le degré zéro de l'écriture: Suivi de nouveaux essais critiques*, Repr. 1972 (Paris: Éditions du Seuil, 1964), 89–104; Roland Barthes, "The Plates of the Encyclopedia," trans. Richard Howard, in *New Critical Essays* (New York: Hill and Wang, 1980). See also André Tavares, *The Anatomy of the Architectural Book* (Zurich: Lars Müller/Canadian Centre for Architecture, 2016), 293–315.

150 Picon, *Claude Perrault*.

151 Picon, *Claude Perrault*, 138, n. 43.

protection of this powerful brother, along with the status Perrault had earned through his scientific work—a status reconfirmed by Colbert's commission to translate the Roman treatise—allowed him some independence from the Académie establishment and the positions taken by its director François Blondel (1618–1686).[152] This independence was asserted in Perrault's later *Ordonnance des cinq espèces de colonnes selon la méthode des anciens*,[153] which put forth his theory of architecture in opposition to the thesis published by Blondel in his *Cours d'architecture* between 1675 and 1683.[154] The quarrel between Blondel and Perrault emulated the "*querelle des Anciens et Modernes*" in literature that had taken place some years earlier between Charles Perrault (1628–1703) and his opponent Nicolas Boileau (1636–1711) over the relevance of antique sources to the development of contemporary culture. Blondel and Perrault used the medium of books as support for their similar dispute over the foundations of architectural theory. The fifth and final volume of the *Cours* was published in 1683, the same year as the *Ordonnance*, and the following year Perrault presented the second and definitive edition of his large folio Vitruvius. In terms of its layout and form, the 1684 edition was close to that of 1673 but the comments were reformulated in response to Blondel's arguments. Nonetheless, this debate was not directly evident in the book but occurs between the lines. The paradox of Perrault's Vitruvius is that, despite his philological care and accuracy in translating the Roman text, he supported the renewal of the conceptual field in which architecture operates, namely the development of a modern architectural theory. Vitruvius granted his translator,

---

152 On the purposes and activities of the French Academy, see Anthony Gerbino, "Blondel, Colbert et l'origine de l'Académie royale d'architecture," ed. Jean-Philippe Garric, Frédérique Lemerle, and Yves Pauwels, in *Architecture et théorie: L'héritage de la Renaissance*, online ed. (Paris: Institut National d'Histoire de l'Art, 2010), 20–25, https://books.openedition.org/inha/3394.

153 Claude Perrault, *Ordonnance des cinq espèces de colonnes selon la méthode des anciens* (Paris: Jean Baptiste Coignard, 1683).

154 François Blondel, *Cours d'architecture enseigné dans l'Academie royale d'architecture* (Paris: Lambert Roulland, 1675–1683).

an outsider, the authority to challenge the higher instances of the Académie d'architecture. As Perrault argued, "the great authority [Vitruvius's] writings have always had, made his precepts the ones that established the true rules of beauty and perfection in buildings," and "if nature does not supply such rules ... human institutions must do so, and in order to accomplish this, agreement must be reached as to some authority which will take the place of positive reason."[155] Hence Perrault's Vitruvius performed various functions: (1) it rescued Vitruvius's text from oblivion after being marginalized by the adoption of the architectural orders as normative precepts; (2) it granted Perrault an authoritative status matching the prestige of the Roman author; and (3) it grounded an intense debate on various aspects of architectural theory, nurturing further writings and publications to sustain the positions of the authors involved.

One year after the publication of his first Vitruvius, Perrault got rid of the most cumbersome parts of the Vitruvian text in a compact octavo edition. The resulting *Abrégé des dix livres d'architecture de Vitruve* was an entirely new construction in which Perrault's appropriation of the text reflects his own ideas, with no apparent concern for the original sense.[156] As Antoine Picon has underlined, the *Abrégé* is a key turn toward the theoretical framework that would later be deployed in the *Ordonnance* and that centers on the distinction between positive and arbitrary beauties. Unlike the typographical achievements of Fra Giocondo, who in 1513 squeezed the contents of his 1511 quarto into an octavo by means of italics and new woodcuts, Perrault took out most of the images and cleaned up the layout of the *Abrégé* to eliminate all the complexity, the multiple layers, and the visual content of its parent.[157]

---

155 Quoted in McEwen, "On Claude Perrault," 323–324.

156 See Olga Medvedkova, "Un *Abrégé* moderne ou Vitruve selon la méthode," in *La construction savante: Les avatars de la littérature technique* (Paris: Picard, 2008), 43–53.

157 An *Abrégé* of Vitruvius was not a complete novelty. In the third century, Cetius Faventinus authored the *Artis architectonicce privatis usibus abreviatur liber*,

As Olga Medvedkova has shown, a sophisticated system of parallel cross-references, brackets, and epitomes reference Vitruvius while allowing Perrault to insert his own arguments in support of an original new narrative. It is not surprising that this concise and affordable octavo of 1674 was Perrault's most successful Vitruvius, more frequently reprinted than the lavish 1673 folio.[158] The first reprint of the octavo was made in Amsterdam in 1681,[159] even before Perrault expanded the large edition with his rebuttal of Blondel's critique.

Perrault died in 1688, and in 1692 his *Abrégé* was translated and published in London as *An Abridgment of the Architecture of Vitruvius*.[160] This English text was based on the Amsterdam reprint, subsequently reorganized for a 1703 edition,[161] and then in 1708 printed together with a translation of the *Ordonnance* as *A Treatise of the Five Orders of Columns in Architecture*.[162] The international travels of the *Abrégé* took it to Italy in 1711—it appeared as the *Compendio dell'architettura generale di Vitruvio* translated by Carlo Cataneo, who

---

which extracted a number of useful points on domestic architecture from its source. There was also, as previously discussed, the French epitome of Jan Gardet and Dominique Bertin. Medvedkova, "Un *Abrégé* moderne," here 43–44.

158 The *Abrégé*'s cover price of 3 livres was likely a factor in its commercial success in relation to Perrault's other books: the *Ordonnance* folio cost 9 livres, and the lavish *Vitruve* sold for 22. The subsequent Amsterdam reprint, soon to serve as the basis of the English and Italian translations, extended its popularity. Medvedkova, "Un *Abrégé* moderne," here 47.

159 The title page mentions 1681, whereas the frontispiece shows 1691. Bibliographers believe the correct date to be 1681. See Frédérique Lemerle, "Une édition de l'Abrégé," ed. Frédérique Lemerle and Yves Pauwels, in *Architectura: Architecture, textes et images (XVIe–XVIIe siècles)*, online (Tours: Centre d'Études Supérieures de la Renaissance, Université François-Rabelais, 2011), http://architectura.cesr.univ-tours.fr/Traite/Notice/PerraultCl1681.asp?param=.

160 Harris and Savage, *British Architectural Books*, 462–463, n. 891.

161 A second printing was issued in 1729. Harris and Savage, *British Architectural Books*, 463, nn. 892, 893.

162 It was translated by John James (ca. 1672–1746). The book was sold by subscription and 269 subscribers were listed, the book being published in March 1707. Robin Middleton, Gerald Beasley, and Nicholas Savage, *British Books: Seventeenth through Nineteenth Centuries*, 4 vols., The Mark J. Millard Architectural Collection, vol. 2 (Washington, DC: National Gallery of Art, 1998), https://www.nga.gov/content/dam/ngaweb/research/publications/pdfs/mark-j-millard-british-books.pdf, 207–209; Harris and Savage, *British Architectural Books*, 368–371, nn. 700, 701.

14 Perrault 1681, frontispiece of pirated French abridged edition published in Amsterdam and used as source for the first English translation

followed the Amsterdam reprint instead of the original Parisian edition, with new editions in 1747 and 1794 enriched by the always appreciated comments of Barbaro—and to Nuremberg, Würzburg, and Prague in 1757—in a German-language triple-location edition set in blackletter with the title *Des grossen und weltberühmten Vitruvii Architectura*. It was then made to speak Spanish by José Castañeda (d. 1766), who translated it from the Italian edition. Published in Madrid in 1761, the text made its return to Paris, where the Spanish edition was reprinted in 1768. It traveled even farther in 1789, when the first Russian translation was published in Moscow.[163]

The international career of the *Abrégé* granted Perrault a wide readership and made Paris the central point of the discussion of the fundamentals of architectural theory. His impact was so strong that some scholars go as far as positioning his Vitruvius editions as the end of a Vitruvian treatise era.[164] It was Perrault's polemic verve and challenging theoretical propositions—backed up by a growing interest in French philosophy and science—that granted him this prominent position. Worth noting is that to some extent, between the large apparatus of the folio edition and the compact octavo version, as Vitruvius's authority increased, the Roman author's actual arguments faded away. The form of the books sustained Per-

---

163 The Russian edition of the *Abrégé* preceded the Russian translation of Perrault's complete Vitruvius, published by the Imperial Academy of Sciences in serial form between 1790 and 1797. Vasily Bazhenov (1737–1799), a leading architect in the service of Catherine the Great, worked on this key Vitruvian translation. Although it was the first Russian Vitruvius to be published, an earlier Russian translation, dating from 1757, exists in manuscript. See Branko Mitrovic, "Studying Renaissance Architectural Theory in the Age of Stalinism," *I Tatti Studies in the Italian Renaissance* 12 (2009): 233–263, https://www.jstor.org/stable/27809576?seq=1#metadata_info_tab_contents, here 247, n. 32.

164 See, for instance, Vaughan Hart, "'Paper Palaces' from Alberti to Scamozzi," ed. Vaughan Hart and Peter Hicks, in *Paper Palaces: The Rise of the Renaissance Architectural Treatise* (New Haven, CT: Yale University Press, 1998), 1–29. On pages 10 and 11, Hart argues that the "gradual loss of vitality in Vitruvian debate" relates to the conflict between the ambiguous proportional systems of the Vitruvian orders and the rise of mathematical knowledge, leading to the idea that the "immutable basis of architecture in universal harmony as recorded by Vitruvius" was "founded on nothing more than human judgement and taste."

rault's ambition to construct an argument that, backed by the classical author, would become more relevant than the original text. Hence the subtle strangeness of the 1946 collector's edition of Perrault,[165] a book which includes just the translation. The editor explained that "the notes, headlines, and figures that comment or illustrate [Vitruvius's text] in the 1673 edition were not added. They are the work of the translator only."[166] It was a curious move, editing Perrault's Vitruvius stripped of Perrault and relaying only his translation of the Vitruvian text.

To underline Perrault's achievement, it is worth comparing his work to some unsuccessful contemporary attempts to translate Vitruvius into English. In 1670, while the French edition was being prepared, Christopher Wase (1625–1690) launched a subscription campaign to fund his ongoing translation. He published the preface and first chapter[167] but could not raise enough funds to proceed. Another failed English Vitruvius was undertaken by Robert Castell (d. 1728),[168] who launched his call for subscriptions in 1728[169] following Lord Burlington's recognition of the need for an English translation.[170] Castell was incarcerated for unpaid debts and tragically died in prison

---

165 Set by hand in Garamond type and printed on laid paper with a limited print run of 115 copies.

166 Perrault 1946, n.p.

167 The only remaining evidence of these chapters is in Christopher Wase, "Certain Humble Propositions", Bodleian MS CCC c 378. Referenced in Harris and Savage, *British Architectural Books*, 462.

168 Sir John Clerk went on an architectural tour from Edinburgh to London in 1727 in the company of his architect William Adam, the father of Robert and James Adams. Clerk visited Lord Burlington and Chiswick, where he must have been encouraged to undertake editorial projects. Through his correspondence with William Aikman, we learn that in the autumn of that year Clerk encouraged his son James, who was then studying in London with Aikman, to buy "a Vitruvius with Barabaro's notes" and translate it into English. The project was dropped once they learned that a translation of Vitruvius was already being "undertaken by the author of Pliny's Gardens," presumably Robert Castell. This abandoned editorial project might have been the seed of William Adam's also failed *Vitruvius Scoticus*, which was nonetheless continued and published later with significant differences. See John Fleming, *Robert Adam and his Circle in Edinburgh & Rome* (London: John Murray, 1962), 28, 48–49.

169 Harris and Savage, *British Architectural Books*, 464.

170 Royal Institute of British Architects, *Early Printed Books*, no. 3507, 2289–2290. On Burlington, see this book's section "Model and Theory".

without ever publishing it,[171] leaving biographers to wonder why Burlington did not come to his rescue.[172] It was not until 1771, almost a century after Perrault's first edition, that William Newton (1730–1798) published an English translation of the first five books of Vitruvius without calling for advance subscription. The edition did not sell well, and a second edition, which comprised all Ten Books,[173] was printed just after Newton's death in a print run equal to the number of unsold copies of the first edition, which received new title pages with a new imprint.[174]

Perrault's authority came from his large folio edition, but it was a translation of his *Abrégé* (from the Amsterdam octavo) that first introduced him to English readers in 1692. In 1703 the text was further abridged by Abel Boyer (1667–1729) to produce a new and even more abbreviated English version, stripped of marginal comments and references to the original Vitruvian structure,[175] and combined, in a tour de force of classical references, with a new printing of Joseph Moxon's (1627–1691) plates for Vignola.[176] The result was an affordable pocket book that addressed a practical readership and aimed to combine theory and practice in a unified corpus. It reflects at once the progressive erosion of Vitruvius's text and the propensity to reduce the orders to a standard method for

171 Many Vitruvian bibliographies feature a reference to Castell's 1730 edition. Nonetheless, the existence of such a book or manuscript has not been verified to date.

172 Harris and Savage, *British Architectural Books*, 464.

173 Newton published *Commentaires sur Vitruve* in 1780, where he discussed Perrault's and Galiani's translations and interpretations. Harris and Savage, *British Architectural Books*, no. 896, 465. On later English publications in French, see Olga Medvedkova, "L'édition des livres d'architecture en français dans l'Angleterre du XVIIIe siècle," ed. Daniel Rabreau and Dominique Massounie, in *Claude Nicolas Ledoux et le livre d'architecture en français, Étienne Louis Boullée: L'utopie et la poésie de l'art* (Paris: Editions du Patrimoine, 2006), 72–85.

174 Harris and Savage, *British Architectural Books*, 463–467, nos. 894, 895.

175 This edition was still available in 1729, and the remaining copies were reissued with a new imprint. Harris and Savage, *British Architectural Books*, no. 892, no. 893, 463.

176 Moxon, the son of a printer, was a distinguished mapmaker and hydrographer who, amongst his publications, translated Vignola into English in 1655, likely from Pierre Le Muet's (1591–1669) 1650 Dutch version. See Harris and Savage, *British Architectural Books*, 324–325, 458–459.

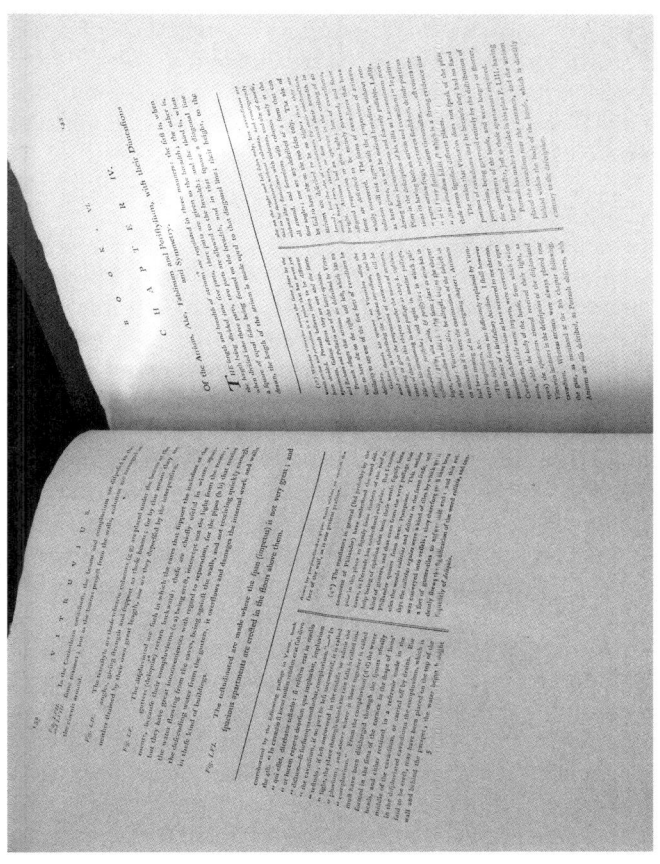

15 Newton 1791, Book VI, Chapter 3. The first printed English translation in 1771 was limited to the first five books, and the edition was completed twenty years later

architectural design, while its compact, portable format accompanied and encouraged these processes. Here, theory and practice meet—an encounter depicted in the frontispiece by means of a smiling bust of Vignola that faces an imposing Vitruvius.

The beginning of the eighteenth century saw Vitruvius's text lose its tightness in successive declensions of the content, but it also gained cultural momentum by means of a renewed presence of theory within architectural practice. It is in this context that the luxurious quality and refined texture of Perrault's folio edition sustained the French writer's authority. If we look carefully beyond the exquisite engravings at its page layout, the sheets are distinct from those of earlier editions in the use of two columns to set the commentary. Each chapter is defined by a centered header followed by a description of the chapter's content in 12-point italics. The main text runs the width of the page from margin to margin and is set at 10 points, with commentary laid out below it in two columns of 9-point text. The inner margins have helpful letter markers that situate the reader within the page (A, B, C, D, E) and lend it a regular rhythm, while the outer margins contain abbreviated references to the chapters, assisting navigation within the book and space for annotations. This complex structure consolidated a system that coherently articulates the various voices within the book, surpassing the subtle distinctions made by Barbaro's dual use of roman and italic type, the independent nature of Philandrier's comments, or the resonances with manuscript culture adopted in Cesariano's dialogue. The engravings were carefully synchronized with the letterpress such that the text and images are printed on the same sheets. These editorial extravagances confer the book with a powerful aesthetic that matches the refinement of the French translation and the incisive comments. Thus it is not surprising that, regardless of the wider circulation of pocket-size translations and other variations of Perrault's editions, the folio editions of 1763 and 1784 have become a key reference in the field.

16 Perrault 1703, Vignola facing Vitruvius in the frontispiece of combined "Theory and Practice." English translation by Abel Boyer

The second half of the eighteenth century brought significant novelty to Vitruvian scholarship. In 1738 King Charles VII of Naples (also Charles V of Sicily and Charles III of Spain, 1716–1788) invested the archaeological excavations of Pompeii and Herculaneum with a relevant political and ideological bias. The antiquities, excavated and displayed in royal collections, gave the monarchy an illustrated prestige and attracted prominent European intellectuals to the Bay of Naples. The unexpected result was the reconfiguration of archaeology as an academic discipline.[177] The excavations were first conducted by Roque Joaquín de Alcubierre (1702–1780), who secured strict royal control over the discoveries, a possessive vision that challenged the idea of the past as collective knowledge and prompted criticism, mainly from foreign visitors. Alcubierre favored the collection of objects that ultimately would become part of the royal collection and published in lavishly illustrated books. One of his assistants, the Swiss Karl Weber (1712–1764), favored a topographical approach that placed the objects within their contexts. This resulted in comprehensive plans being drawn up between 1750 and 1756 that comprise a first portrait of Pompeii, its architecture, and the excavation process, but that remained unpublished until the nineteenth century.[178] Apart from the official teams working on the digs, access to the archaeological sites was restricted to maintain control over the discoveries being made, and those visitors admitted were not allowed to draw or take notes on site. The regulations were not relaxed until the beginning of the nineteenth century, when archaeologists like François Mazois were permitted to produce comprehensive representations of the site and its architecture for publication. This selective

---

177 See Alain Schnapp, "The Antiquarian Culture of Eighteenth-Century Naples as a Laboratory of New Ideas," ed. Carol C. Mattusch, in *Rediscovering the Ancient World on the Bay of Naples, 1710–1890* (Washington, DC: National Gallery of Art, 2013), 13–34.

178 Christopher Charles Parslow, *Rediscovering Antiquity: Karl Weber and the Excavation of Herculaneum, Pompeii and Stabiae* (Cambridge: Cambridge University Press, 1995), 177–198.

and progressive release of findings from Pompeii and Herculaneum explains the relative delay in incorporating newfound archaeological knowledge into commentaries on Vitruvius, with the exception being Berardo Galiani (1724–1774) who first brought Pompeii into the Vitruvian canon.

In 1758, aiming to surpass Perrault in faithfulness to the Roman authority, Galiani's edition proved to be a key turning point in Vitruvian book history. Despite following Perrault's page structure, and praising the merits of his work,[179] he developed his translation and studies in a different direction. Galiani was working in Naples, where he followed the progress of the ongoing archaeological digs, meeting local scholars and international visitors drawn to this significant source of ancient Roman vestiges.[180] Galiani reinvested the Vitruvian agenda with the philological bias that had characterized Giocondo's 1511 edition. Like Barbaro, he developed his own Latin version along with the translation, but instead of publishing it in a separate book he presented the Latin text in italic type on the even pages, facing the translation set in roman type on the odd pages. The commentary, set at the bottom of the page in two columns with smaller type, unifies the page sequence. At the end of each book, the illustrations recall the archaeological evidence that informed the scholarly path followed by the author. Unlike the bridging of theory and practice of architecture being attempted in England, Galiani brought back Vitruvius as a key author through which to rediscover Roman antiquities.

This archaeological trend is confirmed by the Spanish translation of José Francisco Ortiz y Sanz (1739–1822) in 1787, a work sponsored by King Carlos III of Spain, to whom, in his capacity as King of Naples, Galiani had also dedicated

---

179 "Perrault is doubtless the only one who deserves every and until now singular esteem for the the utility of his well-reasoned remarks and for the clarity of his version," Galiani 1758, iv, translated by the author.

180 Galiani encountered the German art historian and archaelogist Johann Joachim Winckelmann while excavating Herculaneum. See Steffi Roettgen, "German Painters in Naples and Their Contribution to the Revival of Antiquity 1760–1799," ed. Carol C. Mattusch, in *Rediscovering the Ancient World on the Bay of Naples, 1710–1890* (Washington, DC: National Gallery of Art, 2013), 123–140, here 126.

17 Galiani 1758, Book VI, Chapter 3, multiple layers of content containing Latin, translation, comments, illustration captions, and navigation cross-references

his impressive Italian edition. After beginning the translation in Spain, Ortiz y Sanz felt the need to experience the material remains of Roman architecture, so he traveled to Rome and Naples to conduct surveys and studies—both at archaeological sites and in libraries—that would inform his work.[181] The translation is similar to Newton's English version in structure and ambition, aiming for an archaeological accuracy that sidesteps the debate over theory and practice. Perrault's influence is also felt. Not only did Ortiz y Sanz replicate the use of a single column for the main text and double columns for the commentary, he managed to make his edition even larger than Perrault's, with pages 48 centimeters high. As such, Ortiz y Sanz's translation belongs to a group of folio editions that includes those of Galiani, Newton, and Perrault—the latter understood as an oeuvre as grand as the French nation—designed to be read on cradles in libraries and meticulously studied along with other books. This scholarly approach was consistent with the practice of the Grand Tour and the study of architectural antiquities, be they Greek, Roman, Egyptian, or Persian.[182] As such, in the library Vitruvius's text would meet volumes that provided a visual record of ancient ruins produced by authors such Julian-David Le Roy (1724–1803), James Stuart (1713–1788), or Nicholas Revett (1720–1804).

It is hard to imagine what would have become of Vitruvius without Perrault. Until the twentieth century's continuous series of editions, Perrault was the most successful and most reprinted Vitruvian author.[183] His work propelled the rediscovery of Vitruvius in various languages, including Italian, and the expansion of its readership as far away as Russia. The

---

181 His edition was laid out with a main text column followed by a double column for commentaries, the plates organized in an independent volume with the captions running on parallel pages.

182 On the Grand Tour and its books, see Robin Middleton, "Introduction," in *The Ruins of the Most Beautiful Monuments of Greece*, by Julien-David Le Roy, 1st ed. 1758 (Los Angeles: Getty Research Institute, 2004), 1–199.

183 He would ultimately be overtaken by Frank Granger in English and by the twentieth-century editions of Ortiz y Sanz and Augustín Blánquez. On later Perrault reprints, see the next section.

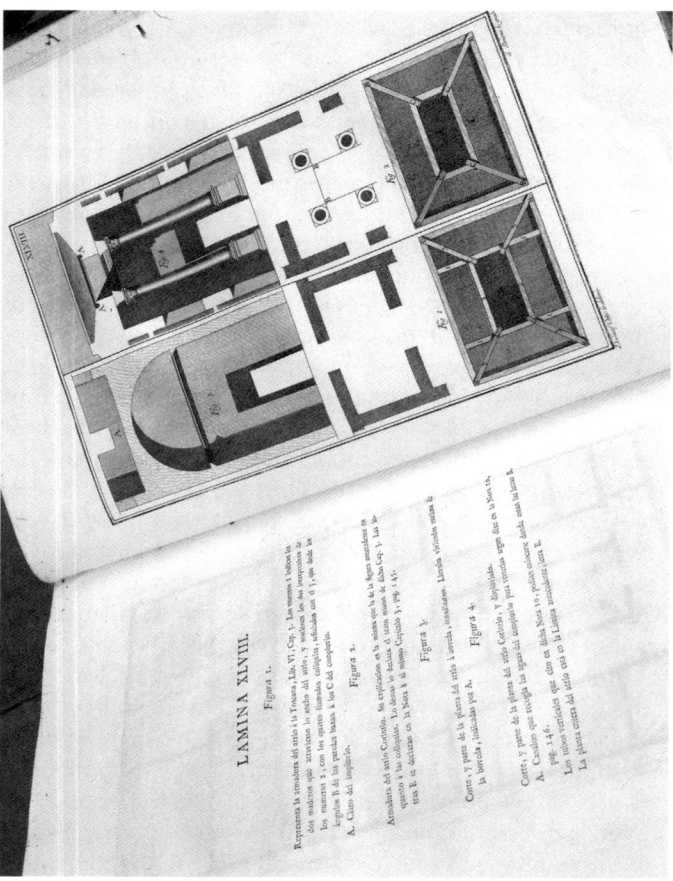

18 Ortiz y Sanz 1787, Book VI, Chapter 3, plate XLVIII, illustration of *cavaedia*

Vitruvian revival inspired by Perrault's successful venture in support of the French Académie accompanied a growing investment in architectural education in France, and beyond that provided a theoretical framework for the transmission of architectural knowledge. Vitruvius's authority, invoked and defended by Perrault to his own benefit, made the Roman author a compulsory reference to be quoted in every architectural argument, from the primitive hut to the origin of the orders. If in the sixteenth century every translator orchestrated the text to suit his own interests, Perrault unabashedly went further, pushing the content well beyond its original purpose while retaining the authority granted by the text's ancient pedigree. This unprecedented flexibility, not so obvious in the sixteenth-century editions, began to be expected in the seventeenth century, and the multiplicity of interpretations of Vitruvius that circulated as a result made it an intricate task—if not an impossible one—to unravel the various meanings assigned to Vitruvius as an authority. Thus for most readers, the purpose of a given edition was intuited not through a demanding critical assessment of its content but by considering its size, layout, and, ultimately, its cover price.

DIFFUSE KNOWLEDGE, 1796–1909

The production of paper in continuous rolls changed the book industry.[184] Steam and steel mechanized the craft-based manufacturing process, replacing the previous single-page printing rhythm with rolling presses. This shift generated a continuous flow of book production, with dramatically expanded print runs, at a scale that implied serious investment and risk.[185] By the 1830s the book trade was dominated by the industrialized book. Printers were now service providers to publishers, and publishers became experts in marketing books by developing a relationship between an author and their readers. This had a tremendous impact upon the trade, with distribution networks placing booksellers in closer contact with new clienteles to take advantage of and encourage expanding markets. There were more books and more readers. In architecture, this shift coincided with the establishment of formal education systems, both Beaux-Arts and polytechnic, that required textbooks and thus amplified the expansion of the readership for architectural books. With his authority renewed by Perrault

---

184 See Mark Kurlansky, *Paper: Paging Through History* (New York: W. W. Norton, 2016).

185 These technical changes in book production cannot be separated from political and geographical shifts that helped to grow the book industry, enlarging readership by means of better public education and higher literacy rates and developing wider and more efficient networks for commercial distribution. See Frédéric Barbier, "L'industrialisation des techniques," in *Histoire de l'édition française: Le temps des éditeurs; Du romantisme à la Belle Époque*, by Roger Chartier and Henri-Jean Martin, 1st ed. 1985, vol. 3 (Paris: Fayard/Cercle de la Librairie, 1990), 51–66.

and his treatise considered the foundational work of architectural theory, Vitruvius enjoyed a nineteenth-century growth.

The three books authored by August Rode (1751–1837) between 1796 and 1801 show the effects of the industrialization of bookmaking.[186] The pages of the 1796 edition, a German translation published in Leipzig, are rather wide, with a 1:1.2 ratio instead of the conventional 1:1.5. More significantly, the paper texture is strange to the touch, denoting a shift from fiber- to pulp-based manufacturing. The format is the same for the 1800 Latin version with a Berlin imprint,[187] but the pulp-based paper is even more precarious, its near-translucent pages a sign of its low quality, a flop for the paper producer. Only the frontispieces to these editions were illustrated, with the "forms" published in a third book featuring a taller 1:1.6-ratio page format, comprising copper engravings with their captions presented on separate letterpress pages. The strange proportions and the non-matching formats—the text volumes being different from the volume of the images—give Rode's edition a singular presence in the history of Vitruvian publishing, presaging the variety of formats and qualities to come. Before Rode, there were three categories of Vitruvius editions, with minor variations: (1) the large folio, like those by Cesariano, Barbaro (the first 1556 edition), Perrault, Galiano, and Ortiz y Sanz; (2) the quarto, like those by Veroli, Giocondo, and the second editions by Ryff and Barbaro; and (3) the octavo, like the second Giocondo, the first Ryff, Philandrier's comments, and the second Perrault. All of these editions had a pre-industrial feeling that was upturned by Rode's books.

As Georg Germann pointed out,[188] Rode's Vitruvius volumes signal a triple allegiance in combining philological re-

---

186 They were reprinted in 1987 in Zurich by Artemis, then in 1995 and 2001 in Basel.

187 Royal Institute of British Architects, *Early Printed Books*, no. 3502, 2283–2284.

188 Georg Germann, "Vitruv, Vitruvianismus und Rodes Übersetzung," in Rode 1987, vol. 1, 7–24.

19 Rode 1801. The nineteenth century was dominated by German editions, a trend set by Rode, which marked Vitruvius's industrialization.

search with recent archaeological evidence and thus achieving the ambitious project of renewing architectural theory and practice. They are indebted to Friedrich Wilhelm von Erdmannsdorff (1736–1800), the subject of a biography Rode published in 1801[189] and to whom the 1796 Vitruvius is dedicated. Erdmannsdorff was a cultivated architect and another aspiring translator of Vitruvius, whose classical knowledge was fostered by time spent in Rome, where he had met the renowed art historian and archaeologist Johann Joachim Winckelmann (1717–1768). The Palladian tones of Erdmannsdorff's Schloss Wörlitz, built near Dessau, established his reputation as being responsible for the resurgence of antique models in the German-speaking world, and this architectural practice in turn inspired the theoretical bias of Rode's work. Rode's is the second German translation of Vitruvius, and he is credited with putting Vitruvius into "the fluent language of Goethe's era,"[190] renewing the interest of German speakers in the Roman author. In fact, these German editions released at the opening of the nineteenth century were of paramount importance to Vitruvian scholarship: Rode's allegiance to Erdmannsdorff gave his enterprise a contemporary architectural pedigree, while the subsequent Latin edition of 1800 highlights his commitment to philology, and the 1801 plates include attempts to update the archaeological surveys of antique architectural design. This triple orientation is to be found again a century later in the 1909 edition by Auguste Choisy.

In the chronology, Rode is followed by Baldassare Orsini (1732–1810), who published his Italian translation as a rather simple and straightforward set of two octavo volumes in Perugia in 1802, with cheap-looking engravings and an unambitious letterpress. The edges of the type on the text pages are blurry due to the ink having been drawn into the ab-

---

[189] Auguste Rode, *Leben des Herrn Friedrich Wilhelm von Erdmannsdorff*, reprint of Dessau: H. Jänzer, 1801 (Wörlitz: Kettmann, 1994).

[190] Beat Wyss, "Editorische Notiz" in Rode 1987, vol. 1, 5, translated by the author.

20 Orsini 1802, a tetrastyle *cavaedium* in a compact octavo edition with cheap-looking engravings

sorbent paper.[191] Prior to his Vitruvius, Orsini had published a treatise on geometry and drafted an architectural treatise in 1778, *Dell'architettura civile*.[192] In the latter work, which remained unpublished,[193] Orsini focuses on the connections between geometrical principles and systems of architectural composition, an approach further developed in his role as director of the Accademia del Disegno in Perugia. This didactic link explains the publication of his translation in an affordable pocket format.

In the following years, Vitruvius was published in a wide range of forms and places. In 1807 two octavo Latin versions were published, both with a rather scholarly apparatus and almost no illustrations: in Strasbourg, by the Bipontina society, and in Lepizig, in the three volumes of Gottlob Schneider (1750–1822). In 1812 William Wilkins (1778–1839) began publishing his English translation—at which we will look in more detail—with Books III to VI. His venture was completed with a reissue including the last plates in 1817. In 1816 Jean-Michel de Moreau (1765–1835), known as Moreau de Bioul, published a French translation in Brussels, the format of which was close to Rode's but with plates integrated into the text volume. In 1823, and again in 1832, Galiani's edition was reprinted in Milan. In 1826 John Weale (1791–1862), one of the major British architectural publishers of the nineteenth century, issued an English translation by Joseph Gwilt (1784–1863) that would be reprinted several times, the last being in 1909. In 1829/1830, in Milan, Carlo Amati (1776–1852) issued a new Italian translation in various installments.[194] Between 1825 and 1830 Simone Stratico

---

191 The two volumes were preceded by a Vitruvian dictionary: Baldassarre Orsini, *Dizionario universale d'architettura e dizionario Vitruviano* (Perugia: Carlo Baduel e Figli, 1801).

192 Baldassarre Orsini, *Della geometria e prospettiva pratica*, 2 vols. (Rome: Benedetto Franzesi, 1771–1772).

193 See Adriana Soletti and Paolo Belardi, *Dell'architettura civile di Baldassarre Orsini* (Rome: Officina Edizioni, 1997).

194 "The fly-title to each book always formed the first leaf of a new fascicle." Royal Institute of British Architects, *Early Printed Books*, no. 3529, 2306.

21 Moreau de Bioul 1816, remake of Tuscan and tetrastyle cavaedia as illustrated by Galiani

(1733–1825) published his eight-volume "acme of all learned editions of Vitruvius,"[195] which continued the strategy of accumulating Vitruvian scholarly apparatuses, including his own detailed comments, the parallel content of the 1649 de Laet edition, and Giovanni Poleni's *Exercitationes Vitruvianae* of 1739 to 1741. But it was Quirico Viviani's (1780–1835) Italian translation, published between 1830 and 1833, that distended the forms of the published Vitruvian body of architecture. His publication was an extended set of eleven volumes with vertically exaggerated pages in a 1:1.7 ratio.[196] The plates are printed on folded pages at the end of each volume with the images offset to leave a large blank space to the left of each sheet, allowing the reader to unfold any image sheet and leave it visible while reading the text.[197] Viviani's edition is distinguished in that it was the first to present each book of Vitruvius as a separate volume—a daring move that challenged the unity of the Vitruvian body.

The nineteenth-century editorial frenzy around Vitruvius was even more intense than that of the hectic decades of the sixteenth century bookended by the publication of Giocondo's illustrations and Barbaro's translations. It was also more geographically and intellectually diverse, which is mirrored in the variety of formats and shapes of the books produced. The two 1836 editions, issued in Leipzig and Rome, offer a sense of the range. The modest Leipzig edition is a single octavo volume of 250 pages in Latin—Viviani's volumes have about 2,000 pages in total—that was issued by Karl Tauchnitz (1761–1836), a publisher known for affordable editions of classical texts. In contrast, its Roman counterpart is a luxury

---

195 Royal Institute of British Architects, *Early Printed Books*, no. 3505, 2287.

196 Viviani 1830–1833. The Werner Oechslin Library copy has eleven volumes, corresponding to the Ten Books plus the indexes. The copy held at the Centro Internazionale di Studi di Architettura Andrea Palladio in Vicenza is bound in five volumes.

197 There is a curious discrepancy between the plates, which were likely printed later than the text: Book III contains the plates related to Book I, and so forth. This complicates the process of unfolding the plates at the end of the volume to juxtapose text and illustration, requiring the reader to match the volume containing the text to that with the corresponding images.

four-volume set in Latin by Luigi Marini (1768–1838), to which three additional volumes in Italian were added the following year. The Italian volumes are elephant folios more than 53 centimeters high, making them the largest Vitruvius books ever published.[198] The grandeur of the complete set of seven volumes is overwhelming: the type, cast specifically for this edition and the letterpress, subdivided sections of text, amendments, and comments on the illustrations, forming an elegant block bounded by vast margins of heavy, smooth paper. From Leipzig in the north to Rome in the south, the 1836 crop of Vitruvius publications were widely contrasting, shaping the content for different purposes and to appeal to different readers.

The 1817 William Wilkins edition, *The Civil Architecture of Vitruvius*, is limited to Books III through to VI and reflects an interest in Greek architecture that was characteristic of the author's generation. Wilkins was an active architect whose education included a Grand Tour between 1801 and 1803.[199] Like many of his peers, Wilkins was drawn to visit Athens. While there, he surveyed various ancient buildings, compiling a portfolio that would later inform his architectural practice in England, including the controversial construction of the National Gallery between 1832 and 1838. An expert in Greek antiquities—he published *The Antiquities of Magna Graecia* in 1807—he criticized his predecessors who grounded their readings of Vitruvius in the assessment of Roman antiquities alone. For the 1812 to 1817 Vitruvius, Wilkins carefully structured the plates in support of his argument by means of detailed engravings that stress an allegiance to Greek architecture. Printed in two sizes,[200] the book was still available in the mid-1820s, and it is significant that John Weale acquired Wilkins's copyrights

---

198 The RIBA Library copy is 43.6 cm tall. Royal Institute of British Architects, *Early Printed Books*, no. 3506, 2288–2289; and no. 3531, 2308–2309.

199 See R. W. Liscombe, *William Wilkins 1778–1839* (Cambridge: Cambridge University Press, 1980). See also the short description of Wilkins's Grand Tour on the website of Downing College Cambridge, https://www.dow.cam.ac.uk/about/downing-college-archive/archives/william-wilkins-grand-tour.

200 Royal Institute of British Architects, *Early Printed Books*, no. 3534, 2310–2311.

22 Marini 1836, a gigantic four-volume edition with deluxe paper and exquisite printing

in 1822. It is not clear what the business between Weale and Wilkins was,[201] but it could be related to the eventual success of Weale's 1826 publication of Gwilt's translation—"the standard translation into English throughout the nineteenth century"[202] —printed in a more economical format. This acquisition of the rights to a refined Greek Revival edition to allow a publisher to create a favorable market for a cheaper edition in a large print run signals the industrialization of Vitruvius. Instead of relying on the agendas or predispositions of authors, publishers now negotiated and speculated on the economics of books based on market predictions.

The first sign of this new business model was the resurgence of previous editions released in updated formats. In France, Perrault was as commercially successful as Gwilt was with English readers. In 1837 Eugène Tardieu and Jean-Antoine Coussin (1770–1849) presented a "rectified" edition of Perrault's full translation and comments that they claimed eliminated the "nonsenses" of the then 150-year-old text.[203] They enriched their edition with some passages from Galiani and separated the text—similar to the latter in its page layout—from the images. Although some new images were added, the sequence was still driven by Perrault's original, with versions of his illustrations freshly engraved in outline form. The result lends the book a very different visual resonance, with the naturalistic images of the buildings stripped of context and detached from their analytical representation. This edition was reprinted in 1859 and again in 1866. Another edition was published in 1846 by Désiré Nisard (1806–1888), whose fo-

---

201 Royal Institute of British Architects, *Early Printed Books*, no. 3534, 2311. The authors of the RIBA catalogue remark that "this purchase may have been motivated by Weale's desire to build up a list of architectural publications in the early 1820s," and that "it is not clear whether the sale was instigated by Wilkins (trying to make some capital from the work before a rival appeared) or by Weale (in order to control a possible competitor to Gwilt's translation)."

202 Royal Institute of British Architects, *Early Printed Books*, no. 3508, 2291. Gwilt's Vitruvius was later reprinted as number 128 of Weale's popular Rudimentary Series, and in 1909 a new reprint of the 1860 edition came out under the imprint of Crosby, Lockwood and Company.

203 Perrault 1837, v.

23 Galiani/Schneider 1854. Scholarly editions were dominated by dense text and commentaries

cus was on classical references. His adaptation of Perrault's translation was published as part of the series *Collection des auteurs latins* in a volume that also includes Vitruvius's usual companion, Frontinus's aqueducts, as well as other Roman authors. Perrault's notes are relegated to an independent chapter at the end of the Vitruvius section, and a Latin version of the text matching the French translation is added to each page. None of the images were reproduced. Nisard's edition was reprinted in 1852, 1857, and 1877.[204] These editions would take over the space Moreau de Bioul had attempted to occupy with his 1816 Brussels edition and proved more efficient than a new translation—also unillustrated and paired with Latin—by Charles-Louis Maufras (1805?–1859) issued by the publishing house of Panckoucke in 1847 and reprinted in 1850.

These two successful editions of Perrault display the duality that Vitruvius acquired during the nineteenth century. On one hand, architects looked to the treatise and the descriptive captions to the illustrations as design references; on the other, scholars preferred to be able to compare the contemporary translation to the so-called "original" Latin text. Continuous book-market growth motivated reprints representing both editorial strategies. As such, publishers began to profile themselves by distinguishing all of these books from one another, and thus the authorial contributions of translators, commentators, and editors began to be overshadowed by the name on the book imprint: readers now asked for "Nisard's Vitruvius" or "Tardieu and Coussin's Vitruvius" rather than for "Perrault's Vitruvius." Thus instead of continuing to consider his work mainly as a reference for a given contemporary theo-

---

204 Perrault's editorial life would continue on into the twentieth century. The Italian version of the *Abrégé* was again reprinted in 1938 and 1943, and the Spanish *Compendio* was also reprinted in 1981. In France, after the 1946 edition, a new edition was organized by André Dalmas in 1965, to be reprinted in 1967 and 1986. In 1979 the Belgian publisher Mardaga undertook a new edition, published again in 1995 as a facsimile.

retical or architectural position, the proliferation of competing versions shifted the focus back to Vitruvius as an author.

This attention to Vitruvius as author pushed scholars to pursue a philological approach to the text in order to establish a precise translation of the original Latin, which of course had to be reconstructed. It was in Germany that this effort began in earnest, where, following Rode's German translation of 1796, two Latin editions were printed in Leipzig, by Schneider in 1807 to 1808 and by Tauchnitz in 1836, followed by a dual Latin and German edition printed in Gotha by Karl Lorentzen (1817–1888) in 1857, and finally another German translation printed in Stuttgart in 1865 by Franz von Reber (1834–1919). Paramount to these editions is the 1867 Teubner Vitruvius by Valentin Rose (1829–1916) and Hermann Müller-Strübing (1812–1893), a meticulous philological reconstruction of the Latin text. The book belongs to the successful and highly respected Bibliotheca Teubneriana, a series initiated in Leipzig in 1849 by Benedictus Gotthelf Teubner (1784–1856) to provide high-standard editions of classical texts in affordable formats. Teubner's books became references and inspired similar collections still in print today, like the Loeb Classical Library, the Collection Budé, and Oxford Classical Texts. Teubner's focus on restoring the original text is evident in the notes, where instead of the erudite or biased comments of previous editors, textual variations between various editions are meticulously indicated, with the need for accuracy trumping legibility. It is also significant that the book opens with a genealogical tree that traces the affiliation of various families of manuscripts, shedding light on the circulation of the text before its printed life began.

The last quarter of the nineteenth century was marked by a scattering of reprints of previous editions and by the first Hungarian version, translated by Béla Fuchs with commentaries by Jusztin Bódiss (1863–1921), in 1898. Rose continued to work on German versions of the text, but these, according to critics, did not have the quality and the fluency of his

24 Rose 1867, a successful establishment of the Latin text accompanied by precise cross-references and accurate footnotes with editorial variations

first celebrated Teubner edition.[205] At this point, while Vitruvius advanced to become a major theoretical reference in the academic teaching of architecture, a breach emerged between the scholarly attention devoted to his text—more and more focused on language—and the practical irrelevance of his treatise to contemporary building. This was the gap that Auguste Choisy (1841–1909) attempted to bridge in his unique edition[206] by integrating an accurate Latin edition, a precise French translation, and a new set of plates that provided methodological hints for contemporary architectural design.

Choisy's edition was organized into four volumes: the first, *Analyse*, is dedicated to detailed explanations by the author, the second and third, *Texte et traduction*, comprise the original Latin text and its French translation, and the fourth, *Figures*, contains ninety-five plates with 379 illustrations and their respective captions. The paragraphs in volume one seldom have more than three lines, and many sentences are shorter than thirty words.[207] The pages of volumes two and three, where the original text appears alongside the translation, are set in two columns, each of no more than forty characters, or seven words, wide. As the author warns the reader, "the translation, strictly literal, is set, phrase part by phrase part, in relation to the text."[208] Each sentence begins on an independent line, which is numbered, and paragraphs are double-spaced. Reading becomes a ponderous task; the for-

---

205 The authors of the Italian reference edition of 1997 comment that for the Vitruvian editions "the fundamental one is that edited by V. Rose and H. Müller-Strübing (Leipzig, 1867), philiologically more reliable in terms of the subsequent Teubner editions (edited, respectively, by V. Rose, 1899, and F. Krohn, 1912)." Gros-Corso-Romano 1997, "Nota critica," vol. II, 1437, translated by the author. Ingrid D. Rowland also praises the 1867 edition, arguing that its "extensive apparatus of alternative manuscript readings is still indispensable for anyone undertaking a serious examination of the text." Rowland, "Vitruvian Scholarship to Vitruvian Practice," here 16.

206 Choisy 1909; Choisy 1971.

207 The writing strategy stands for a "refusal to do literary work." Thierry Mandoul, *Entre raison et utopie: L'histoire de l'architecture d'Auguste Choisy* (Wavre: Mardaga, 2008), 67.

208 Choisy 1909, vol. II, n.p.

25 Choisy 1909, a rigorous parallel between Latin and French to be read line by line

mat sets the pace required to consider the weight of every word and grasp its implications. The slow pace of reading is also encouraged by the plethora of numbered cross-references mapping out relationships between the two central volumes: the one containing the analysis, which follows the sequence of words in the text; and the volume of illustrations referring both to the text and the analysis. Hence, a careful reader needs to have at least three volumes open simultaneously: the Latin text supports both the reading and verification of the French translation; cryptic words and passages in the text are explained verbally in the analysis and visually in the cross-referenced illustrations; and the captions relate back to Choisy's contemporary analysis of the text. The references—to books, chapters, paragraphs, lines, plates, illustrations, and captions—employ a complex and structured numbering system to guarantee that each detail is properly connected to the others. Despite its telegraphic quality, the form given to Choisy's minute exegesis of the Latin text imposes a slowness that the early printed editions with their extra-long lines and massive text blocks cannot match.

Choisy took a very long time to complete his edition of Vitruvius because he developed it alongside his other work, both pedagogical and editorial. He taught at the École Nationale des Ponts et Chaussées from 1876 until 1901. His magnum opus, the *Histoire de l'architecture*, was first published in 1899, the success of which would later be extended by its recognition by the avant-gardes of modern art and architecture.[209] He would often refer to the Vitruvius as a life-long journey—"I continue to stupify myself over this caustic [work], which will enrage me"[210] —and it was. Sadly, Choisy died after falling

---

209 Notably Le Corbusier and Sergei Eisenstein. On Eisenstein and Choisy, see Yve-Alain Bois, "Montage and Architecture," *Assemblage: A Critical Journal of Architecture and Design Culture*, no. 10 (December 1989): 110–131, 111–115, 130–131.

210 Choisy, quoted in Fernand Dartein, "Notice sur la vie et les travaux de M. Auguste Choisy," *Annales des ponts et chaussées* 3 (May 1910): 7–46, here 12; quoted in Mandoul, *Entre raison et utopie*, 31; translated by the author.

from a bus in September 1909[211] and never experienced the joy of seeing his exquisite Vitruvius in print.[212]

Choisy's plates for *Vitruve*—like those of the *Histoire*—result from obsessive and detailed work.[213] The buildings described are drawn in telling axonometries, often seen from below, providing the reader with decomposed and analytical views.[214] Such textual and visual analysis encompassed a specific design rationale: that the same logic used to pictorially represent past architectural accomplishments was easily translatable into contemporary building design practice. This characteristic positions Choisy's edition as the last Vitruvius edition to take a design-oriented approach in that he expected that architect readers would use the book to engage with the rationale of the Roman author, presented as a methodology for classical architectural design. Published at the beginning of the twentieth century, when the theory and practice of architecture were being completely redefined, it closed the door on an era of Vitruvian publications with multiple purposes—from design-oriented to philologically inquisitive editions.

---

211 Mandoul, *Entre raison et utopie*, 35.

212 In 1911 it was possible to acquire Auguste Choisy's Vitruvius for sixty francs. See "Bibliographie," *Construction Moderne* 26, no. 31 (April 29, 1911): 371–372.

213 Mandoul, *Entre raison et utopie*, 136–139.

214 "Wishing, above all, irreproachable illustrations, he proceeded as follows with the drawings: executed in large format, using photography, they were scaled down to the desired size and then etched in metal; and it was the prints of these engravings that we then used for the zinc plates for the reproductions in the print run." Dartein, "Notice sur la vie et les travaux de M. Auguste Choisy," 41, quoted in Mandoul, *Entre raison et utopie*, 137.

AUTHOR OF THE TWENTIETH CENTURY, 1914-1964

From 1486 to 1909 one hundred editions and reprints of Vitruvius were published, all in Europe. In contrast, the following one hundred years, ending with the 2016 Danish translation by Jacob Isager, produced a complex inventory of 183 editions, prints, and reprints across the globe from the Americas to Asia. No century had seen more Vitruvian editions written and printed than the twentieth. Moreover, the fields in which the Roman author was examined broadened well beyond those of design methodology and architectural theory to establish the text in subjects ranging from archaeology to philology and linguistics, with the result being a scholarly devotion that ultimately stripped the work of its architectural significance. Despite the sheer number of Vitruvian editions published in the past century, Vitruvius never came to be considered an author of the twentieth century, primarily because most of the architects of the previous centuries had so thoroughly imbibed his theory. While Vitruvius was published more than ever, he was as an authority of the past.

To an architect of the twenty-first century, and although featured in the reading list of almost every first-year architecture student, Vitruvius is barely readable. His message, enounced on the first pages of the first book, remains bound to the principles of order, proportion, and composition, the qualities of sites and the broad super-human knowledge an architect was said to have to possess. Nonetheless, Vitruvius is still the author most quoted in architectural lectures from Álvaro Siza to Rem Koolhaas, for first-year students to structural engineers. The triad of Vitruvian architectural qualities—*firmitas, utilitas, venustas*—has conquered the heart and the reason of every architectural discourse. Ironically, the formulation owes much to Alberti who, in his own treatise and wrestling with Vitruvius's cumbersome syntax, updated a marginal remark to establish one of architectural history's most powerful aphorisms.[215] This encapsulation of the treatise in a few words turned out to be a highly effective ingredient in maintaining Vitruvius's ubiquitous presence in architectural discourse. The treatise's circulation as a book allowed owners the illusion of possessing an idea along with the physical object. Hence, the presence of the ghost of Vitruvius on architects' shelves populated by the 183 post-1909 editions operated in parallel with the legacy of the one hundred pre-1909 editions, a legacy that inscribed their profession within a tradition of architectural discourse that had begun in the Renaissance.

As book history demonstrates, reading practices changed over time. The Vitruvius editions of the first half of the twentieth century, after Choisy, take one of three approaches to the source: the first is scholarly and oriented to classical studies, a traditional approach renewed by Morris Hicky Morgan's (1859–1910) posthumous edition of 1914; the second is ideological, of which Erich Stürzenacker's monumental German edition in 1938 stands out; and the third, for lack of better designation, can be called editorial, referring to the variety of translations and editions that produced a diversity of book forms that effectively and surprisingly maintained

---

215 In the second chapter of Book I, Vitruvius mentions his triad as subordinate to the six fundamental principles of architecture: order, arrangement, eurythmy, symmetry, propriety, and economy. Alberti moved the triad to the first lines of his Prologue and adjusted the concepts of *firmitas, utilitas,* and *venustas* to *necessitas, commoditas,* and *voluptas*—the fundamental needs of humanity fulfilled by architecture. See Françoise Choay, *La règle et le modèle: Sur la théorie de l'architecture et de l'urbanisme*, 1st ed. 1980 (Paris: Seuil, 1996), 92–94.

Vitruvius as the key textbook of a profession in permanent transformation.

Morgan's is the first non-European Vitruvius edition. Published in 1914 by Harvard University, where Morgan was professor of classical philology, it benefited from its prestigious academic pedigree. Beyond the sophisticated and readable English prose[216] —a translation of the acclaimed Rose edition of 1867—Morgan's book is prominent in its use of photography to illustrate the text. It is noteworthy that it took more than half a century for Vitruvius editions to incorporate photographic illustrations, especially considering the relevance of the technology to architectural publishing. As early as 1851 James Ferguson (1808–1886) praised the advantages photography could bring to the discussion of ancient buildings from all over the world, and in 1866 he included printed photographs in his books on Indian architecture.[217] From the late nineteenth century, architectural books had been populated with photographs, both printed as independent plates and mixed in with the text. But the model for Morgan's Vitruvius was the archaeological book, not the architectural one. In archaeological publications, the use of photography was rather obvious, illustrating the examples quoted in the text by means of immediate and faithful images. This tactic is challenging to adapt to Vitruvius, because instead of referring to precise examples he describes ideal models. Nonetheless, Morgan went ahead, and the first illustration shows Giocondo's illustration of *caryatids* alongside photographs of examples from Athens, Delphi, and Rome.[218] The rest of the illustrations continue to be an as-

---

216 Richard Schofield, the most recent English translator, expressed doubt that Morgan's "dignified and intelligent prose could be surpassed" in his translator's note to the Penguin pocket edition. Schofield 2009, xli.

217 On Fergusson, see A. Tavares, *Anatomy of the Architectural Book*, 48–49. See also Nikolaus Pevsner, "James Fergusson," in *Some Architectural Writers of the Nineteenth Century* (Oxford: Clarendon Press, 1972), 238–251; Maurice Craig, "James Fergusson," ed. John Summerson, in *Concerning Architecture: Essays on Architectural Writers and Writing Presented to Nikolaus Pevsner* (London: Allen Lane the Penguin Press, 1968), 140–152.

218 The book was posthumously edited by his colleague Albert Howard, who followed Morgan's annotations to the manuscript and suggestions of which illustrations

sortment of images taken from previous editions of Vitruvius, the majority of them drawings that convey the proportions of columns and temples. The several photographs scattered throughout the text remind the reader of buildings currently in existence that comply with Vitruvian precepts.

Some of Morgan's images were taken from August Mau's (1840–1909) *Pompeii: Its Life and Art*, published in 1899. More significant than the photographs he borrowed from Mau are the survey drawings of ruins used to illustrate the passage on *cavaedia* in Book VI, Chapter III, Paragraph 1. While the use of surveys to illustrate Vitruvian passages was far from new, Morgan's unprecedented choice to show detailed plans of specific houses that vary significantly in their configuration distorted the expectation of a geometrically perfect outcome encouraged by the text. By referring to archaeological knowledge and to a reality that was far from being a paradigmatic reflection of the Vitruvian ideal rather than as a tool to shape contemporary architecture, Morgan's edition draws the reader's attention to the text's significance as a reference for archaeological studies and the history of architecture.

Morgan's edition was reprinted in 1926, but its authoritative status was edged out, beginning in 1931, by the success of the scholarly edition by Frank Granger (1864–1936), a professor of classics and philosophy at the University of Nottingham. Published in two paperback volumes in 1931 and 1934 as part of the prestigious Loeb Classical Library,[219] the Granger

to use. Morgan's colophon indicates that the illustrations and original designs were prepared under the direction of Harvard architecture professor Herbert Langford Warren.

219 Originally distributed in the United States by the New York publisher G. P. Putnam's Sons and in London by William Heinemann, who organized the content. Heinemann was James Loeb's partner in publishing the Loeb Classical Library, an intercontinental venture that since 1911 has produced a series of translations of works by classical authors. The two Vitruvius volumes are numbers 251 and 280. Reprints of volume I were issued in 1944, 1955, 1960, 1970, 1983, 1995, 2002, and 2014; volume II was reprinted in 1944, 1956, 1962, 1970, 1985, 1998, 2002, and 2014. The last reprints coincided with the release of the online versions of both volumes, at which point the publisher stopped listing previous reprints.

26 Morgan 1914, August Mau's archaeological survey of a tetrastyle cavaedium used as illustration to the first American edition

edition translated the Latin text of the British Library's Harleian 2767 manuscript into a new English version.[220] The book has few illustrations—what is there is a varied mix of reproductions of historical engravings, photographs, and schematic references, all of unremarkable quality—inserted at the end of each volume. The volumes were reprinted first in 1944, then in 1955/1956, and from then on the two volumes (volume one for Books I to V, volume two for Books VI to X) seem to have led separate lives, each of them regularly reprinted every ten to twelve years. Eclipsing the previous English translations by Newton, Wilkins, and Gwilt, as well as Morgan's translation (which was published as a low-cost Dover paperback[221]), Granger assumed the position of the primary reference in the English Classical Library for the remainder of the twentieth century, structuring readings of Vitruvius in powerful English-speaking academic circles.

The second thread of Vitruvian editions that weaves its way the first half of the twentieth century reveals an opposite usage to scholarly reading and study, instead reflecting the authoritarian bias of European governments and their imperial visions, whereby architecture and its theory were part of a larger cultural ideology. It is telling to compare—if not to juxtapose—the small compact size and long print-life of Granger's two-volume set to the large size of Erich Stürzenacker's edition, printed only once on the eve of World War II.[222] Where the first is practical, portable, and easily readable, the second is a tabletop book made to assert an argument—a book to be admired rather than studied.

Published in 1938 in Essen, Stürzenacker's Vitruvius is a black-cloth volume bound in hard cover. The only text on

---

220 On how Granger might have used Vitruvian sources, see Rowland, "Vitruvian Scholarship to Vitruvian Practice," here 16.

221 In 1960 it was reprinted unabridged in paperback by Dover, a classic edition that is still in print. This Dover version was the source for the updated 2003 edition by Thomas Gordon Smith.

222 Granger's two volumes, taken together, measure 17 × 10.8 × 4.3 cm, compared to 32 × 23 × 3.2 cm for Stürzenacker's book.

27 Stürzenacker 1938, a Vitruvius illustrated by Third Reich contemporary monuments to demonstrate the genetic lineage of Teutonic culture

the outside, in embossed roman serif capital letters, is the author's name in German: Vitruv. Inside, the title page, in gothic letters, gives the German title, *Über die Baukunst*, and the presumed extended name of the Latin author, Marcus Vitruvius Pollio.[223] The treatise is also set in gothic type, and the illustrations are a mix of drawings that had first appeared in various classic editions from Cesariano to Barbaro, including Rusconi and even Newton. It also reproduces the title page of the 1548 German edition, with *Vitruvius Teutsch* in gothic type, asserting the pedigree of the work in the Germanic realm and thus framing its reading.

Significantly, the question of type was subject to a controversial ideological discussion in early twentieth-century Germany, the diametrical opposition of roman to gothic fraktur linked to conflicts of "Rationalism against Romanticism, progress against reaction, internationalism against nationalism."[224] Nonetheless, this ideological schism was not so absolute in practice, where the two types coexisted in the print realm. Although in 1933 the National Socialists declared fraktur as the "German type," in 1941 the Nazi Party issued a circular prohibiting its use due to its purported Jewish roots, instead favoring roman type.[225] Reflecting this ambivalence, Stürzenacker's Vitruvius used both roman and fraktur types, although it is the Germanness of the blackletter that most characterizes the book.

For the distracted reader, a preface by Adolf Hitler reiterates the heroic pedigree of classical architecture, a genetic lineage that purportedly connected ancient Greek and Roman to contemporary Teutonic cultures. The page is excerpted from the infamous 1933 political speech "German Art as the Proud-

---

223 On Marcus and Pollio as Vitruvius's presumed names, see Jacques Gubler's "Préface du traducteur" in Germann, *Vitruve et le vitruvianisme*, x–xi.

224 Hans Peter Willberg, "Fraktur and Nationalism," ed. Peter Bain and Paul Shaw, in *Blackletter: Type and National Identity* (New York: Princeton Architectural Press, 1998), 40–49, here 42.

225 See Robin Kinross, *Modern Typography: An Essay in Critical History*, 1st ed. 1992, 2nd revised ed. 2004 (London: Hyphen Press, 2010), 121–123.

est Defence of the German Nation,"[226] in which Hitler called for the arts to emulate ideal pre-existing models rather than pursue innovation—and set the tone for the book's remarkable series of rotographic images.

Rotographs are photographs printed using a luxurious technique rare in books on architectural theory, which betrays the nature of the edition as a book to be shown rather than a book to be read. The layout of the photography spreads is also daring. The images fill the right-hand pages in full bleed, and the near-blank facing pages further emphasize the presence of the photographs. Just a few lines of text in fraktur are set at the bottom of the left-hand pages, along with an image caption in a counterintuitively light sans-serif type. The wide letter-spacing of the text loosens the characteristically compact form of the blackletter, challenging the balance of the layout. The void whiteness of the empty upper page plays with the sans-serif caption, the loose block of blackletters generating an asymmetrical and dynamic modern composition. This powerful design decision disputes the architectural idea the photographs seem intended to convey. The latter present a sequence of classical references, beginning with the Athens Acropolis, in images that emphasize the formal qualities of the buildings: their shapes, their presence in the landscape, and the ancient materiality of their stones. The rotographs, with their characteristic deep darks and powerfully nuanced contrasts, underline the dramatic qualities of the antique examples. The sequence then jumps from the ancient to the contemporary, with images of the monumental architecture of the Third Reich, from the Ehrentempel on Königsplatz and the Haus der Deutschen Kunst in Munich to the Olympic Stadium in Berlin. Despite the modern page layout, the classical architectural lineage of the rising Nazi empire is made abundantly clear—one does not need to read Vitruvius to find it.[227]

---

226 Adolf Hitler, *Die deutsche Kunst als stolzeste Verteidigung des deutschen Volkes: Rede, gehalten auf der Kulturtagung des Parteitages 1933* (Munich: Zentralverlag der NSDAP, Franz Eher Nachfahren, 1934), translated by the author.

227 It comes as a surprise to find a similar visual strategy in a 1956 Polish

The evocative power of Vitruvius's treatise does not only recall ancient Rome—an affiliation exploited by Stürzenacker to link the imperial architectural ambitions of his time with those of the past—but also the entire European tradition of classical architecture. Thus, considering Japan's will to uphold traditional national values in the context of its involvement in World War II after 1941, it is surprising to find a Japanese translation published in Tokyo in 1943. The translator was Morita Keiichi (1895–1983), an architect who in the 1920s was involved in a theoretical renewal of Japanese architecture[228] as part *Bunriha Kenchiku Kai*, a group that presented avant-garde designs in Japan and pled for a modern architecture based on European references.[229] In 1922 Morita began teach at the Imperial University of Kyoto, and it is perhaps this work that compelled him to read and teach Vitruvius.[230] During a trip to Paris in 1934 he studied classical architecture treatises and worked on a translation of Paul Valéry's (1871–1945) *Eupalinos ou l'architecte*. Despite its academic tone, the publication of his Japanese Vitruvius in 1943 is intriguing. Why present this European reference at a time when Japan was keen to affirm itself as an Eastern imperial power?[231]

---

edition. Despite using a more modest offset printing technique for the illustrations, the Warsaw edition uses the same full-page black-and-white photographs as its Essen predecessor. See, for example, the photograph of the remains of the Olconio house in Pompeii featured in both editions. Stürzenacker 1938, n.p., and Kumaniecki 1956, 105.

228 See Amanai Daiki, "The Founding of Bunriha Kenchiku Kai: 'Art' and 'Expression' in Early Japanese Architectural Circle, 1988–1920," *Aesthetics*, no. 13 (2009): 235–248.

229 See Benoît Jacquet, "Between Tradition and Modernity: The Two Sides of Japanese Pre-war Architecture," ed. Susanne Kohte, Hubertus Adam, and Daniel Hubert, in *Encounters and Positions: Architecture in Japan* (Basel: Birkhäuser, 2017), 226–237; Benoît Jacquet and Nicolas Fiévé, *Vers une modernité architecturale et paysagère: Modèles et savoirs partagés entre le Japon et le monde occidental* (Paris: Éditions Collège de France, 2013).

230 According to Hui Zou, Morita's translation was made from the Valentin Rose version. Hui Zou, "China (Sixteenth to Eighteenth Centuries): Renaissance Humanism and Chinese Architecture," ed. Nicholas Temple, Andrzej Piotorwski, and Juan Manuel Heredia, in *The Routledge Handbook on the Reception of Classical Architecture* (London: Routledge, 2019).

231 The refined 1943 edition can only be found in some library catalogues.

Attempts to ascribe ideological motivations to specific editions of Vitruvius, like the Japanese translation, usually yield equivocal results. Nonetheless, Vitruvius's treatise did interest several authoritarian powers. In Italy, Vitruvius's birthplace, just two editions were published during the Mussolini era. The first was by Ugo Fleres (1857–1939), comprising two small volumes published in 1933 in a limited print run of two hundred copies, reprinted in 1947. The second is a peculiar booklet edition by Giuseppe Guenzati (1902-?). Printed near Milan in 1943, it is a stapled reprint of the Italian translation of Perrault's *Abrégé*, done, as the editor states, in a "fast and furious" manner after a manuscript got lost "because of the war."[232] Such a small Italian output might be explained by the origin of the aesthetic of Italian Fascism in the modernist avant-garde, or instead by the long lineage of Vitruvian editions already available in Italy, although there had in fact not been a new one since 1854.[233]

More telling, in this respect, is the significant Vitruviana gathered by the Milanese architect Giovanni Muzio (1893–1982). Going beyond the eclecticism of Milanese *fin-de-siècle* architecture, Muzio championed a return to the classical, from building design to urban form. His powerful constructions, in particular the Cassa di Risparmio delle Provincie Lombarda (1937–1941) and the headquarters of Mussolini's newspaper *Il Popolo d'Italia* (1938–1942), helped to shape an image of the modern Fascist city.[234] Not surprisingly, Muzio possessed more than fifteen editions of Vitruvius in his library, from Fra Giocondo to Ortiz y Sanz, a collection

---

Easier to find are the 1969 and 1979 editions, which have a format and expression that corresponds to their academic purposes.

    232 Giuseppe Guenzati, "Avvertimento dell'editore," in Guenzati 1943, n.p.

    233 The last Italian edition before the 1933 Ugo Fleres was the 1854 Galiani-Schneider published in Venice.

    234 See *L'architettura di Giovanni Muzio* (Milan: Abitare Segesta Cataloghi, 1994); Giorgio Ciucci, *Gli architetti e il Fascismo: Architettura e città 1922–1933* (Turin: Enaudi, 1989).

that underlines the affiliation of his own architectural practice with the Vitruvian tradition during the Fascist regime.[235]

The conundrum of the ideological bias given to Vitruvius can be further assessed in three editions published in the Soviet Union, giving us a glimpse as to how they fit into a complex network of ideas so often obscured by the common association of monumentality with totalitarianism.[236] For example, as Jean-Louis Cohen points out in his discussion of the national pavilions Germany and the USSR built for the Paris exhibition of 1939, the rhetorical monumentality of state-sponsored architecture is compromised by the internal displays—including suprematist decor and a functionalist presentation of Mercedes products—that are more representative of industry's technological drive.[237] Analogous conflicting interests shape the Soviet Vitruviuses, which cannot be read simply as representing the official turn from constructivism to classicism in the early 1930s. Instead, in their balancing of ideology and scholarship, architectural practice and aesthetic theory, the history of architecture and literary criticism, they underline the intricate network of the claims at stake in the highly sensitive cultural context of Stalinism.

Three Vitruvius editions were printed in the USSR in the 1930s: two of them appeared in Moscow, in 1936 and 1938, under the aegis of the Academy of Architecture, and another was published in Leningrad in 1936.[238] While the Leningrad edition was an isolated venture, the Moscow editions were produced as part of a larger plan to renew architectural education

---

235 This collection is now kept at the Getty Research Institute, Los Angeles, whose catalogue lists the following editions with Muzio's *ex-libris*: Giocondo 1511; Cesariano 1521; Giocondo 1522; Giocondo 1523; Durantino 1524; Martin 1547; Durantino 1535; Barbaro 1556; Barbaro 1567; De Laet 1649; Perrault 1673; Ryff 1614; Perrault 1684; Galiani 1758; Ortiz y Sanz 1787.

236 On the fascination of Stalinist architects with Italian architecture, see Élisabeth Essaïan, *Le Prix de Rome: Le "Grand Tour" des architectes soviétiques sous Mussolini* (Paris: Éditions B2, 2012).

237 Jean-Louis Cohen, "Retro-grad ou les impasses du réalisme 'socialiste' en URSS," in *Les années 30: L'architecture et les arts de l'espace entre industrie et nostalgie* (Paris: Éditions du Patrimoine, 1997), 163–179, here 163.

238 Mishulin 1936; Petrovsky 1936; Zubov 1938.

28 Morita 1943, a Japanese Vitruvius printed during World War Two

and to revive the serious study of Renaissance architectural culture. It was not only Vitruvius that was translated into Russian, but also Barbaro's comments on Vitruvius, as well as the treatises of Alberti, Palladio, Vignola, and others. Branko Mitrovic, in his analysis of the genesis and outcome of this venture, traces the project's origin to a decision of the Central Committee of the Communist Party and identifies three of the key authors who worked on it: Vasily Pavlovich Zubov (1900–1963), Aleksander Georgievich Gabrichevsky (1891–1968), and Ivan Vladislavovich Zholtovsky (1867–1959).[239] Zubov, whose main achievement was the translation of various treatises by Alberti, including *De re aedificatoria*, is often credited with the 1938 Moscow Vitruvius; Gabrichevsky supervised the project, edited the volumes, and was responsible for their prefaces; and Zholtovsky, who was a leading figure in the Soviet architectural scene, was responsible for the translation of Palladio's *I quattro libri*.[240] For the Vitruvius editions, two other authors were fundamental: Fyodor A. Petrovsky (1890-1978), who translated the Vitruvian text, and Aleksey Venediktov, who translated the Barbaro's commentaries on Books I to VI.[241]

Zholtovsky was the architectural mastermind of the venture, as well as a professional architect. The apartment building he inaugurated on the Mokhovaya in 1934—the same year that Le Corbusier's Centrosoyuz was completed[242] —is the built counterpart of his scholarly Renaissance revival project. Zholtovsky's building is a sophisticated iteration of Palladio's Loggia del Capitano in Vicenza, deftly avoiding both eclectic pastiche and the monumentality of constructivist and Stalinist beacons. Its significance in Soviet architectural history is as a hinge between the avant-garde quest for the new and the

---

239 Mitrovic, "Studying Renaissance Architectural Theory."

240 Andrea Palladio, *Tchetyre knigi ob arkhitektoure*, ed. A. Gabritchevky, trans. Ivan Joltovski (Moscow: Akademii Arkhitektoury, 1937). See Essaïan, *Le Prix de Rome*, 13, n. 13.

241 Zubov translated the commentaries of Books VII to X.

242 See Selim O. Khan-Magomedov, *Pioneers of Soviet Architecture*, 1st ed. 1983, ed. Catherine Cooke, trans. Alexander Lieven (London: Thames; Hudson, 1997), 265, illustration 699: "Today's Marx Prospect, Moscow, 1932–1934."

Stalinist turn of the 1930s and might suggest an affiliation between the Soviet interest in Vitruvius and the search for a new monumentality.[243] As Katerina Clark has emphasized, Vitruvius was part of a discourse that sought to present "the new Moscow as heir to the architectural greatness of ancient Rome"[244] in the context of the ongoing "battle of the styles" that accompanied the growth of Soviet cities in the 1930s and 1940s, and translations of Western sources fed the development of "social realist" architecture.

While Zholtovsky was influential and well-connected in the architecture world, Gabrichevsky and Zubov were independent intellectuals with backgrounds in literature and history who had to navigate the uncertainties of the high surveillance and the repressive ideology of the Stalinist regime.[245] Their contributions gave this Renaissance project, initiated for the purpose of architectural education, a significant scholarly bias. It is telling that the 1938 Russian translation also comprised a translation of Barbaro's comments that includes the variations between the 1556 and 1567 commentaries. This led Ernst Gombrich to characterize the achievement—in a 1968 review of an English translation of a book by Zubov on Leonardo da Vinci—as one of "cloistered scholarship," pointing out the awkwardness of "a commentary on a commentary published in the worst period of Stalinist terror."[246] It was Zubov, the translator of part of Barbaro's commentary and Alberti's *Da re aedificatoria*, who, in 1945, wrote an account of the project in which

---

243 Zholtovsky: "I chose Vitruvius as my teacher and guide," quoted in Katerina Clark, *Moscow, the Fourth Rome: Cosmopolitanism, and the Evolution of Soviet Culture, 1931–1941* (Cambridge, MA: Harvard University Press, 2011), 98–99, n. 55.

244 Clark, *Moscow, the Fourth Rome*, 97.

245 It is worth recalling that Gabrichevsky was incarcerated three times over the course of the project, once for three years in the Urals. Mitrovic, "Studying Renaissance Architectural Theory," 242–243.

246 Ernst Gombrich, "Leonardo in the History of Science," ed. Richard Woodfield, in *Ernst Gombrich, Reflections on the History of Art: Views and Reviews* (Los Angeles: University of California Press, 1987), 68–73, quoted in Nadia Podzemskaia, "Publication of Renaissance Architectural Treatises in the Soviet Union in the 1930s: Alexander Gabrichevsky's Contribution to the Theory and History of Architecture," *Journal of Art Historiography*, no. 14 (June 2016): 1–14, here 13 n. 44.

he dismissed the idea that they were devising a normative canon for architecture and specified that the books were "intended for architectural historians, not for archaeologists or architects."[247] Despite its origin in a discussion on the direction of contemporary architecture, the scholarly approach of the Soviet Vitruvius puts it closer to the *Vitruvius Academicus* of the second half of the twentieth century.

Meanwhile, before and after the two World Wars, Vitruvius continued to be published in less ideologically charged contexts. These books helped shape a third distinctive thread of twentieth-century editorial strategies that had been timidly initiated before the wars.[248] Apart from the German reprints of editions edited by Jakob Prestel (1847–1930) and the abridged version by Bodo Ebhardt (1865–1945), most of the new publications were translations. A Dutch version of 1914, by J. H. A. Mialaret, was reprinted in 1920. In France, shortly after World War II ended, Perrault's translation was printed in a luxurious 1946 collector's edition stripped of the commentary. In 1953, the Ten Books were translated into Czech by Alois Otoupalík, subsequently reprinted in 1979, 2001, and 2009. In 1955, a new Spanish edition by Agustín Blánquez (1883–1965) appeared and was reprinted many times. In 1956, a Polish translation by the philology professor Kamizierz Kumaniecki (1905–1977) and the architect Piotor Biegański (1905–1986) came out, reprinted in 1999. In 1960 came Silvio Ferri's (1890–1978) new Italian translation, reprinted in 2008. In 1964 there was a posthumous Romanian translation by the Beaux-Arts-trained modern architect George Matei Cantacuzino (1899–1960). To some extent, this linguistic and geographical diversity reinforces the idea of a diffuse bibliographic panorama in the era of mass publishing, with specialized publishing houses that cater to the interests of limited circles coexisting with powerful publishers whose editions

---

247 Mitrovic, "Studying Renaissance Architectural Theory," 253.

248 Still during the war, in 1944 a small booklet containing Vitruvius's section on theaters was published in Prague in a Czech translation by Jaroslav Pokorny (1920–1983), who later became an important figure in Czech theater.

dominate the international distribution market, as Harvard University Press has done for Granger's Vitruvius. This varied scene, with a growing scholarly tone, continued in the editions published after 1964.

VITRUVIUS ACADEMICUS, 1964-2016

Over the last half century, the number of Vitruvian editions has continued to grow, populating various editorial genres: textbooks for young architecture students to read as fundamental bibliography; scholarly books, mainly new translations, to further Vitruvian and classical studies; historic manuscripts, printed and edited to shed light on specific aspects of architectural history and theory; and reprints of past editions to satisfy bookish curiosity and feed scholarship. The borders between these genres are blurry, with student textbooks being developed by meticulous scholars[249] and older editions recycled without a clear audience in mind.[250] All of this editorial activity is fueled by the relentless work of scholars who gather in specialized conferences, the published proceedings of which analyze the Roman text in infinite detail.[251] Among all these Vitruvian books, one project stands out: the ten-volume *Collection des Universités de France* or Budé edition, a product of forty years of collective intellectual labor initiated by Jean

---

249 Rowland 1999.
250 Dalmas 1965 and 1967.
251 See *Le projet de Vitruve: Objet, destinataires et réception du De architectura* (Rome: École Française de Rome, 1994), the proceedings of a conference held in Rome in 1993. McEwen references additional conferences held in Rome 1980, Darmstadt 1982, Berlin 1983, and Leiden 1987. See McEwen, *Vitruvius: Writing the Body of Architecture*, 4, n. 24.

Soubiran and published by Les Belles Lettres between 1969 and 2009.[252]

Today's Vitruvian research is highly interdisciplinary, gathering art historians, linguists, archaeologists, architects, and others in pursuit of the most accurate reading of the text and its variants. They draw on previous research, such as Hermann Nohl's (1850–1929) terminology,[253] while engaging with new digital tools for language analysis.[254] Louis Callebat and Pierre Fleury's *Dictionaire*, and especially the 1984 *Concordance*,[255] with over a thousand pages reconnecting every variant of each word to trace the original concepts embedded in the text, is a majestic product of the postmodern effort to provide the ultimate rational reading of the text.

This intensification of specialized scholarly reading can be traced back to two significant publications of 1964. That year, the American publisher Gregg Press presented a facsimile edition of Jean Martin's long-forgotten 1547 French translation. Made possible by advancements in photographic offset printing—by then both easy to do and relatively inexpensive—the reprint signaled a revival of interest in the original editions of Vitruvius. Facsimiles of Martin, Cesariano, Rusconi, Choisy, Ortiz y Sanz, and Urrea soon followed, published in the United States and across Europe.[256] The newfound accessi-

---

252 Publication dates and authors are as follows: Book I, Philippe Fleury, 1990; Book II, Louis Callebat, Pierre Gros, Catherine Jacquemard, 1999; Book III, Pierre Gros, 1990; Book IV, Pierre Gros, 1992; Book V, Catherine Saliou, 2009; Book VI, Louis Callebat, 2004; Book VII, Bernard Liou, Marie-Thérèse Cam, Michel Zuinghedau, 1995; Book VIII, Louis Callebat, 1973; Book IX, Jean Soubiran, 1969; Book X, Louis Callebat, Philippe Fleury, 1986.

253 Hermann Nohl, *Index Vitruvianus*, facsimile reprints of Leipzig: Teubner, 1876 (Darmstadt: Wissenschaftliche Buchgesellschaft, 1965 and 1983).

254 Sonia Maffei, "Il progetto di una 'concordanza storica vitruviana': Un approccio metodologico per il trattamento informatico di varianti testuali," in *Le projet de Vitruve: Objet, destinataires er réception du* De architectura (Rome: Ecole Française de Rome, Palais Farnèse, 1994), 231–245.

255 Louis Callebat, Philippe Fleury, Pierre Bouet, and Michel Zuinghedau, eds., *Vitruve: De architectura; Concordance. Documentation bibliographique, lexicale et grammaticale*, 2 vols. (Hildesheim: Olms-Weidmann, 1984); Callebat and Fleury, *Dictionnaire des termes*.

256 Martin 1964; Cesariano 1968; Rusconi 1968; Choisy 1971; Ortiz y Sanz 1974; Urrea 1978.

bility of these original editions propelled a growing interest in other historic editions, variations of the text, and unpublished manuscripts. A new German edition by Curt Fensterbusch (1888–1978) was published in 1964, which brought Vitruvian discussion and debate to a highly sophisticated level. Noting the deficiencies of previous editions in terms of their knowledge of Roman antiquity, and thus the text's cultural and technical context, Fensterbusch conducted a careful and clarifying reading of the manuscripts, which included a palaeographic analysis. Not only did this result in a new and more accurate Latin text, one that challenges Alberti's assertion that Vitruvius was a bad writer, but Fensterbusch's contextual assessment of the content resulted in a more conscious reading that propelled new translations and renewed interest in the text itself. Despite the groundbreaking content, the book itself is packaged as a conventional academic text, without any distinctive features.

Following the Fensterbusch edition, a group of scholars was formed to critically assess the Roman source, recalling the work of the sixteenth-century Accademia della Virtù in breaking the tradition of lone Vitruvian scholarship. The ultimate result of this intense collaboration is the French Budé edition, published in individual volumes, book by book, from 1969 to 2009. In addition to being a collective endeavor, its many coauthors recognize the contributions of an even wider circle of scholars whose work was critical in reaching a detailed understanding of the text. The compact edition that followed in 2015, edited by Pierre Gros (the most prolific and prominent Vitruvian scholar of the Budé group), was equally reliant on collaboration: the title page acknowledges nine other scholars who contributed to the editing, translation, and commentary.[257] Before this, Gros had edited a massive new Italian translation that came out in 1997 with commentary by Antonio Corso and Elisa Romano, a project closely linked in authorship

---

257 Gros 2015.

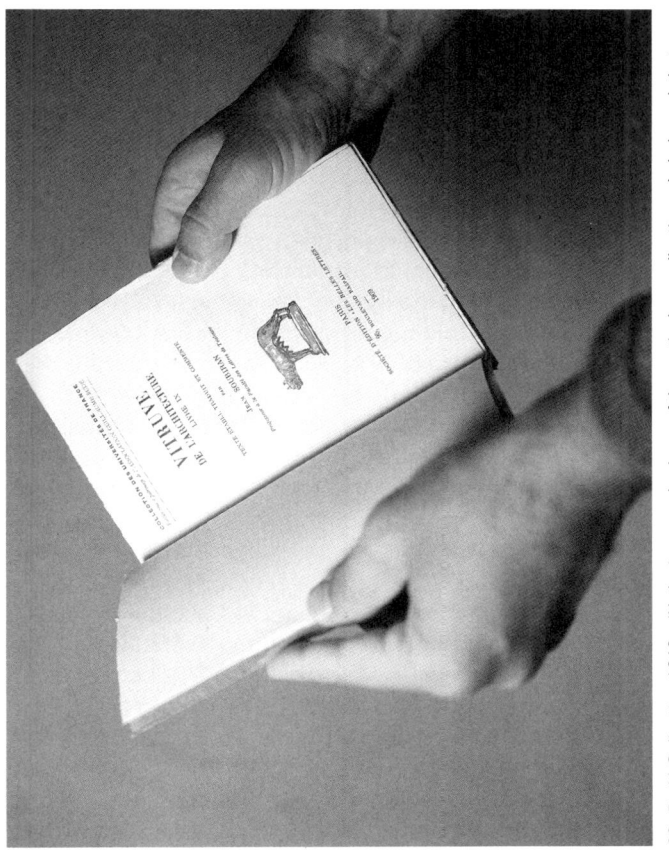

29 Budé Collection 1969 ± IX, the inaugural volume of the meticulous collective scholarly work that rejuvenated twentieth-century Vitruvius

and methodology to the scholarly French editions.[258] Together, its two volumes comprise over 1,500 pages, with a critical apparatus of introductions, comments, annotations, essays, and a wealth of illustrations.

To get a sense of how these scholarly editions are organized, it is worth taking a look at how each of them presents the tetrastyle *cavaedium* of Book VI, Chapter III, Paragraph 1. In the Italian book, the passage appears in a two-page spread on pages 836 and 837, in Latin on the left side with the Italian translation facing it on the right.[259] While the Latin text flows uninterruptedly, the Italian paragraph generates a parade of endnotes numbered from 79 to 92. The associated thirteen notes are found from pages 894 to 908, interspersed with black-and-white illustrations. A related colored illustration features in a separate unpaginated sequence of images printed on glossy paper, an option that guarantees a better print quality than the uncoated paper used for the rest of the book. This complex system of cross-references relates multiple layers of content and, in doing so, traces the scholarly effort to get as close as possible to the two-thousand-year-old source and to clarify how its meanings were construed over its long existence. In the multivolume Budé edition, Book VI was translated by Louis Callebat and published in 2004. The translator's introduction and extensive commentary bracket the Vitruvian text. The *cavaedium* sentence is on spread 14 (the left- and right-hand pages share a number) with the French on the left and the Latin on the right. Callebat's footnotes reference textual variations in the manuscripts to establish his version. Things were done a little differently in the compact edition of 2015. There, after a 105-page introduction, the Latin text is set on the left-hand page and the French on the right, and although the footnotes only refer to the French text they are distributed across both sides of the spread. The *cavaedium* sentence sends the reader to footnotes 39 to 43 and to figures 1 and 2.

---

258 Gros/Corso/Romano 1997.
259 The Latin takes twelve lines, whereas the Italian takes fourteen lines.

These figures are full-page illustrations placed among a set of images at the end of the section on Book VI and dedicated to that part of the treatise. A set of color photographs on glossy paper, independent of the page sequence, is bound between pages 408 and 409.[260] The extensive textual content of these recent editions is evident in their mass alone, but when one adds to that their sophisticated structures and high production quality, their academic purpose and scholarly refinement is unquestionable.[261]

Within an equivalent academic context, the 1999 Cambridge University Press edition, translated by Ingrid D. Rowland with commentary and illustrations by Thomas Noble Howe, adopted a different strategy. After explanatory introductions, the text flows regularly from the beginning of Book I on page 21 to the end of Book X on page 134. Although a few footnotes provide comments on the wording—such as "an unusually convoluted sentence"[262]—or on textual variations between editions, most references come in the form of asterisks that mark words and phrases discussed in the commentary. This restrained reference apparatus and the strategy of minimal textual interference encourages an uninterrupted reading, as if there were nothing to add to the fluent translation. The commentary, which begins on page 135, is organized under the

---

260 Their position, between pages 512 and 513 in the volume (the initial 104 pages are numbered independently in roman numerals) reveals the printing technique of assembling the book in thirty-two-page signatures.

261 At the opposite end of the spectrum of academic ambition is the 1998 Italian edition of Book VI, published with the evocative title *Case d'aria e terra acqua e fuoco*, or *Houses of Air and Earth, Water and Fire*. Migotto 1998 + VI ab. The stapled booklet is part of the series *Piccola biblioteca dell'architetto* (the small library of the architect). The translator is not named, and the only mention of the source of the text is in the promotional blurb, which contains a short biography of Vitruvius and mentions that the content is the sixth book of his architectural treatise. The edition is illustrated with original hand-drawings, and its format and lightness suggest that the goal is to introduce classical authors to a wide audience. The publisher is the same for the 1993 and 2008 editions authored by Luciano Migotto (Migotto 1993 and 2008), where for the Latin version a facsimile of Fensterbusch's 1976 edition was used. In the "Nota Critica" of the authoritative 1997 edition by Gros, Corso, and Romano, the authors assert: "The Italian editions edited by L. Cherubini (Pisa 1975) and L. Migotto (Pordenone 1988) are deprived of textual value." Gros 1997, 1437.

262 Rowland 1999, VI, 6, 77.

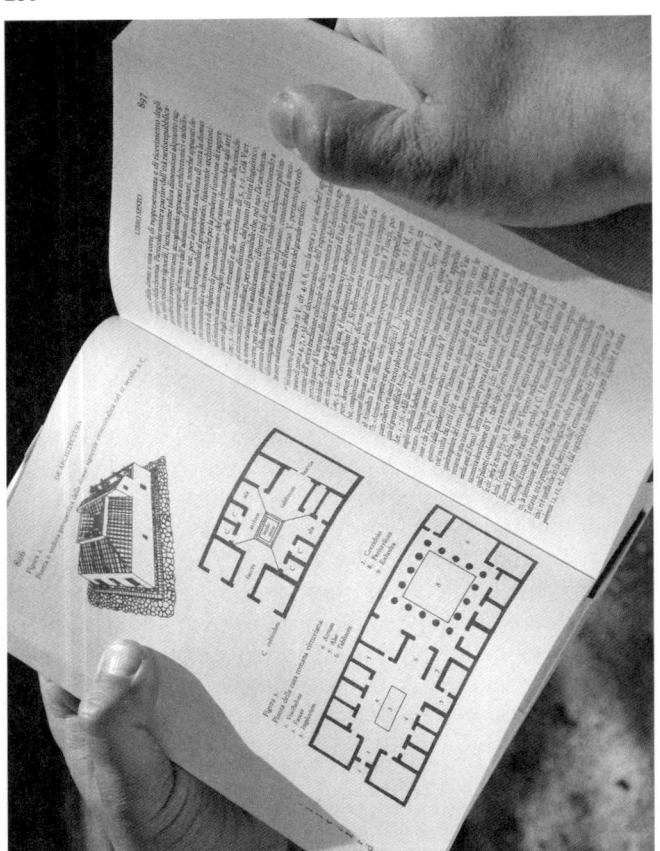

30 Gros/Corso/Romano 1997, a detailed 1,500-page edition, combining introductions, comments, annotations, essays, and a wealth of illustrations

headings of the words and passages marked with asterisks in the translation, thus suggesting an independent rereading of the text, this time accompanied by the same knowledgeable source who produced the pedagogical illustrations. Noble Howe explains that illustrating the work was an opportunity to "investigate the possibility of a consistent design approach in Vitruvius,"[263] and indeed this edition has a unity and readability rare in twentieth-century editions, with complex imagery hand-drawn from multiple sources. The unified aesthetic of Noble Howe's illustrations and the fluidity of Rowland's syntax suggest that the main purpose of their millennial English translation was to divulge the meaning and content of the text rather than meticulously documenting the process of their scholarly work.

If the burgeoning market for academic editions was already a factor in nineteenth-century publishing, the increased accessibility of higher education after World War II stimulated a boom in Vitruvian reprints and new editions. Cheap reprints aiming to meet demand from students buying compulsory readings flooded the book market, and publishers continue to compete for a share of it. For example, as recently as 2009, only ten years after Rowland's successful Cambridge translation, Penguin published a new pocket-sized English translation by Richard Schofield. These academic text books have proliferated in most of the Vitruvian languages: in French, André Dalmas' edition of 1965 began a thread of editions;[264] in Italian, there has been a diverse series of reprints, manuscript facsimiles, and new translations;[265] in Spanish, the market is

---

263 Thomas Noble Howe, "Illustrator's Preface," in Rowland 1999, xv.

264 The first edition by Dalmas, who reviewed Perrault's translation, was published in 1965 in landscape format with a luxurious variety of illustrations, including pasted colored prints, reproductions of figures from previous editions, and contemporary photographs of buildings such as Pier Luigi Nervi's sports hall dome in Rome, built in 1957. It had a print run of 2,000 numbered copies "reservés aux membres du Club des Libraires de France." The book had a parallel unnumbered print run with a similar layout, but in a normal portrait octavo format. In 1986 the edition was further simplified by a new publisher, Errances.

265 Cherubini 1975; Florian 1978; Migotto 1988; Gros/Corso/Romano 1997; Bossalino 1998.

31 Rowland 1999, a fluid translation with minimal editorial interference to encourage an uninterrupted reading

dominated by the ten editions of the 1955 translation by Augustín Blánquez;[266] in German, it is dominated by Fensterbusch with seven reprints;[267] and in English, where reprints of Granger were paramount until 1999. These and other editions ensured a massive circulation of the text as a perennial reference for both the architectural field and for classical studies. However, within the colossal growth of book printing that took place in the second half of the twentieth century, the interests of commercial publishers inolve profit: an edition is considered successful when its sales figures are on par with bestseller lists.

This allegiance between academia and the book trade also characterizes the growth of Chinese editions—encouraged by a new foreign affairs policy—from 2001 on. In 1956 Gao Lütai, who had been a student of Morita in Tokyo, made a Chinese translation from Morita's Japanese edition using Granger's Loeb Classical Library volumes as a supplemental reference. As Hui Zou has pointed out, the foreword emphasizes the discipline as a "building science" and insists on a "scientific attitude" for modern architecture.[268] Lütai's translation was eventually published in 1986 and was then used as the basis for a 2001 edition that was reprinted until it was eclipsed by the careful translation of Ping Chen in 2001. Published as part of a series of scholarly Chinese translations of "landmarks in art history" alongside Palladio's *I quattro libri* and works by Alois Riegl, Henri Focillon, and Heinrich Wölfflin, Ping Chen's Vitruvius in turn follows Rowland's suc-

---

266 The 2007 edition is labeled the tenth, although we were only able to locate nine editions: 1955, 1970, 1980, 1982, 1985, 1991, 1995, 2000, and 2007.

267 The first edition of 1964 was revised in 1976 and then reprinted in its updated form in 1981, 1987, 1991, 1996, 2008, and 2013/2014.

268 Zou, "China (Sixteenth to Eighteenth Centuries)." Vitruvius was first brought to China by Jesuit missionaries in the seventeenth century. While early Chinese adaptations of classic Western works by authors like Euclid, Agostino Ramelli, and Andrea Pozzo exist from that period, Vitruvius was not translated then. Nonetheless, as Hui Zou has shown, there are traces of Vitruvian ideas and concepts in some traditional Chinese architecture of the seventeenth and eighteenth centuries, evidence of a cultural adoption that went much deeper than the exotic importation of classical models in the 1980s.

cessful 1999 English version and includes the illustrations and commentary by Noble Howe. It also features cross-references to Rowland's original edition, with page references in Arabic numerals placed alongside the text plus an index to the English book—an inventive feature that expands the book's already intertwined system of references and facilitates comparative reading.

The history of architectural theory in China follows a different pattern than its European or American counterparts, but the reliance on a printed source as a reference for professional practice sets a parallel between Vitruvius and a twelfth-century Chinese construction manual, the *Yingzao Fashi*.[269] Although no copy of the original woodblock printing of 1103 has survived, the *Yingzao Fashi* later circulated in manuscript and, as might be expected, the various copies have a complex history. A careful lithographic edition was produced in 1920 to restore traditional knowledge threatened by modernization, followed by an annotated and further illustrated edition in 1925 by Tao Xiang (1870–1940). A smaller and more commercially viable version was reprinted in 1954, followed in 1984 by an annotated and newly illustrated version. If the *Yingzao Fashi* is the primary reference for local technical and historical building knowledge, the existence of a Chinese Vitruvius represents an attempt to bring architectural education in twenty-first-century China in line with the standards and references used in Europe and North America. Indeed, it is significant that in the years since the first Chinese Vitruvius appeared there have already been more Chinese editions of Vitruvius than of the *Yingzao Fashi*.

Spain offers another case where, as in China, editions of Vitruvius have followed political change. The twentieth-

---

[269] I am grateful to Shen He, who introduced me to the *Yingzao Fashi* and its various editions during a seminar at the Institute for the History and Theory of Architecture (gta Institute) at ETH Zurich in 2018. Further remarks by Christian Gänshirt were helpful in understanding the manual within the Chinese context. See also Jiren Feng, *Chinese Architecture and Metaphor: Song Culture in the Yingzao Fashi Building Manual* (Honolulu: University of Hawai'i Press; Hong Kong University Press, 2012).

century Agustín Blánquez edition, first published in Barcelona in 1955, marked the return of Vitruvius to the Iberian Peninsula 168 years after the Ortiz y Sanz translation, and it quickly became the standard reference in Spanish.[270] In 1973, the year *El Caudillo* General Franco resigned as president, Carmen Andreu published a new translation in Madrid. The next year, in Oviedo, a reprint of Ortiz y Sanz signaled the growing autonomy of the various Spanish regions, a political ambition repressed under Franco's vision of a centralized state. After several additional editions appeared in Madrid, Barcelona, and Toledo, a virtual explosion of Vitruvian editions followed across the country in response to the organization of professional architects into regional *colegios*, a change allowed by the democratic regime post-Franco: in 1978 a new reprint of Urrea was published in Valencia, in 1981 a Spanish translation of Perrault was published in Murcia,[271] in 1989 a new Ortiz y Sanz was published in Lugo, and in 2000 a Basque translation by Xanti Iruretagoiena was published in Bilbao. In these cases, the Vitruvian editions seem to have operated symbolically as a means for the architects of the various regions to express their professional identity.

Generally, the number of translations continued to expand in the late twentieth century, when Vitruvius was rendered into Greek, Portuguese, Turkish, and Danish. In the chronology of its various publications, the Greek translation project explicitly shows how the translators worked to manage the text in progressive steps. To begin with, the ten prefaces were translated by Pavlos Mylonas and published in 1986.[272] The scholarly operation involved interpreting the nuances of Vitruvius's Hellenistic sources. Mylonas experimented with putting

---

270 Iberia's 1970 reedition of Blánquez was the point of departure for subsequent Spanish editions.

271 Beyond Vitruvius, the Colegio Oficial de Aparejadores y Arquitectos Técnicos de Murcia distinguished its regional identity by means of careful editions of various classical treatises, including Sagredo, Alberti, and Vignola, among others.

272 Published as an 81-page offprint out of the four-volume work Φίλια Έπη *in Honour of G.E. Mylonas* (Athens: Archaeological Society of Athens, 1986–1990).

the Greek passages in both ancient and modern Greek in order to determine "the proper Greek version to be used for the translation, so as to translate the text substance and to convey the essence of Latin 'language-physiognomy.'"[273] This initial step was followed by a first complete translation by Stelios Zerefos in 1998.[274] A second two-volume edition, a more refined translation with scholarly annotations, was published between 1997 and 2009 by Pavlos Lefas.[275]

While records point to the existence of a Portuguese translation from 1541 by the scholar Pedro Nunes,[276] the manuscript was ultimately lost. As such, a Portuguese translation did not see print until the late twentieth century, the product of an enterprise that followed the Greek model, beginning with the prefaces published in 1995 by Justino Maciel.[277] In 1998, in Lisbon, Maria Helena Rua published a complete translation based on Perrault's 1673 French edition. Then, in 1999, another complete translation was published in São Paulo by Marco Aurélio Lagonegro and quickly reprinted in 2002. Maciel completed his accurate translation in June 2006, and the book was immediately reprinted in November of the same year. After a new Brazilian edition of Maciel's Vitruvius was released in 2007, a third Lisbon reprint came out in 2009, to be again reprinted in 2015. Instead of resorting to historical illustrations, photographs, or new drawings, Maciel's edition is distinguished by its use of the complete set of illustrations by

---

273 Paul M. Mylonas, "The Affinity between Greek and Roman Cultures, as Revealed through a Research Translation of Vitruvius into Greek, and Commentary," in *Research Reports and Record of Activities, Washington, National Gallery of Art Center 6*, May 1985, 71–72, here 71.

274 Zerefos 1998.

275 Lefas 1997–2009.

276 Henrique Leitão, "Sobre as 'obras perdidas' de Pedro Nunes," ed. Henrique Leitão and Lígia Azevedo Martins, in *Pedro Nunes, 1502–1578: Novas terras, novos mares e o que mays he; Novo ceo e novas estrellas* (Lisbon: Biblioteca Nacional, 2002), 45–66.

277 M. Justino Maciel, "Os *Prooemia* vitruvianos," in *Estudos de arte e história: Homenagem a Artur Nobre de Gusmão* (Lisbon: Vega, 1995), 345–371. In 1996, Book V was published by Maciel in a collective title, M. Justino Maciel, "O livro quinto do *De Architectura* de Vitrúvio," in *Miscellanea em Homenagem ao Professor Bairrão Oleiro*, vol. V (Lisbon: Colibri, 1996), 285–329.

Noble Howe from 1999, lending the book a visual coherence that matches the historical rigor of the translation. Meanwhile, in 2007, the São Paulo publisher Martins Fontes brought the Lisbon edition to Brazil, putting it in direct competition with Lagonegro's version.[278]

A Turkish translation was first published in Istanbul by Suna Güven in 1990, with a second translation by Çiğdem Dürüşken published in 2017. Güven's version is a translation of Morgan's American text, itself a translation of Rose's 1867 Leipzig edition, and is thus the product of a singular combination of intercontinental movements by the Roman author via Germany to the United States and then to the Bosporus. The connection to Morgan is emphasized on the cover of the 2005 reprint, which reproduces, in a reduced format, the cover of the Dover reprint of Morgan from the 1960s with its duotone orange image of the interior of the Pantheon in Rome—a curious choice considering that the cupola is not mentioned in the book, likely because the Pantheon as we know it was not yet built when Vitruvius completed his treatise. Nonetheless, the choice to reuse the cover of the American book for the Turkish translation suggests that the publisher wanted to keep production costs low to appeal to a student market. It is thus markedly different from editions that are crafted carefully by their authors as a means to articulate the textual content through a well-designed object.

In 2016 Jacob Isager's Danish translation was published. As a book, it is a compact scholarly edition, with illustrations consisting of reprints of illustrations from Renaissance editions, contemporary photos of Roman antiques, reconstructions, and informative maps—an apparatus that secures an insightful introduction to Vitruvius in a unique and specific contemporary language.

---

278 The fact that the 2006 Maciel edition was republished in Brazil in competition with the home-grown Lagonegro edition attests to a commercial rivalry between Brazilian publishers. Despite the physical and cultural distance between Portugal and Brazil, a great deal of mutual interest and respect connects the Portuguese-speaking Vitruvian community on both sides of the Atlantic.

Another genre of recent Vitruvian books focuses on the publication of the prior manuscripts. In 1975 Vincenzo Fontana and Paolo Morachiello brought a translation by the Renaissance scholar Fabio Calvo (1450–1527) to print. Theirs is an accurate critical edition, contextualizing the author and considering the various versions of the manuscript kept in Ravenna. The rigorous page layout articulates the footnotes, comments, and cross-references in a clear system that combines several layers of scholarship into a readable whole. Another Renaissance translation, by Francesco di Giorgio Martini (1439–1501), has received similar significant attention: Gustina Scaglia's edited version of the *Vitruvio magliabechiano* was published in 1985. It was followed in 2002 by Marco Biffi's edition based on another Martini manuscript kept in Florence and, in 2003, by Massimo Mussini's comparative edition that references the three known surviving Martini manuscripts: the Zichy, Spencer, and Magliabechiano versions. In 2004 Claudio Sgarbi edited and published a manuscript kept in Ferrara, probably a transcription by the Renaissance librarian Pellegrino Prisciani (1435–1518), with original illustrations significant in that they are independent of the corpus established by Giocondo and thus offer an alternate Renaissance vision of the treatise.

These historical editions were produced in a spirit similar to that in which the Milanese Il Polifilo has published its well-known series of carefully edited Renaissance treatises. Among the Scritti Rinascimentali di Architettura series of the 1970s is a 1978 volume that includes parts of Cesariano's Vitruvius. In 1981 Il Polifilo edited and reprinted Cesariano's entire Vitruvius and in 1987 produced a version of Barbaro's with critical contributions by Manuela Morresi and Manfredo Tafuri.[279] Il Polifilo's activity coincides with the sustained scholarly attention paid to Renaissance architecture by art historians, of which the most comprehensive outputs are the unique series of yellow monographs published by Electa on architects from

---

279 Reprinted in 1994.

Raphael to Michelangelo and the ongoing work of the Palladio Museum in Vicenza.[280]

It is not by chance that Venice is a center for this resurgence of Renaissance studies. In 1980 the city inaugurated the architecture Biennale, which in its first edition showcased postmodern architecture under the motto "The Presence of the Past."[281] For architects, the exhibition was proof that the long-lived interest of their profession in classical architecture had been rekindled following the modern architectural orthodoxy of the first half of the twentieth century, and especially since Robert Venturi (1925–2018) identified Rome as a reference for contemporary architecture. American postmodernism was the most visible outcome of this flirtation, in which skyscrapers and public buildings were flooded with columns and pediments. However, since the postmodern sources were mostly built examples of classical architecture, Vitruvius seems to have been relatively marginal to this euphoria.

It was not until 2003 that the American architect and educator Thomas Gordon Smith published what we might call a postmodern Vitruvius. In it he explicitly addresses practitioners in the commentary, arguing that "although materials and methods of construction have changed, the core concerns of the profession remain unaltered. Vitruvius's recommendations are still germane to solving problems of strength, function and beauty in modern circumstances.'[282] Gordon Smith's edition is limited to Books I, III, IV, V, and VI. The text is based on Morgan's translation of 1914 but with updates to vocabulary and syntax made with the help of the linguist Stephen Kellogg. Throughout the book, new technical drawings and illustrations demonstrate the continuity between Vitruvius's

---

280 The Centro Internazionale di Studi di Architettura Andrea Palladio, Vicenza. Founded in 1958, the center promotes research, stages exhibitions, publishes books, and organizes courses and seminars in which Vitruvius is a frequent subject, directly or indirectly.

281 See Léa-Catherine Szacka, *Exhibiting the Postmodern: The 1980 Venice Architecture Biennale* (Venice: Marsilio, 2016).

282 Gordon Smith, "Commentary," in Gordon Smith 2003 ± I, III–VI, 10.

examples and contemporary practice, with aquarelles of Vitruvian façades, details, and plans represented in equivalent fashion to Gordon Smith's postmodern buildings. In addition to promoting the applicability of Vitruvius's proportional system and design methods in architectural practice, Gordon Smith also envisions the book's academic use in providing a suitable disciplinary and moral framework for the education of future architects. He claims that "Vitruvius's call for an education both intellectual and tangible, and his plea for an ethos of accountability among architects in their role as civic leaders, continue to be appropriate admonitions."[283]

Today, the digital turn has brought the catalogue of Vitruvius editions to another level of complexity, with books metamorphosing as dramatically as they did in the fifteenth century when manuscript culture was transformed by print. Digital versions of the Granger and the Rowland editions can be bought online and read on screen. The Morgan edition of 1914 is available for free on the Project Gutenberg website. Similarly, many libraries have digitized their old Vitruviuses, providing easy access to the content of most editions published before 1909. Even as the production of new print editions continues to accelerate, it seems that the future of Vitruvius is in the digital world, where it will face new and different challenges.

---

283 Gordon Smith, "Commentary," in Gordon Smith 2003 ± I, III–VI, 10.

THE TETRASTYLE HYPOTHESIS

How does a sentence from a theoretical treatise materialize as built architecture? The question is an unsolvable enigma. Nonetheless, the pursuit of links between Vitruvius's descriptions of tetrastyle rooms and their built counterparts offers glimpses of the convoluted paths linking theory and practice. Vitruvius is quite specific in describing the structure and purpose of a tetrastyle *cavaedium*: the four columns relieve the load on the beams and shorten their span.[284] Such a space, a feature of domestic architecture, seems close to what today we call an atrium: a transitional room that mediates between the entrance to the house and its internal functions.

While there are not as many built tetrastyle spaces as one might imagine, they exist everywhere, a few of them scholarly references to the Vitruvian tradition but many more that seem to have slipped away from it. To find them, I broadened the definition of an atrium to include living rooms, bathrooms, and even cafés. This enlargement runs parallel to the evolution of the tetrastyle concept from Vitruvius's sentence into real building; the words seem prescriptive, but the meaning is open.[285]

My search for tetrastyle rooms began with the aim of assessing correspondences between how the sentence is presented in various iterations of the book and contemporaneous architectural solutions. As the work went on, it became clear that such a parallel was near-impossible to establish, but that other paths were more promising. Rather than establishing direct commonalities between text and built work, the resulting collection of tetrastyle rooms suggests an intricate web of connections—explicit and implicit—between the Roman treatise, its editions, and the practice of architecture.

---

284 Vitruvius, VI, 3, 1. See "Prologue", notes 2 and 3.
285 Francisco Mario Grapaldi (ca. 1464–1515) pointed out the ambiguous nature of Vitruvius's distinction between atrium and *cavaedium* in 1494 in a publication addressing the parts of the Roman house. Francisci Marii Grapaldi, *De partibus aedium libellus: Cum addita mentis emendatissimus*, 1st ed. 1494 ([Parma]: [F. Ugoletto], [1501]).

THE TETRASTYLE HYPOTHESIS

In the following pages, I explore some of these connections between the book and buildings along five of these paths: the first looks at the book's illustrations, where the exact passage is transformed into representation; the second discusses a series of enigmatic Renaissance tetrastyle rooms in Tomar, Portugal; the third presents the Roman reference as an ideal to which the most precise tetrastyle *cavaediae* correspond; the fourth considers Pliny the Younger as a literary source for restitutions of possible ideal Roman villas; and, finally, the fifth describes a series of tetrastyle spaces whose connection to Vitruvius is likely accidental but is nonetheless revealing of the threads that tie books to practice.

PROPORTIONAL DEADLOCK

In 1914 Harvard University Press published the first American edition of Vitruvius by Morris Hicky Morgan. To illustrate Book VI, Chapter III, Paragraph 1, he used plans from August Mau's reference book *Pompeii: Its Life and Art*.[286] With this straightforward option, Morgan offered historically accurate illustrations of the *cavaedia* Vitruvius was referring to, replacing the architectural interpretations of his predecessors with factual examples. The plans show the ancient Roman houses as complex systems, their distortions exposing the intricate reality of construction rather than designs produced according to ideal principles. Thus the houses that were unearthed over a century of continuous archaeological work at Pompeii, allowing Vitruvius's descriptions to be experienced as built form, were transported as images into his book. Before Pompeii, illustrating the passage on *cavaedia* involved an adventurous incursion into architectural design, since the text's vague terms left open a wide range of possibilities.

Various editions of Vitruvius include such original speculative designs for tetrastyle rooms: by Fra Giocondo, Cesare Cesariano, Andrea Palladio (for the second editions of the Italian and Latin versions of Daniele Barbaro's Vitruvius), Claude Perrault, Berardo Galiani, William Newton, Baldassare Orsini, Quirico Viviani, Luigi Marini, and Auguste Choisy. In other editions, the illustrations are either copied or the text is left without

---

286 August Mau, *Pompeii: Its Life and Art* (New York: Macmillan, 1899).

a visual counterpart.[287] The original designs vary significantly, and as such demonstrate both their authors' independent reading of the canonic text and the volatility of architectural prescriptions. Overlooking the architectural orders adopted that are seldom visible or explicit, the most direct way to compare them is to follow Vitruvius's descriptions and assess the method used to fix their spatial proportions. This, however, is made difficult because the designs do not reflect the method explicitly and because the method itself leaves open most of the other crucial decisions required to shape architecture, as evident in that even by following the same steps the various authors arrived at different results. Additionally, most of the authors, despite knowing and understanding Vitruvius's recommendations, deliberately selected different principles on which to base their designs. This divergence between the argument and the architecture is visible in the options presented by the various authors for the proportions of the plans, but also in the variety of heights adopted. These discrepancies might be attributed to the fundamental ambiguity of Vitruvius's treatise, the book being somewhere in between a prescriptive set of norms and a system of architectural principles. Thus each architectural design for the tetrastyle room displays its author's allegiance to a particular reading of Vitruvius, a reading that is moreover anchored in a precise context of book production and usage.

In the first paragraph of Chapter III, Book VI, after describing the types of *cavaedia*, Vitruvius offers three possible ratios for the rectangular plan of the atrium—5:3, 3:2, or 1:$\sqrt{2}$—and specifies that the *compluvium* should be proportional, occupying 1/4 or 1/3 of the overall width. The fourth paragraph defines the height of the space—3/4 of the width—and discusses how to determine the dimensions of the aisles (or *alae*), acknowledging that there is no precise proportional system for doing so since the aisles should be balanced with the size

---

287 For example, Durantino used Giocondo's drawing, and Ryff adapted Cesariano's. Rode, for his part, illustrated *cavaedia* but not tetrastyles.

1511 Giocondo

1521 Cesariano

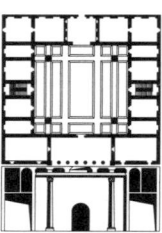
1567 Barbaro

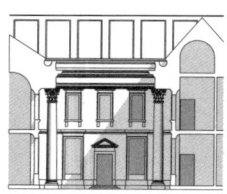
1673 Perrault

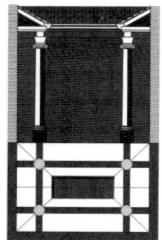
1758 Galiani

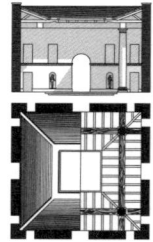
1791 Newton

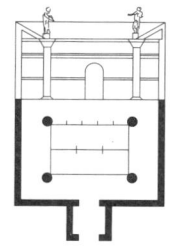
1802 Orsini

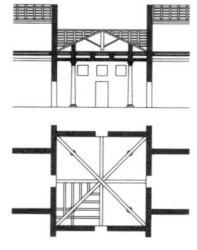
1830-33 Viviani

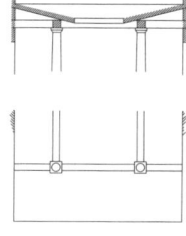
1909 Choisy

32 Nine Tetrastyle *cavaedia* from Vitruvius editions

PROPORTIONAL DEADLOCK

33 Proportions of nine Tetrastyle *cavaedia*

of the rest of the construction. He suggests possible ratios for atria of lengths of 50 feet, of between 60 and 80 feet, and of between 80 and 100 feet, and concludes by stating that the "lintel beams should be placed high enough to make the height of the alae equal to their width."[288] Despite the proportional system, the effective dimensions change everything, and it is worth noting that almost all authors avoided giving their designs precise dimensions, leaving them as abstract principles instead of building plans.

The first published illustration of a tetrastyle *cavaedium* is a woodcut in the 1511 edition by Fra Giocondo. It represents a two-level courtyard with a one-story-high *compluvium* formed by a light wooden roof structure resting on a beam above the columns. Four windows are visible on the upper floor, but there are no openings at ground level. The absence of openings gives the space a somewhat abstract appearance.[289] The perspective drawing is rather coarse, making the precise proportions of the space and its elements hard to establish, but it is evident that Giocondo did not follow any of the three sets of proportions Vitruvius suggests. Instead, if we translate his perspective drawing into orthogonal projections, a less Vitruvian system based on a square plan divided into a nine-part grid seems to emerge. The columns have a ratio of 1:9, with an intercolumniation of four columns and an aisle width equivalent to three columns, whereby the module is established by the column diameter. Giocondo's perspective of the testudinate atrium—a 14-module square with a regular two-module spacing for both the aisles and intercolumniation—is easier to read. The grid on the floor is a helpful guideline that makes it possible to confirm the hypothesis of the square plan in the tetrastyle atrium. Giocondo also used square plans for his Tuscan and displuviate designs. Only the Corinthian

---

288 Morgan 1914, VI, 3, 3, 178.

289 The illustration suffered adaptations in the 1513 pocket edition and in the 1523 Lyon edition. In both, the general scheme of the original is retained; the differences are in the lesser technical quality of the later illustrations, not in the content. Giocondo's illustration was later adopted and reused by many editors of Vitruvius.

is rectangular, stretched to accommodate an additional row of columns. The relationship of height to width reflects a ratio of 3:4, and in the illustration that follows it, dedicated to Paragraph 4, Giocondo shows how to proportion the atrium according to the ratios specified by Vitruvius. But why did he not use Vitruvius's proportional system for all the *cavaedia* he designed? Was the square plan an awkward compromise because it allowed the foreground of the perspective to be omitted for better visibility?

The 1521 tetrastyle room designed by Cesare Cesariano has square Corinthian piers—an exception to the round columns standard in his other *cavaedia*—that resonate with its quasi-square plan. The grid inscribed on the floor indicates a 15:17 ratio, and the sectional perspective through the *compluvium* accentuates the space's depth. In comparison to other tetrastyle *cavaedia*, the most distinctive characteristic of Cesariano's design is the treatment of the upper floor, with obvious functional spaces placed above the aisles. The piers coincide with the edges of the *compluvium*, echoing Vitruvius's comment on how the four vertical elements offer the structural advantage of supporting an upper floor, thereby gaining additional space. The elaboration of the design seems an attempt to resolve the contradiction between the *cavaedium*'s openness and the desire to enclose the upper level, contrasting with Giocondo's version in which the colonnade supports a simple wooden roof attached to the peripheral walls. The proportions of the piers have a 1:10 ratio with an intercolumniation of approximately six columns and an aisle depth of four columns. Each of the ground-floor walls has two high windows and a central door with a decorated entablature. There is one window on the visible short side of the upper floor and two on each of the longer sides, reinforcing the idea of a rectangular space and differentiating it from Cesariano's other illustrations of *cavaedia* that seem to be square in plan. Again, it is the use of perspective that renders ambivalent the proportions of the spaces and the methods for their design.

Andrea Palladio's tetrastyle atrium for 1567 Daniele Barbaro's Vitruvius is a key moment in the history being traced here.[290] This is because Palladio soon expanded the scope of his theoretical proposal by reproducing two similar drawings in his own *I quattro libri*,[291] and also by building spaces that recreate his interpretation of Vitruvius's description of the room type. In this, its original context, it is hard to distinguish whether the design should be credited to the architect Palladio or to the author Barbaro. The design is of a square space, with a rectangular *compluvium*—on a 1:2 ratio—aligned with the entrance. The four columns are placed in between the perimeter walls and the *compluvium*. The coffered ceiling reinforces the longitudinal perspective of the space, underplaying its square shape. But is it an inside room or an open *cavaedium*? The space's interior character reflects Palladio's preference for covered spaces while retaining an ambiguity about its function as either an atrium or as an enclosed room, a distinction that has consistently troubled readers of Vitruvius. The design also differs from earlier illustrations in that the columns are independent of the *compluvium*, a choice that accentuates the presence of the ceiling. The height of the space is guided by the 1:9 ratio of the columns and is thus lower than the dimension of three quarters of the width suggested by Vitruvius.[292] Another difference lies in the presentation of the design. While earlier editors chose the more illustrative perspective, here a combination of plan and section is used, suggesting that the operative function of the image is as a design reference. Therefore, the persistence of the square space seems not to be a fortuity but a deliberate divergence from the ancient treatise's recommendations.

290 Palladio's tetrastyle rooms are discussed below in the section "Model and Theory." The 1556 illustrations to Book VI comprise just a plan and section of a "private house" featuring a monumental *cavaedium* with two parallel rows of six Corinthian columns that rise the full height of the two-story building. The tetrastyle *cavaedium* is not illustrated until the 1567 Italian and Latin editions.

291 Palladio, *I quattro libri*, 27–28, 36–37.

292 He uses the 3:5 ratio for the *testudinate* and the $1:\sqrt{2}$ ratio for the Tuscan *cavaedia*.

Palladio and Barbaro's tetrastyle room is quite different from those of Giocondo and Cesariano in that it is conceived of as belonging to the scheme for the Roman house as a whole. As such, it is clear that the room is part of a larger project to update the ancient source as a reference for contemporary design. Where the earlier authors illustrated independent ideal spaces, Palladio and Barbaro's atrium belongs to an interlocking system with correlated elements. This seems to be an exception to the general rule, since the editions that follow theirs return to describing the ideal tetrastyle room without considering the rest of the house, which is an approach implicit in the structure of Vitruvius's text itself, subdivided as it is into discrete chapters and paragraphs that accentuate the independent nature of the architectural illustrations. Each image thus seems a design for a singular space—matching each separate paragraph—instead of a component of an overall system for designing a balanced structure.

The next new tetrastyle design did not appear until Claude Perrault's French translation of 1673, more than a century after Palladio's illustration. Perrault acknowledges the difficulty of following Vitruvius's argument, calling his description of the tetrastyle "obscure and corrupted," and explaining that he had had to add words to the sentence to make sense of it.[293] Perrault understands the *cavaedium* to be a court inside a house, formed by "multiple parts of lodgings that enclosed a square or any other figure."[294] Although they both use the square, this clarification allows him to distance his proposal from Palladio's, in which atria and *cavaedia* are spaces sometimes open to the elements and sometimes indoors. Perrault stresses the function of the gutter element around the roofs—the *cheneau*—giving a pretext for a massive entablature supported by the four corner columns. Unlike Perrault's Corinthian court, where the alignment of the columns

---

293 Perrault 1673, VI, 3, 3, n. 3, 198.
294 Perrault 1673, VI, 3, 3, n. 1, 195, translated by the author.

"creates a corridor that runs covered along the walls"[295] on all sides, in his tetrastyle court the four columns just support the entablature without covered galleries. He does not provide a plan, but assuming he intended a square plan like his other *cavaedia*, his tetrastyle atrium would be a cube within a cube. The inner cube corresponds to the *impluvium*: the space is as wide as it is high, the intercolumniation matching the height of the columns. A second abstract cubic shape is formed around it with the addition of aisles one-column-diameter deep on each side, and the entablature, which is two diameters high. Despite the abstraction of the figure, this cube within a cube demonstrates a compositional rationale that goes well beyond Vitruvius's description of the tetrastyle room.

Printed in Naples as Karl Weber was making progress on the excavation of Herculaneum and Pompeii,[296] Galiani's 1758 design for a tetrastyle cavaedium reflects a newfound understanding of the architecture of the Roman villa. An illustration at the end of Book VI that shows a stone fragment inscribed with plans of ancient Roman houses reinforces the author's intentions to provide a more accurate assessment of ruins and factual information than that afforded by the antiquarian culture that grew out of the Renaissance. Galiani acknowledges his limitations, in particular a lack of factual knowledge of ancient remains that renders "the understanding of this chapter slightly grueling."[297] Nevertheless, his tetrastyle atrium avoids the square plans of his predecessors and adopts the Vitruvian ratio of $1:\sqrt{2}$, with the *compluvium* centered proportionately and the four columns distributed at the intersections of two pairs of perpendicular axes. The columns are a half module in diameter, and their 1:9 ratio determines the height of the space—an option that, diverting from the treatise's recommen-

---

295 Perrault 1673, VI, plate LI, 197, translated by the author.
296 See Carol C. Mattusch, ed., *Rediscovering the Ancient World* (Washington, DC: National Gallery of Art, 2013), 3–4. On Pompeii see the sections "Grounding Theory" above and especially "Shifting Type" below.
297 Galiani 1758, VI, 3, 1, n. 2, 228, translated by the author.

dations, enhances the vertical development of the space. This proposal finds an echo in the design Ortiz y Sanz published in his Spanish translation of 1787. Despite significant differences from Galiani—in his composition of columns the fact that he does not show a tetrastyle atrium, and in the difficulty in linking any proportional system to his design—both authors extend the space vertically (Ortiz y Sanz going as high as five modules).[298]

The 1771 English translation by William Newton presents a design that updates the Palladian tetrastyle model but adopts a much more generous opening and a different language for the architectural elements. The main difference is that Newton's *compluvium* is designed as a concentric square within a square that reinforces the centrality of the space. Its overall height derives from the 1:9 ratio of the four columns, set back in the centers of the corner squares of a nine-square plan. Despite the reference to the nine squares decipherable in Giocondo, it is an obvious divergence from other Vitruvian designs. Since the beams are laid over the columns, they are far from the center of the *compluvium* so to allow for the roof to extend father inward, with Newton using what he believed were Vitruvius's *interpensiva*. Following Philander, Newton defines the *interpensiva* as "joists projected beyond the beams" that, in this case, bridge the distance from the beams resting on the columns to the outer edge of the roof, in turn comprising a large gutter. Another distinctive feature of his design are the two floor levels surrounding the *cavaedium*—an option already adopted by Perrault—which, since the *compluvium* is limited to the central square, creates a rather ambiguous perception of the space as an inner court.

Nineteenth-century tetrastyle designs come closer to the Vitruvian proportions. The 1802 edition by Baldassarre Orsini presents a humble set of illustrations that combine, in a pe-

---

[298] Despite the similarities between Ortiz y Sanz's and Galiani's designs for a *cavaedium*, Ortiz y Sanz argues that the *interpensiva* beams only need to be anchored in the walls in the Tuscan, the columns providing the necessary structure to avoid the use of such long wooden beams. Ortiz y Sanz 1787, V , III, 1, 145–146.

culiar way, Newton's elevations with Galiani's proportions. Orsini's image is rather coarse, and the clumsy distribution of the drawings within the plate results in a lack of clarity about whether the relatively low height of the *cavaedium* is intentional or an adjustment required to squeeze the drawing into the available space within the upper border. The columns seem to approximate to a ratio of 1:9, but because of the low roof they look rather slim. Unlike the previous designs, Orsini leaves some small lines in the plan that hint at its proportions. They indicate that he used either three or five parts to devise the length of the *compluvium*, but since he adopted a 3:2 ratio for its shape the relevance of the five parts indicated in the plan is uncertain as they seem not to relate to any of the other elements of the design. This 3:2 *compluvium* is again an unexpected option, and it occupies an area significantly larger than the maximum 1/3 suggested by Vitruvius. Although the design follows the Vitruvian recommendation to establish a proportional relation between *cavaedium* and *compluvium*, it seems that Orsini did this backwards, beginning with the six-square *compluvium* and determining the dimensions of the *cavaedium* by adding aisles exactly one-*compluvium*-square-deep around the perimeter of the central space. Like those of Giocondo and Cesariano, his columns are aligned with the gutters of the *compluvium*, again deviating from the Vitruvian description but in this case to reflecting the archaeological evidence that was emerging from the work at Pompeii and Herculaneum.

Luigi Marini's tetrastyle *cavaedium*, published in 1836, is the only one to adopt a 5:3 ratio in plan, and again diverting from Vitruvius he inserts the *compluvium* as the middle module of the three that determine the width of the space in his compositional scheme. He then divides each corner module into four to set the columns apart from the gutters of the *compluvium* and leave a half module on each side for the aisles. The height of the space follows the 3:4 rule and leads to a 1:9 ratio for the Doric columns. Marini explicitly relates his abstract Vitruvian design to real Roman tetrastyle atria by pairing it with a plate reproducing a "Pompeian House with Tetrastyle Cavaedium and Square Peristyle,"[299] specifically the house of the general Championnet as illustrated by François Mazois (1783–1826) in the second volume of *Les ruines de Pompéi*.[300] Along with the tetrastyle atrium, Marini illustrates a tetrastyle *oecus*, a space Vitruvius mentions in Paragraph 8 of the same chapter of Book VI. Based on a square plan, its double height is covered with a non-Vitruvian dome. This proposal raises the recurrent puzzling question of the relationship between the definitions of atrium and *cavaedium*, one that Palladio had explored in his own treatise in developing his tetrastyle *cavaedium* as an interior tetrastyle room.[301]

Bringing us into the twentieth century, Auguste Choisy's 1909 edition offers a rather schematic system of design in which the *cavaedium* is presented as an assemblage of different components rather than as a unitary space. Its openness is suggested by the incompleteness of the plan and section, and to grasp the overall design one must consider multiple illustrations that accompany the figure of the tetrastyle room. Although this combinatory system was not new, in earlier editions it was always complemented by a complete view of the *cavaedium*. To make sense of the elements of the tetrastyle *cavaedium* presented in plate 60 of the Choisy edition, the reader must retain the proportions of the plan in plate 61 and the height ratio defined in plate 62. In this way, instead of offering a clearly defined and illustrated architectural concept, Choisy dissects Chapter III of Book VI into a series of ideas about how to compose a space. He attempts to transform the Vitruvian sentences into geometrical forms and places a great deal of emphasis on the actual dimensions of the space.

---

299 Marini 1836, plate CIII, translated by the author.

300 François Mazois, *Les Ruines de Pompéi: Seconde partie; Édifices privés. Précédé d'un essai sur les habitations des anciens Romains* (Paris: Firmin Didot, 1821–1824), plate XXI. See further below in the section "Shifting Type."

301 The same is true of Thomas Gordon Smith's house in Indiana, discussed below in the section "Vitruvius by Accident."

Where Vitruvius was vague, suggesting a flexible method of distributing the various elements in relation to the adopted dimensions, Choisy attempts to nail down a progressive ratio that interlocks the sizes of all of the parts by means of a mathematical equation. This focus on the dimensions—a theme essentially ignored by his predecessors—points to the importance of his edition to architectural practitioners.

Choisy's was the last tetrastyle *cavaedium* intended to establish a conversation with practicing architects. Most editions subsequent to the 1914 edition featuring Mau's surveys of Pompeii would follow Morgan's lead and provide archaeological references rather than illustrating the treatise with a tetrastyle room intended to be adaptable for new projects. The examples described above, spanning four hundred years of Vitruvian publications, highlight the collective ambition to complement the ancient text and enhance its reading with factual and palpable examples of architectural form. What becomes evident when studying this group of designs is that a dependence on proportional systems can result in an architectural deadlock. In the end, although Vitruvius suggested some flexibility in the proportions of the tetrastyle space, the various architectural translations of the text end up being guided by elements other than their proportions, among them the relationships between open and closed areas, the design of the beams and how they define the ceiling, the form and style of the columns, the presence of the *impluvium* in the space, and the positioning of the windows and doors. Although the various designs follow the same rules, it is symptomatic that the most similar element between them is the 1:9 ratio of their columns, regardless of whether the order is Doric, Ionic, or Corinthian. Nonetheless, the effort made by each author to produce an original design lends every one of these editions a singular quality, with the various architectural cultures it relates to legible in the design.

THE TOMAR ENIGMA

In May 1547, King John III of Portugal (1502–1557) wrote to Friar António de Lisboa (1484–1551), prior of the Order of Christ in Tomar. Friar António had initiated a strategic reform of the Order of Christ in 1529 and, at around the same time, led the expansion of his order's conventual facilities at Tomar—a unique complex that can be traced back to the city's ancient kasbah and, later, to the Templars and their Romanesque church—by building the connected cloisters of the so-called New Convent, a major cultural achievement of the reign of John III.[302] The supervisor of works was João de Castilho (1470–1552). Castilho's career bridges two traditions: he began as a medieval master builder and emerged as an intellectual Renaissance architect, moving from an intertwined practice of imagining and building to one in which the conceptual work and the actual construction were separate.[303] He thus worked in both aspects of the trade, sometimes acting as a contractor on the designs of others—he built the citadel of Mazagão in Morocco, conceived by Miguel de Arruda (d. 1563), Diogo de Torralva (1500–1566), and Benedetto de Ravena (ca. 1485–1556) between 1541 and 1542, some-

---

302 Paulo Pereira, "O 'Convento Novo' (1529–1551)," *Monumentos*, no. 37 (November 2019): 100–119.

303 See Ricardo Jorge Nunes da Silva, "O paradigma da arquitetura em Portugal na Idade Moderna: Entre o tardo-gótico e o Renascimento; João de Castilho 'o mestre que amanhece e anoitece na obra'" (PhD diss., Faculdade de Letras da Universidade de Lisboa, 2018).

times taking credit for the entire work, as at Tomar.[304] There, Castilho built the first stages of the Main Cloister—transformed and completed by Diogo de Torralva in 1562—and other important parts of the monastery structure, including the refectory, the dormitory, and the Raven's Cloister. With a few circumstantial exceptions, Castilho managed the construction work within the complex until his death in 1552, executing the royal contracts accepted by Friar António de Lisboa.

The short letter conveys several directives regarding the monastic works and mentions the presence of an António Rodrigues (ca. 1525?–1590) on the building site:

> *António Rodrigues has shown me the letter you wrote with the information that he gave you about these works. I am sending him back to you with the drawing of them. The works are to be done in accordance with the said drawing, and you will now be able to have António Rodrigues there for as long as you think necessary. This time will be as short as possible for João de Castilho, once he has seen the papers and their information, and with the practice that they have both had, to be more certain about what has to be done and the way that he has to do it, as you will write and tell me what is necessary.*[305]

The passage is clear: Castilho, then seventy-seven years old, should follow a drawing carried by Rodrigues. A few months earlier, Castilho had been told by the king to "practice"[306] the construction alongside Miguel de Arruda. Arruda had been the principal architect of the crown since 1543, and his sophis-

---

304 See Maria Ealo de Sá, *El arquitecto Juan de Castillo: El construtor del mundo* (Santander: Colégio Oficial de Arquitectos de Cantabria, 2009).

305 Letter from King John III to Friar António de Lisboa on the works of Christ Convent in Tomar, May 6, 1547, transcribed by Silva, *O paradigma*, vol. II: 193; and Rafael Moreira, "A arquitectura do Renascimento no sul de Portugal: A encomenda régia entre o moderno e o romano" (PhD diss. Faculdade de Ciências Sociais e Humanas da Universidade Nova de Lisboa, Lisbon, 1991), vol. II: 106–107.

306 The Portuguese word used is *praticase* according to Silva, "O paradigma," vol. II, 198, doc. 93.

ticated signature distinguishes the most exquisite Portuguese Renaissance spaces.[307] This explains the usual and eventually accurate attribution of the Noviciate area of the Convent of Christ, built between 1546 and 1551, to both Castilho and Arruda,[308] who had already worked together on Mazagão. But who was Rodrigues? Today António Rodrigues is a ghostly character, often absent from the main historical narratives.[309] According to the authoritative dictionary of Portuguese architects, Rodrigues took over Arruda's position as royal architect following the latter's death in 1564 and later also became the crown's head of fortifications, retaining both titles until his own death sometime before February 1590.[310] This means he would have been an important figure in the country's building culture.

The exceptional mention of a young Rodrigues carrying architectural drawings to Tomar in May 1547, likely for the purpose of participating in the first steps of the construction of the Noviciate, is of great interest to our Vitruvian history. According to Rafael Moreira's thorough assessment of a forgotten manuscript,[311] in 1576 Rodrigues authored and edited a complete original architectural treatise.[312] The presence in Tomar

---

307 See Rafael Moreira, "Arquitectura: Renascimento e classicismo," in *História da Arte Portuguesa, Do "Modo" Gótico ao Maneirismo*, vol. 1 (Lisbon: Círculo de Leitores, 1995), 302–375. The main English source for Portuguese Renaissance architecture remains George Kubler, *Portuguese Plain Architecture: Between Spices and Diamonds, 1521–1706* (Middletown, CT: Wesleyan University Press, 1972).

308 Silva, "O paradigma," vol. I, 412.

309 Excepting the art historical work of Rafael Moreira, who places Rodrigues in the epicenter of the royal works. My father's synthesis of Portuguese Renaissance architectural history picks up this thread. See D. Tavares, *António Rodrigues*.

310 Sousa Viterbo, *Dicionário histórico e documental dos arquitectos, engenheiros e construtores portugueses ou a serviço de Portugal*, 1st ed. 1899-1922, 3 vols. (Lisbon: Imprensa Nacional Casa da Moeda, 1988), vol. 1 1st ed. Imprensa Nacional, 1899–1922; vol. 2 Lisbon 1904 ed., 385-86; vol. 3, Lisbon 1922 ed., 97. This source is provided by Moreira, "Um tratado português," here 375.

311 Moreira, "Um tratado português." Also on the manuscript and the use of perspective drawing in Portugal, see João Pedro Xavier, *Sobre as origens da perspectiva em Portugal: O "Livro de Perspectiva" do Códice 3675 da Biblioteca Nacional, um Tratado de Arquitectura do século XVI* (Porto: Faup Publicações, 2006).

312 A 1579 version of this treatise, edited and bound but also incomplete, has also been identified. See Moreira, "Um tratado português," 393-397.

of this future theorist is thus highly significant in that within the Noviciate are three carefully tailored tetrastyle rooms.

Tomar's tetrastyle rooms were built in parallel with an intellectual movement that bridged Portuguese culture and European architectural theory. In 1547 André de Resende (ca. 1500–1573) completed his Portuguese translation of Alberti's *De re aedificatoria*[313] to accompany the successful Lisbon edition of Diego Sagredo's *Medidas del Romano*, printed in 1541 and 1542,[314] and a translation of Vitruvius by the eminent scholar Pedro Nunes (1502–1578)[315] in a trio of theoretical works commissioned by John III. The translations by Resende and Nunes were never published, and Nunes's Vitruvius manuscript, first mentioned in 1541 and referred to by Ryff in the 1548 *Vitruvius Teutsch*,[316] is thought to have been lost after being carried to Madrid in 1581 by Juan de Herrera along with other works from the king's library.[317]

Another important theorist of the period was Francisco de Holanda (1517–1585),[318] whose position as a star of

[313] *De re aedificatoria* was finally published in a Portuguese translation. See Krüger's introductory essay: Mário Krüger, "As leituras da arte edificatória," trans. Arnaldo Espírito Santo, in *Da arte edificatória*, by Leon Battista Alberti (Lisbon: Fundação Calouste Gulbenkian, 2011), 17–129. On Nunes's translation, see 83–85.

[314] Diego de Sagredo, *Medidas del Romano agora nueuamente impressas y añadidas de muchas pieças e figuras muy necessarias alos officiales que quieren seguir las formaciones delas basas, colunas, capiteles, y otras pieças de los edificios antíguos* (Lisbon: Luis Rodrigues, 1541), reprinted in 1542.

[315] Rafael Moreira, "Reflexos albertianos no Renascimento Português: A descriptio urbis romae, o matemático Francisco de Melo e um mapa virtual de Portugal em 1531," ed. Mário Krüger, in *Na génese das racionalidades modernas II: Em torno de Alberti e do Humanismo* (Coimbra: Imprensa da Universidade de Coimbra, 2015), 427–442, http://dx.doi.org/10.14195/978-989-26-1015-3_22.

[316] Xavier, *Sobre as origens*, 20 n. 8. Julian Jachmann, *Die Architekturbücher des Walter Hermann Ryff: Vitruvrezeption im Kontext mathematischer Wissenschaften* (Stuttgart: ibidem, 2006).

[317] Leitão, "Sobre as 'obras perdidas' de Pedro Nunes," here 65–66.

[318] Holanda was the author of *Da pintura antiga* (1548) and *Dialogos em Roma* (1548), soon expanded with *Do tirar polo natural* (1549). In 1571 he completed *Da fábrica que falece à cidade de Lisboa*, which was given publishing permission by the censor in 1576, although it remained unpublished until 1879. Holanda's status as a major European intellectual was only acknowledged in the nineteenth century with the translation of the Roman Diálogues. In that volume, Michelangelo Buonarrotti (1475–1564)—whom Holanda had met in Rome—features as respondent in the dialectic structure of the text. For the Portuguese editions, see José da Felicidade Alves,

34 Diogo de Castilho and Miguel de Arruda, Noviciate Chapel, Convent of Christ, Tomar, 1546–1551

Portuguese Renaissance culture was recognized in the nineteenth century with the rediscovery of his manuscript *Da pintura antiga*, a treatise on painting dating from 1548.[319] This was in part due to the work's connection with Michelangelo Buonarrotti (1475–1564), the second part of the treatise being set up as a dialogue with the Italian master. Silvie Deswarte argues that Holanda modeled the first part of his treatise on Vitruvius—whom he quotes on various occasions—and points out the distinct resemblance between the second part, the *Dialogos em Roma,* and Sagredo's dialogues, which Holanda does not mention.[320] Not only is this treatise, with its Vitruvian connection, contemporary to the construction of the Noviciate rooms, but both Holanda and Vitruvius were well known in Portuguese intellectual circles. António Prestes even used Holanda as the basis for his portrayal of the Devil in his play *Auto de Ave Maria*, written in the 1560s.[321] In it, the Devil intervenes to ensure the success of an ongoing building project, boasting that he can be Vitruvius whenever he wants to establish his legitimacy as an architect.[322] The play stresses the conflict between local traditions and the international fashion for new classicizing designs, personified in the Devil architect claiming that his works are inspired by Serlio and

---

Introdução ao estudo da obra de Francisco de Holanda (Lisbon: Livros Horizonte, 1984); and the set of five volumes containing transcriptions of the sourced texts.

319 Sylvie Deswarte, "Franscisco de Holanda, teórico entre o renascimento e o maneirismo," ed. Vítor Serrão, in *História da Arte em Portugal*, O Maneirismo, vol. 7 (Lisbon: Alfa, 1986), 10–29, here 15.

320 Deswarte, "Franscisco de Holanda," here 24.

321 António Prestes, "Auto de Avé Maria," in *Teatro de autores portugueses do séc. XVI: Base de dados textual* (Lisbon: Centro de Estudos de Teatro, 2000), http://www.cet-e-quinhentos.com/obras.

322 "In the shadow of Your Grace, this sketch I have done. When I want, I am Lucio Vitruvius; it does not leave me." Prestes, "Auto de Avé Maria," line 1215, translated by the author.

Villalpando[323] and venturing as far as taking credit for the Pantheon, using Serlio's treatise as proof.[324]

This criticism of the Italianate character of contemporary architecture reflects a political swing that undermined further developments of Portuguese Renaissance culture. As is shown in the play, when Holanda's progressive approach fell from royal favor, so did the fashion for references to antiquity among Portuguese intellectuals. Rodrigues too was affected by the shift of official taste, and although he retained his titles as royal architect and master builder, his commissions dwindled as those given to Filippo Terzi (1520–1597) rose. Rodrigues retreated to Alcácer do Sal, where he built the chapel and mausoleum of D. Pedro Mascarenhas (1484–1555), the politician whose embassy in Rome Holanda had joined in 1538. An expansion of an existing church, the domed chapel is built of smooth marble masonry on a square plan in proportions that evoke the musical qualities of an elaborate mathematical system.[325] As João Pedro Xavier has shown, Rodrigues epitomized the geometrical logic of the design in his 1576 treatise, in which, following the Vitruvian principle of the proportions of an ideal man, a synthesis of the square and the sphere is presented as key to the creation of a perfect centralized space.[326]

Proposition 35 of Rodrigues's treatise presents an example of a square space defined as a tetrastyle room. The figure

---

323 "In very plain Tuscan I have written, it should not be presumed. Of it the great Serlio was the ink, I the quill. And in centuries of the Golden Age, by Villalpando in Spain it was translated and seized from the Tuscan. Its translation is a sublimated, strange thing." Prestes, "Auto de Avé Maria," lines 1779–1788, translated by the author.

324 "The other ancient building, the Pantheon, who has sketched it? Who? My hand. Who has toiled on it? My craft proves my Serlio." Prestes, "Auto de Avé Maria," line 1835, translated by the author.

325 João Pedro Xavier has thoroughly analyzed Rodrigues's geometrical precepts and his use of mathematical proportions in theory and practice. See Xavier, *Sobre as origens*; João Pedro Xavier, "Geometria e proporção," ed. Domingos Tavares, in *António Rodrigues: Renascimento em Portugal* (Porto: Dafne Editora, 2007), 103–119, 103–119.

326 Xavier, "Geometria e proporção," here 106; [Rodrigues, António], "Tratado de arquitectura."

evokes the tetrastyle illustration in Cesariano's Vitruvius—an image that, according to Rafael Moreira, served as reference for the façade of the Nossa Senhora da Conceição Hermitage in Tomar, designed by Castilho and Arruda in parallel with the ongoing works at the convent.[327] A similar scheme is evident in the church of Santa Maria do Castelo in Estremoz, again connected to Arruda.[328] Considerable matching evidence points to the presence of Vitruvianism in Portuguese architectural culture in the mid-sixteenth century. Buildings and theoretical works of the time echo elements of the printed editions of Cesariano and Giocondo and of the various editions of Sagredo's dialogues, intermingled with the influence of Serlio. This leads one to wonder to what extent the Vitruvius passage was used as either reference or authority in the design of the tetrastyle rooms in Tomar.

The three tetrastyle rooms in the Noviciate section of the Convent of Christ are located on the upper floor of Micha's Cloister, above an older bread oven and adjacent to the Necessaria block, accessible through the mezzanine of the original Noviciate area linked to the Santa Barbara Cloister. From the exterior courtyard, the three rooms are defined by three continuous cubic volumes of masonry. Each has an independent roof with gabled ends forming tailored pediments with figurative medallions and windows. The austerity of this exterior is paralleled in the first two interior spaces, which served as dormitories for the novices. These rooms are organized into three aisles of equal width defined by ceiling beams that rest on four Ionic columns. These beams create a strong longitudinal emphasis, highlighted by the path of the light cast by high oval windows at both ends of the side aisles. The third room—square in plan and the last to be accessed when following the main circulation path—served as a chapel and has

---

327 Moreira, "A arquitectura do Renascimento," 560, 566. Moreira quotes illustrations from Book IV, 52, and Book VI, 67.

328 See Francisco Bilou, "Miguel de Arruda, entre Évora e Estremoz: Novos documentos (1532–1562)," *Boletim do Arquivo Distrital de Évora*, no. 3 (September 2015): 53–57.

a rich wooden double-barrel-vault system. The central bay rests upon four Corinthian columns with delicate composite capitals. As opposed to the dormitories, the diffuse orientation of this space is striking, emphasized by the presence of lunette windows at the center of each wall and by the set of twelve engaged columns regularly spaced around its periphery.

Were the tetrastyle rooms of the Noviciate designed in conscious emulation of Vitruvius Book VI, Chapter III, Paragraph 1? This possibility is unlikely. Even though they each have four central columns, as illustrated in Giocondo, there are significant differences between the Noviciate rooms and the Vitruvian sources. First, they are not *cavaedia*, as both their position within the building and their utilitarian program differ from the atria Vitruvius was referring to. Second, they do not reflect the ideal Vitruvian proportions in plan.[329] Moreover, nowhere in Vitruvius's rather laconic description or in any of the published illustrations[330] do we find the twelve engaged columns used in the chapel. Rather, this feature is likely the product of an innovative spatial idea that developed locally, drawing on work done at the Convent of Christ by João de Castilho just before the unique Noviciate tetrastyle rooms were built. Castilho's New Convent contains at least four precedent-setting tetrastyle rooms: the kitchen, a space that for convenience we will call a storeroom,[331] a study room in the Raven's Cloister, and the court of the Necessaria block.

---

329 While the chapel is practically a square, measuring 13.5 × 14.5 meters, the first two rooms are 10.3 and 9.3 meters wide by 13.3 meters deep, far from the Vitruvian proportional rules of 2:3, 3:5 or 1:1√2.

330 Rafael Moreira stresses the autonomous column as an innovative conceptual development in Portuguese architecture and affiliates the Noviciate rooms with Cesariano's 1521 illustration. In Cesariano, the columns are square piers, whereas in Giocondo they are round and Ionic, not unlike the Ionic columns of the two first Noviciate rooms. Moreira also invokes Cesariano as the source for the Santa Maria do Olival chapel, built synchronously by Castilho and Arruda as part of their work on the Convent of Christ. Moreira, "A arquitectura do Renascimento," 560, 566, where Moreira quotes illustrations from Book IV, 52, and Book VI, 67. Coincidences in proportions and details led him to presume that these illustrations were the source for the elevation of Santa Maria da Conceição Church. The same does not apply for the Noviciate.

331 We are not aware of the original purpose of this space. Today it is known as the "olive oil storage," which corresponds to how it was used in the nineteenth century.

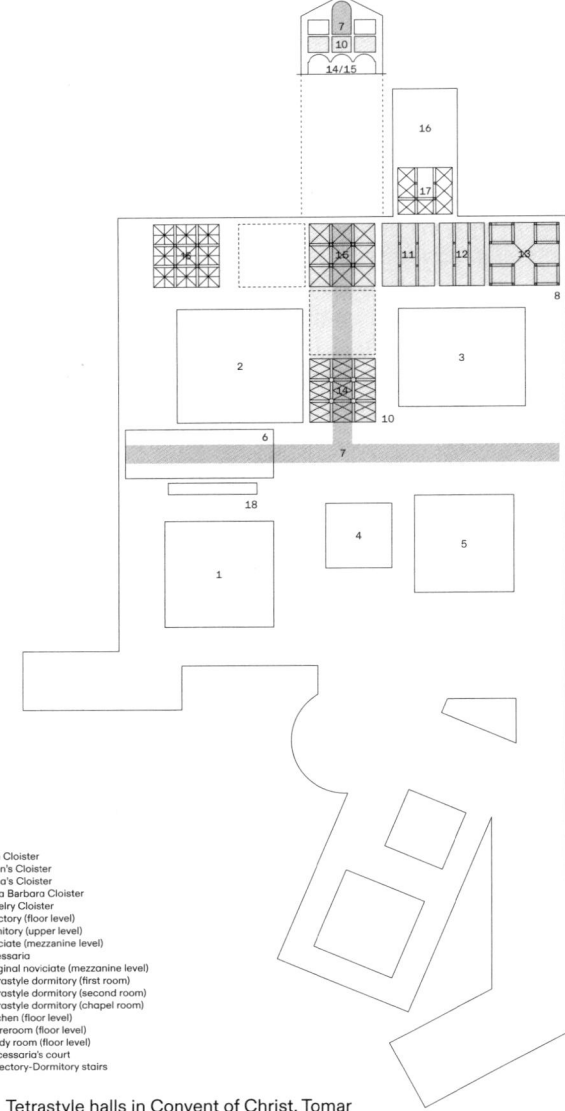

1 Main Cloister
2 Raven's Cloister
3 Micha's Cloister
4 Santa Barbara Cloister
5 Hostelry Cloister
6 Refectory (floor level)
7 Dormitory (upper level)
8 Noviciate (mezzanine level)
9 Necessaria
10 Original noviciate (mezzanine level)
11 Tetrastyle dormitory (first room)
12 Tetrastyle dormitory (second room)
13 Tetrastyle dormitory (chapel room)
14 Kitchen (floor level)
15 Storeroom (floor level)
16 Study room (floor level)
17 Necessaria's court
18 Refectory-Dormitory stairs

35 Tetrastyle halls in Convent of Christ, Tomar

If we follow the chronology—sometimes uncertain due to lacunae in the convent's history[332] —the kitchen and the storeroom were the first tetrastyle spaces laid out by Castilho. After the principal contract was signed in 1533,[333] which required the new spaces to be built *all'antica*,[334] construction started on the Main Cloister, likely completed in 1545 (and later demolished by Diogo de Torralva). The next section begun was the Santa Barbara Cloister, completed in 1543, followed by the Hostelry Cloister, which was built between 1540 and 1543 at the same time as the T-shaped dormitory. The dormitory's south wing rests on the refectory (the two are linked by a bold straight flight of stairs that parallels the main axes of these rooms); its north wing upon the service spaces associated with the functioning of the eastern Hostelry Cloister; and its west wing on two lower levels, namely a mezzanine comprising dormitories for the Noviciate, and below that the storeroom at its west end and the kitchen near the transept foundations. These last two spaces are the earliest tetrastyle rooms in the Convent of Christ.

The dormitory's west wing has a rectangular plan roughly made up of three squares. At ground level, the kitchen and the storeroom occupy the outer squares while the central square is bisected by a bracing wall. The supporting walls that enclose these spaces are not continuous with those of the mezzanine and dormitory floors above it, as one might expect of a straightforward, load-bearing construction.[335] Instead, when the loads of the long corridor walls that define the cells of the dormitory

---

332 For the most accurate and detailed chronology, see Silva, "O paradigma," 625–740.

333 Another figure mentioned in the 1533 contract and throughout the New Convent works is Bartolomeu de Paiva (d. 1536). According to Paulo Pereira, although Paiva oversaw Castilho's activity, he never acted as a designer or architect. Pereira, "O 'Convento Novo' (1529–1551)," n. 66.

334 "*Ao romano*" according to Silva, "O paradigma," vol. I, 693. Silva quotes the 1533 building contract. Arquivo Nacional Torre do Tombo, Ordem de Cristo/Convento de Cristo, liv. 263, fl.

335 In the mezzanine, the low-rise vaults rest on load-bearing walls contiguous with those on the floor above, so the loads are discharged directly from the upper to the lower floor.

and mezzanine reach the ground floor, they are directed into massive supports—four in the kitchen and four in the storeroom—by means of rib vaults and low arches. In the kitchen, the supports are thick columns with squashed proportions, deviating from the strictures Vitruvius laid out. The storeroom has massive square piers with peculiar capitals reminiscent of modern steel structural joints, as if the vaulting fluctuates upon them. The arches of the vaulting span from the piers to corner corbels and to eight pilasters—different in style to the piers—on the peripheral walls. In the kitchen there are no pilasters; all the arches spring from corbels. The elaboration of these two spaces, with their carefully crafted masonry, seems to justify the structural adventure required to place them under the dormitories, with loads traveling along the rib vaults to the peripheral pilasters and corbels. Nothing, however, points to Vitruvius as a possible reference for the tetrastyle design of the kitchen and storeroom, despite the pervasive architectural references to Sagredo throughout the New Convent.

The tetrastyle study room in the Raven's Cloister, built between 1543 and 1546, follows the same design principles as the kitchen. However, this space has a more generous vertical development due to fewer structural constraints—above there are only a few adjunct rooms for elderly friars. The position of the study room in the plan is rather unbalanced: although the overall proportion of the cloister seems to be based on multiple squares, and the room itself is also square, its position is neither central nor terminal. Instead it is shifted far enough away from the southwest corner of the building to allow its axially placed entrance to open directly onto the cloister without having to abandon the square shape of the room.

Two additional tetrastyle spaces are found in the Necessaria, which hosts the convent latrines. This independent functional block, several stories high, is linked to the dormitory wing by discrete passages at both upper and mezzanine levels.[336] The formal and technical sophistication of the carved

---

336 See Ana Carvalho Dias and Renata Faria Barbosa, "O primitivo sistema

THE TOMAR ENIGMA

36 Diogo de Castilho, kitchen, Convent of Christ, Tomar, ca. 1533

stone canals and ventilation ducts suggests an attentive study of hydraulic treatises like Vitruvius's. The block has two areas organized to keep the hygienic facilities as far as possible from the main building. The most distant section, to the west, contains the latrines on the upper floors and two chimneys rising from the cesspool in the basement (from which underground canals drain the wastewater below the outdoor space enclosing the convent). The closer eastern section comprises a veranda on the upper floor that allows outdoor access to the latrines. The first of the Necessaria's two tetrastyle spaces is a reservoir at basement level, in which Doric columns secure sturdy low-rise arches and a rib-vaulted ceiling. Above it, on the ground floor, is the second, a small cloister that, like the upper veranda, provides a transitional outdoor space between the latrine section of the wing and the dormitories. It is organized around a central *impluvium* that conducts rainwater into the reservoir. This feature replicates the ambience of a tetrastyle *cavaedium*, with diffuse light cast from above. The peculiar U-shape of the vaulted covering around the edges leaves one peripheral module of the nine-square plan open and thus bears a remarkable resemblance to the many Vitruvian illustrations of tetrastyle *cavaedia* that show them in a central perspective with an absent side. Nonetheless, the reference to a treatise model here is likely illusory, in part because the space has such a marginal position within the hierarchy of the convent and because the design options seem to result more from practical concerns than from intellectual considerations of the principles of architecture.

Castilho's tetrastyle rooms instead had a different precedent: the local synagogue.[337] Tomar had a thriving Jewish

---

hidráulico do 'convento novo': Contributo dos trabalhos de arqueologia no Convento de Cristo, Tomar," *Monumentos*, no. 37 (November 2009): 162–171.

337 See Fernando Sanches Salvador and Margarida Grácio Nunes, "A Sinagoga de Tomar e o Museu Luso-Hebraico Abraão Zacuto Projecto de conservação e reabilitação," *Monumentos*, no. 37 (November 2019): 178–187. See also J. M. Santos Simões, *Tomar e a sua Judiaria* (Tomar: Museu Luso-Hebraico, 1943); F. A. Garcez Teixeira, *A antiga Sinagoga de Tomar* (Lisbon: Tipografia do Comércio, 1925).

37 Diogo de Castilho and Miguel de Arruda, Necessaria Court, Convent of Christ, Tomar, ca. 1533

community from the 1430s until 1497, when Portuguese Jews were expelled from the country. Dating from this brief period, the synagogue is a square building (9.5 × 8.2 meters) covered by nine brick groin vaults. The four columns, in contrast to their squashed counterparts in the convent kitchen, have elegant Vitruvian proportions with a ratio of 1:9, extending the restrained space up into the vaults. The original entrance (later moved to an axial position) led through an antechamber to a lateral door that would have created a dynamic perspective when entering the room. Historians see a relationship between this construction and other important building sites in the region, extending from the works on the Convent of Christ to the prominent Batalha Monastery and the castle of Ourém, where the crypt presents several formal similarities to Tomar's synagogue. Nonetheless, it is hard to conceive a genealogical chain establishing a lineage between the Vitruvian tetrastyle room, the synagogue, and the various examples in the convent that preceded the three Noviciate rooms because, unlike the others, the synagogue is a sacred space.

The three tetrastyle rooms of the Noviciate reflect an intellectual frenzy in Portugal that looked to Roman antiquity as a model for the architecture of a new-born empire. Rodrigues, the young carrier of drawings and future author of a treatise, would come to embody the ideal of the architect as an intellectual, following the Vitruvian precept of architecture as a liberal art. Nonetheless, a connection between these rooms and Vitruvius eludes us—despite the architects' and builders' knowledge of his treatise and its importance in the intellectual context of the time—and the work seems more likely to be a refinement of previous local experiments.[338] In fact, all of the Tomar tetrastyles discussed make it difficult to connect the treatise to the practice of architecture. This is equally true of a final piece of the puzzle found in Tomar's downtown Café

---

338 In many ways, the tetrastyle precedents of the Noviciate recall the capitular rooms of Italian abbeys preceding Andrea Palladio's tetrastyle spaces that are analyzed below in the section "Model and Theory."

THE TOMAR ENIGMA

38 Tomar Synagogue, ca. 1490

Paraíso, inaugurated in 1911 and refurbished in 1946.[339] The café is a large tetrastyle hall, an elegant and practical solution to reconcile the need for an open space and the structural requirement to support the beams of the residential upper floors. There is no plausible connection between this modern tetrastyle and the fifteenth-century synagogue, two blocks away, or to the various tetrastyle spaces in the Convent of Christ. Nor can it be linked to Vitruvius. In its simplicity, it confronts us with the elusive nature of the tetrastyle enigma and the relationship between reality and the realm of architectural theory.

---

339 The 1946 renovation was conducted by the architect Francisco Granja.

THE TOMAR ENIGMA

39 Francisco Granja, Café Paraiso, Tomar, 1946

MODEL AND THEORY

Of that of all architects, the work of Andrea Palladio permits the most effective assessment of the passage between book culture and building practice. To produce his famous figures for Daniele Barbaro's Vitruvius, Palladio surveyed Roman antiquities and carefully read the relevant passages of the text.[340] Barbaro's first translation of Vitruvius was published in 1556, but the tetrastyle *cavaedium* is only illustrated in the 1567 Italian and Latin editions.[341] Its absence from the first edition confirms the tetrastyle's marginal status as a variation on the Corinthian entrance chosen to illustrate Book VI, Chapter III, Paragraph 1. In the second expanded Italian and Latin editions of 1567, the luxurious Corinthian court is accompanied by woodcuts showing modest *testudinatum*, *displuviatum*, *tuscanicum* and *tetrastylon cavaedia*, a sequence conceived in a crescendo of increasing complexity from the uncovered and austere *displuviatum* to the covered and austere *testudinatum*, the half-covered *tuscanicum* with a coffered ceiling, and finally the tetrastyle, its coffered ceiling and Corinthian capitals ranking it high in the hierarchy of these alternative *cavaedia*.

---

340 See Cellauro, "Palladio e le illustrazioni." See also my argument on the relation between the plan–section–elevation system of representation and the structure of book pages in the chapter "Surface" in A. Tavares, *Anatomy of the Architectural Book*, 210–229.

341 On Barbaro's editions and Palladio's illustrations, see the preceding sections "The Age of Orders, 1556–1649" and "Proportional Deadlock".

MODEL AND THEORY

While collaborating with Barbaro on the Vitruvius editions, Palladio was building his own tetrastyle spaces in urban palazzi and villas in and around Vicenza. In 1570 he published in his own *I quattro libri*, with both an update of the ideal Vitruvian tetrastyle illustration[342] and drawings of a selection of his built works that include revised versions of tetrastyle constructions. Palladio is the ultimate example of a reader who produced original illustrations of tetrastyle spaces for Vitruvius's text, built his own work based on the illustrations, and subsequently produced illustrations of his own built work. In so doing he completed the circle from the book to architecture as representation, from architecture to the built realm as building practice, and from the building back to the book as theory. And if that was not enough, his book became a reference for many other architects who ruminated on Vitruvian examples as points of departure for the invention of new architectural forms.

The passage in Book VI, Chapter III, Paragraph 1 challenged Palladio's imagination. His introduction to tetrastyle construction was the Palazzo Thiene in Vicenza, a prestigious commission inherited from Giulio Romano (1499–1546), for whom he had worked as on-site assistant beginning in 1542.[343] The Palazzo Thiene has a tetrastyle entrance hall with a groin-vaulted ceiling that rests on four columns connected to the peripheral walls by means of lintels, as in a *serliana*. The rather expressive rough-hewn columns have bases and capitals narrower than their shafts, breaking with the Vitruvian canon. Romano built an earlier and quite different tetrastyle entrance for the Palazzo Te in Mantua that functions more simply as a passage to the large inner courtyard.[344] The rough finish of the

---

342 Palladio, *I quattro libri*, "Dell'Atri di Quattro Colonne," 27–28, and "Delle Sale di Quattro Colonne," 36–37.

343 See Howard Burns, "Giulio Romano and the Palazzo Thiene," ed. Guido Beltramini and Howard Burns, in *Palladio* (London: Royal Academy of Arts, 2009), 40–43; Howard Burns, "I progetti vicentini di Giulio Romano," in *Giulio Romano* (Milan: Electa, 1989), 502–505.

344 It was built from 1527 to 1532. See Amedeo Belluzzi and Kurt W. Forster, "Palazzo Te," in *Giulio Romano* (Milan: Electa, 1989), 317–335.

columns is similar to that at Thiene, but the Te columns rest on heavier square bases.[345] The most significant difference, however, is in the vaulting. At Te, the sides have flat, coffered ceilings framing a central barrel vault that emphasizes the path leading to the courtyard, in a direction perpendicular to that created at Thiene where the atrium runs parallel to the street. Nonetheless, both reinterpretations adapt the ideal Vitruvian *cavaedium* to evoke the ritual of passage between exterior and interior spaces.

Palladio's involvement in the Palazzo Thiene must have made him attentive to the relation between Romano's tetrastyle entrances and the Vitruvian prescriptions for houses. His Palazzo Barbarano, completed in 1575, five years after the publication of the *I quattro libri*, also has a tetrastyle entrance.[346] The existing palazzo results from an enlargement of the property after construction had already begun—the earliest drawings for the initial design date back to 1568. When the site was enlarged, the idea of creating a sequence of exterior spaces like a Vitruvian house became more obvious, and Palladio added a peristyle following the tetrastyle entrance that reflects a plan he had drawn for the 1556 edition of Vitruvius. Howard Burns has pointed out how Palladio's four-columned entrances represent a synthesis of his Roman archaeological surveys, his Vitruvian readings on domestic architecture, and his consideration of local references.[347] In the case of the Palazzo Barbarano, the local reference is the Oratory of San Cristoforo in Vincenza,[348] a fifteenth-century tetrastyle space with four Corinthian columns and

---

345 Belluzzi and Forster argue that the scheme "derives from a misreading of the ambiguous Vitruvian text." Belluzzi and Forster, "Palazzo Te," here 321.

346 Guido Beltramini, "Palazzo Barbarano," ed. Guido Beltramini and Howard Burns, in *Palladio*, vol. 6 (London: Royal Academy of Arts, 2009), 208–215.

347 See Howard Burns, ed., *Andrea Palladio, 1508–1580: The Portico and the Farmyard* ([London]: Arts Council of Great Britain, 1975), 230–231. See also Guido Beltramini and Howard Burns, eds., "Andrea Palladio 1508–1580," in *Palladio*, vol. 6 (London: Royal Academy of Arts, 2009), 6.

348 This chapel, known today as the Oratorio dell'antico Ospedale di San Marcello, is located at the intersection of Contrà S. Marcello and Contrà Pasquale Cordenons and is part of the Liceo Statale Antonio Pigafetta.

MODEL AND THEORY 179

40 Andrea Palladio, Palazzo Barbarano, tetrastyle entrance, Vicenza, 1568–1575

a groin-vaulted ceiling.[349] We find the same groin-vaulted ceiling at Barbarano, although, like at Thiene, the columns carry lintels connecting to the peripheral walls that result in a less centralized perception of the space. In accordance with Vitruvius's remark about the structural advantage of tetrastyle rooms to support loads from the upper floors, both of these Palladian ground-level tetrastyles are placed beneath the large room of the *piano nobile*. Guido Beltramini points out that Palladio referred to such a space as an "*entrata*," or entrance, whereas in classical *compluvium* configurations he would use the Vitruvian term "*atrio*," or atrium, as for the monastery of the Carità in Venice.[350] In contrast to Vitruvius's ambivalent terminology, this subtle distinction conveys Palladio's sensitivity to the types of spaces he built and to the range of functions each part of his buildings had to perform—a sensitivity that resulted in a wide range of built iterations of Vitruvius's tetrastyle passage.

In Book II of the *I quattro libri*, an illustration of the yet-to-be-completed Palazzo Barbarano entrance precedes a series of designs for atria that draw heavily, as Palladio acknowledges in the text, on those he produced for the 1567 Vitruvius.[351] His Vitruvian illustrations are ambiguous on the presence of the *compluvium* in that the choice to abut the sections and plans prohibits a clear reading of the opening in the ceiling—an ambiguity reflective of the passage in Vitruvius's text stating that the columns allow a convenient usage of the upper floor. The first drawing in the *I quattro libri* is much more

---

349 Other Italian Gothic references, likely unknown to Palladio, were the tetrastyle capitular rooms of abbeys such as Sant'Andrea di Vercelli and Morimondo, both close to Milan, and the abbey of Casamari in Veroli on the outskirts of Rome. The capitular rooms of these three complexes all have a square plan and vaults with pointed arches. Another parallel can be made with the distant groin-vaulted ceiling of the tetrastyle synagogue in Tomar (see the section "The Tomar Enigma" above), although a direct relationship between the two is unlikely.

350 Guido Beltramini, "Study for the Plan of Palazzo Barbarano (Alternative B) 1568–1569," ed. Guido Beltramini and Howard Burns, in *Palladio*, vol. 6 (London: Royal Academy of Arts, 2009), 213–221, here 213–214. The Venetian atrium for the monastery of the Carità is illustrated in Palladio, *I quattro libri*, 29–31.

351 Palladio, *I quattro libri*, 24.

obvious in showing an open ceiling above the tetrastyle atrium. A few pages later, Palladio introduces a similar illustration, this time for a category of enclosed interior space he refers to as "*sale*," or halls, with four columns. Again, he makes an explicit reference to Vitruvius in explaining the structural soundness of the disposition: the "built columns are there in order to make the breadth proportionate to the height and to make the structure above stable."[352] Thus, whereas Vitruvius does not clearly define the *cavaedium* as either atrium or courtyard,[353] Palladio shows it as both and adapts the configuration to entrances and halls—two novel room types that take their form from antiquity but reflect contemporary needs in their actual structure and use. As such, Palladio's architectural imagination absorbs Vitruvius's words, which then re-emerge as a host of different types of spaces—from a faithful *cavaedium* to an atrium, from an atrium to an entrance, from an entrance to a hall—a slippage that operates both in Palladio's building practice and the representation of it in his book.

In Palladio's built work, an example matching the tetrastyle hall from the *I quattro libri* exists at the Villa Cornaro in Piombino Dese, whose construction was already underway in 1553. The square room is the core of the villa—in many aspects a predecessor of the quintessential round central hall of the Villa Rotonda[354] —and although it is located on the ground floor it has a ceiling height more typical of the *piano nobile* level.[355] Below the flat ceiling, the distance between the four columns is equal to their height, a ratio that generates an abstract cubic volume within the parallelepipedal space of the hall. The square plan differentiates the hall from both

---

352 Palladio, *I quattro libri*, 36. Translation from Andrea Palladio, *The Four Books on Architecture*, 1st ed. 1997, trans. Robert Tavernor and Richard Schofield (Cambridge, MA: MIT Press, 2002), 112.

353 See the prologue section "The Volatile Word."

354 See Wolfram Prinz, "La 'sala di quattro colonne' nell'opera di Palladio," *Bollettino del Centro Internazionale di Studi di Architettura Andrea Palladio di Vicenza*, no. 11 (1969): 371–387.

355 Antonio Foscari, *Andrea Palladio: Unbuilt Venice* (Zurich: Lars Müller, 2010), 104.

41 Andrea Palladio, Villa Cornaro, tetrastyle hall, Piombino Dese, 1552–1588

Vitruvian *cavaedia* and Palladio's entrances, and instead of marking a regular nine-square division of the plan, the proximity of the four columns to the peripheral walls distances it from the capitular halls and oratory that might have served as references. The structural columns support a similarly proportioned room on the upper floor that reflects the need of the proprietor for one grand hall in which to host private functions (on the upper floor) and another for public ones (on the ground floor).[356]

Palladio's extensive activity provided plenty of occasions to experiment with variations on the models later codified in the *I quattro libri*. Two other tetrastyle entrances he built are those of the Villa Pisani in Montagnana, from around 1552, and the Palazzo Iseppo da Porto, built in Vicenza between 1546 and 1552. The Villa Pisani tetrastyle must have been modeled on the Thiene entrance as it shares the system of the four columns carrying lintels connecting to the façade and inner walls. At Pisani, instead of a groin-vaulted ceiling, the Doric columns support a central barrel vault running parallel to the façade that intersects with three lower transversal barrel vaults. The result is a spectacular structure to welcome the visitors. A different approach was taken in the Palazzo Iseppo da Porto, where, because the entrance only occupies half of the ground-floor plan, the four columns are stripped of their primary function as load-bearing supports for the upper floor. Instead of the one-directional lintels used in other entrances, here Palladio emphasizes the central plan of the room by means of a groin vault that defines squares with lower ceilings

---

356 Palladio used a tetrastyle hall to again support a stacked *piano nobile* in a unique unbuilt project for standardized urban houses (Beltramini and Burns, "Andrea Palladio," 169–171. Drawing: RIBA Library, Drawings and Archives Collection, SC225/XVI/9v and 9b. Note the drawing sequence is not reproduced in the Palladio exhibition catalogue.) All three drawings are likely variations of the ground-floor plan, rather than representing superposed levels, but the presence of symmetrical staircases hints at an important upper floor. Again we see Palladio following Vitruvius's advice on the structural advantage of the tetrastyle room, this time in a project meant to accommodate noble living spaces within the tight dimensions of an urban site. Another documented design that would also use this model is the unbuilt Palazzo Garzadori in Polegge, near Vicenza, ca. 1555–1556. Palladio, *I quattro libri*, II, 77.

42 Andrea Palladio, Villa Pisani, tetrastyle entrance, Montagnana, ca. 1552

in the corners. The configuration in plan and section of the formal apparatus of the tetrastyle entrance lends a sense of unity to this space, which works as a constituent part of the ensemble of the Palazzo Iseppo da Porto but is designed according to its own internal rules.[357]

The groin-vaulted ceiling of Palazzo Iseppo da Porto affiliates it with a group of tetrastyle rooms that include the Noviciate Chapel at Tomar described in the previous chapter[358] and iterations on Palladio such as the one built by Ottone Maria Calderari (1730–1803) in the Palazzo Cordellina in Vicenza between 1786 and 1790.[359] Most intriguing of all are the illustrations by Sebastiano Serlio for the unpublished *Sesto libro d'architettura*, titled *Delle habitationi fuori e dentro delle città*.[360] The manuscripts, executed in France between 1541 and 1549, show three remarkable tetrastyle rooms, all with groin vaults. One is in project X 21,c "Large Dwelling for a Prince," where the tetrastyle configures an entrance in a similar position to Palazzo Te.[361] Another is a square tetrastyle room at the center of a square pavilion, part of project 28; and the last is two symmetrical ground-floor vestibules adjacent to a "*gran sala del principe*" in project V. These designs are all found in the Avery manuscript, the earliest of the three versions of Serlio's *Sesto libro*. The Munich version, drawn later,

---

357 The plan published in *I quattro libri* was improved in relation to reality with the addition of a monumental peristyle after the entrance that resembles the illustration of the ideal Roman villa, a sequence that does not exist in the actual building.

358 See the section "The Tomar Enigma" above.

359 See Werner Oechslin, *Palladianesimo: Teoria e prassi*, trans. Elena Filippi (Verona: Arsenale, 2006). The original German text was published in an enlarged version as Werner Oechslin, *Palladianismus: Andrea Palladio; Kontinuität von Werk und Wirkung* (Zurich: gta Verlag, 2008). Notable Palladian tetrastyle entrances in Vicenza include an exquisite example by Francesco Antonio Muttoni (1669–1747) at the Palazzo Trento Valmanara in Contrà S. Faustino and an austere rendition from the 1830s at the Palazzo Piovene in Corso Andrea Palladio, attributed to A. Piovene.

360 Myra Nan Rosenfeld, *Serlio on Domestic Architecture*, 1st ed. 1978 (Mineola, NY: Dover, 1996).

361 For project X 21, "Casa di un principe coppiosa di loggiamenti fuori della città." Rosenfeld, *Serlio on Domestic Architecture*, plate XXVI. A similar variant can be found within the far more ambitious scheme devised in project W, plate LXXI.

has but the one tetrastyle entrance shown in plate XIX,[362] and in the set of printing proofs for the illustration woodcuts kept in Vienna[363] only the "Large Dwelling for a Prince" retains its tetrastyle entrance.[364] The *Sesto libro* contains complete designs, and thus could function as a pattern book to satisfy potential clients—a different approach from the way Serlio's book on the orders and his *Livre extraordinaire* on doors and window frames present elements for use in different configurations. Its structure, based on social hierarchies, is similar to the *recueil* format in which entire buildings, rather than their component parts, are presented as models. It is perhaps not a coincidence that the Avery manuscript was later owned by Jacques Androuet du Cerceau, himself an author of a famous pattern book on houses of varying sizes.[365] Despite Serlio's key position within the history of Vitruvianism, and despite the soundness of the groin-vaulted tetrastyle rooms he designed to illustrate his sixth book (just as in Vitruvius, his Book VI is on houses), his examples have remained part of a forgotten history, and this may be in part because of the book's format. Palladio, whose Book II on houses provided a rich combinatory system, never fell into such oblivion because his tetrastyle atria, entrances, and rooms were more conducive to incorporation in future designs.[366]

One might rightly expect to find some of these Palladian tetrastyle elements in Britain, and indeed there are, but few of them were built. An early point of contact was Inigo Jones

---

362 Sebastiano Serlio, *Sesto libro d'architettura: Delle habitationi fuori e dentro delle città*, Bayerische Staatsbibliothek, cod. icon. 189 (Lyon, 1547–1550), https://www.digitale-sammlungen.de/en/view/bsb00018617?page=1.

363 Francesco Paolo Fiore, ed., *Sebastiano Serlio, architettura civile: Libri sesto settimo e ottavo nei manoscritti di Monaco e Vienna* (Milan: Polifilo, 1996), 29–31.

364 Fiore, *Sebastiano Serlio*, 51 recto.

365 On this relation, see the section "The Age of Orders" above. The works of Du Cerceau, a prolific author, are treated in detail in Jean Guillaume, ed., *Jacques Androuet du Cerceau: 'Un des plus grands architectes qui se soient jamais trouvés en France'* (Paris: Picard/Cité de l'architecture & du patrimoine, 2010).

366 Maria Beltramini, "Palladio e il *Sesto Libro* di Sebastiano Serlio," ed. Franco Barbieri, in *Palladio 1508–2008: Il simposio del cinquecentenario* (Venice: Marsilio, 2008), 187–188.

(1573–1652), an initiator of the British classical tradition who traveled to Italy with a copy of the *I quattro libri* that he annotated while visiting the actual buildings and discussing them with fellow architects. Among those he met was Vincenzo Scamozzi (1548–1616), whose 1615 treatise *L'Idea dell'architettura universale* Jones also owned.[367] Nonetheless, it took a generation before a British architect would pay careful attention to the passage in Vitruvius and to Palladio's related drawings in the person of Jones's former pupil and son-in-law John Webb (1611–1672), whose tetrasyle *démarche* has been described thoroughly by Esther Eisenthal.[368] In 1638, ten years after he first began to work with Jones, Webb produced a set of architectural studies that constitute a contemporary response to the program of the English noble home. These designs relied heavily on books in Jones's library (a collection he would later inherit), and among the designs are a tetrastyle atrium and a hall that correspond to the illustrations in the *I quattro libri*. But instead of adopting the proportions and details suggested by Palladio, Webb drew on the design method set out in Scamozzi's treatise.[369] Rather than using a module based on column diameter, he adjusted the Vitruvian ratios for the columns to use whole numbers and organize the plan according to a grid aligned with the walls and column centers. Eisenthal argues that Webb "refer[s] to Vitruvius as the ultimate authority"[370] but that his reliance on other authors to interpret Vitruvius overwhelms the sense of the original source. Webb's use of Jones's library demonstrates how, as the canonic status of Vitruvius led it to become more and more idea than substance, the accumulated experience transmitted through books—either in printed form or by means of handwrit-

---

367 Christy Anderson, *Inigo Jones and the Classical Tradition* (New York: Cambridge University Press, 2007), 64.

368 Esther Eisenthal, "John Webb's Reconstruction of the Ancient House," *Architectural History* 28 (1985): 7–18, 20–31, https://doi.org/10.2307/1568524.

369 Eisenthal, "John Webb's Reconstruction," here 9. Eisenthal refers to Vincenzo Scamozzi, *Dell'idea della Architettura Universale* (Venice: Expensis Auctoris, 1615), 47–48.

370 Eisenthal, "John Webb's Reconstruction," here 10.

ten annotations—began to prevail over the word. In the British context, this process was likely encouraged by the fact that the first English Vitruvius was not published until 1692, being a translation from Claude Perrault's abridged edition.

The pace of British echoes of the tetrastyle passage accelerated following the printing of this English-language Vitruvius. Between 1715 and 1717, the Scottish architect Colen Campbell (1676–1793) published by subscription an extensive compilation of drawings of classicizing British architecture. Although in naming it *Vitruvius Britannicus* Campbell borrowed the authority of its Roman namesake,[371] the work is more pattern book than treatise, closer to the books of engravings of French building designs by Jean Marot (1619?–1679) than to Vitruvius.[372] In the second volume, Campbell's plans include two tetrastyle rooms of his own design,[373] both of them ground-floor entrances to homes that use the form's convenient layout to reinforce the structure supporting the upper floor. The book's success led to a third volume, published in 1725, where another tetrastyle room appears in the plate dedicated to Marble Hill House, a Palladian villa in Twickenham, London.[374] The compact Marble Hill, which differs from many neo-Palladian villas in that it has no exterior portico, was built between 1724 and 1727 for Henrietta Howard (1689–1767), mistress of the Prince of Wales and future King George II (1683–1760).[375] The

---

371 Colen Campbell, *Vitruvius Britannicus; or, The British Architect: Containing the Plans, Elevations and Sections of the Regular Buildings, Both Publick and Private in Great Britain, with Variety of New Designs, in 200 Large Folio Plates, Engraven by the Vest Hands, and Drawn Either from the Buildings Themselves or the Original Designs of the Architects* (London, 1717). See further Harris and Savage, *British Architectural Books*, 139–148. In 1715 Giovanni Leoni's first English edition of Palladio's *I quattro libri* helped convince the publishers to complete the ambitious editorial enterprise under the Vitruvian patronym.

372 On Marot's *Grand* and *Petit* engraving series, see A. Tavares, *Anatomy of the Architectural Book*, 345–346.

373 Campbell, *Vitruvius Britannicus*, vol. II, plate 89: "Plan of the First Story of My Design for Mr. Secretary Methnven;" vol. II, plate 98: "Plan of the Fist Story of my Invention for the Lord Cadogan."

374 Campbell, *Vitruvius Britannicus*, vol. III, plate 93, "A house in Trittenham Middlesex near the River Thames."

375 See John Moses, "The Builders of Marble Hill" (Talk to the Marble Hill

design is attributed to Roger Morris (1695–1749), cousin of the Robert Morris (1703–1754) who later published an important volume of Palladian theory.[376] Morris's tetrastyle is a ground-floor entrance hall, placed between the pedimented façade that faces the river Thames and a central mahogany staircase that leads to the upper floor. The four Ionic columns reinforce crossed beams that support a cubic[377] hall on the *piano nobile* above. As at Palladio's Villa Cornaro, the tetrastyle lends the ground-level public space an appropriate scale and dignity without compromising structural soundness or the grand dimensions of the room upstairs.

From the cubic geometry of the upper hall to the façade pediment and the absent portico, Morris's Marble Hill was part of a careful strategy to adapt Palladian design to the cultural requirements and climactic conditions of British life. It is not by accident that Alexander Pope (1688–1744), a close friend of Henrietta Howard and a neighbor of Marble Hill, dedicated a verse to the chilling arcades of British Palladianism:

> *Or call the winds through long arcades to roar,*
> *Proud to catch cold at a Venetian door;*
> *Conscious they act a true Palladian part,*
> *And, if they starve, they starve by rules of art.*[378]

This reference to the Venetian "rules of art" features in an epistle addressed to Richard Boyle, Lord Burlington (1694–1753).

Society, March 3, 2013), https://friendsofmarblehill.org.uk/article/the-builders-of-marble-hill/. On Henrietta Howard and her adventurous life, see Tracy Borman, *King's Mistress, Queen's Servant: The Life and Times of Henrietta Howard* (London: Vintage Books, 2010), especially pages 133–137 on the Marble Hill project.

376 Robert addresses Roger in the second part of his lectures, acknowledging the latter's contribution to his own ideas on architectural design. Robert Morris, *Lectures on Architecture, Consisting of Rules Founded upon Harmonick and Arithmetical Proportions in Building*, 1st ed. 1734–1736 part II (London: R. Sayer, 1759), iii–iv. See further Harris and Savage, *British Architectural Books*, 317–323.

377 In Campbell's plate, the hall caption reads "A Cube of 24." Campbell, *Vitruvius Britannicus*, vol. III, plate 93.

378 Alexander Pope, "'Epistle IV, to Richard Boyle, Earl of Burlington: Of the Use of Riches.' In *Moral Essays*, 1731," in *Poetical Works of Pope*, vol. 2 (Edinburgh: Nichol, 1856), https://www.gutenberg.org/files/9601/9601-h/9601-h.htm#link2H_4_0005.

Burlington acquired and circulated Palladio drawings in England, and, following Jones, Webb, and Campbell, expanded the presence of classical culture in England. As discussed in the section "Grounding Theory" in the previous chapter, after Perrault's *Abrégé* was translated into English in 1692, Burlington was close to various failed attempts to translate the entire Ten Books of Vitruvius. In the end, the Palladio drawings he owned, as measurable models, had a far wider reach than the theoretical abstractions of Vitruvius. But despite his interest in Palladio, Burlington did not pay much attention to tetrastyles, and Marble Hill's entrance remains a rare built example from the British Palladian Revival.

Still in England, Sir John Soane (1753–1837) designed and built two tetrastyle experiments—the entrance to Tyringham House in 1796[379] and the dining room for the renovation of Moggerhanger House in 1808[380] —that diverge from the Palladian models and instead draw directly on Soane's knowledge of Roman antiquity. These two homes, built for clients who were bankers and directors of the Bank of England, resonate with the architecture of the Bank itself, the masterpiece to which Soane dedicated forty-five years from 1788 to 1833.[381] The Bank of England's offices along Threadneedle Street and Bartholomew Lane were populated with tetrastyle-like halls,[382]

---

379 See Margaret Richardson, "Tyringham," ed. Margaret Richardson and Mary Anne Stevens, in *John Soane Architect: Master of Space and Light* (London: Royal Academy of Arts, 1999), 128–141.

380 See Sir John Soane's Museum Collection Online, catalogue record by Jill Lever, "Moggerhanger, Bedfordshire: (Executed) Alterations and Additions for Godfrey Thornton, 1790–1799 and Stephen Thornton, 1806–1811," 2012. Between 1790 and 1792, Soane designed alterations for Godfrey Thornton, and, after continuing work on the estate, he planned and executed a major intervention for Stephen Thornton between 1806 and 1811. The tetrastyle experiments at Moggerhanger are from this second phase.

381 See Daniel Abramson, *Building the Bank of England: Money, Architecture, Society, 1694–1942* (New Haven, CT: Yale University Press, 2005).

382 The Old Four Per Cent Office, New Four Per Cent Office, Bank Stock Office, Four Per Cent and Five Per Cent Office, and Consols Transfer Office. See plan and names in Daniel Abramson, "Bank of England," ed. Margaret Richardson and Mary Anne Stevens, in *John Soane Architect: Master of Space and Light* (London: Royal Academy of Arts, 1999), 208–251, here 213.

albeit with the columns supporting rounded arches under domed ceilings rather than an upper floor. While these spaces were not conceived as domestic, nor imagined from the Vitruvian or Pompeian sources, they do attest to Soane's pursuit of an architectural language expressive of Roman magnificence. Soane's adaptation of ancient Roman sources—evocative of the grandeur of the past—is done to create a novel language for the future—a language that envisions the prospect of future ruins. Soane's vision of a circular trajectory from ruins to construction, from construction to ruins, is evident in the famous cut-away perspective of the bank as a gigantic building site by Joseph Gandy (1771–1843)[383] that recalls images of the archaeological excavations at Pompeii. Soane visited the recently accessible ruins of Pompeii several times in 1779 as part of his Grand Tour.[384] He ignored the local ban on note-taking to register the ongoing excavations in his sketchbooks, drawing carefully measured surveys of temples and houses.[385] This makes it clear that Soane, who amassed a significant collection of Vitruvius editions throughout his life,[386] would have been familiar both with Vitruvius's passage on *cavaedia* and ancient built examples of the form when he came to design his own tetrastyle rooms.

Soane's Tyringham House is a compact volume along the lines of neo-Palladian models such as Marble Hill. Its tetrastyle

---

[383] As Daniel Abramson notes, Joseph Gandy's grandiloquent rendering of the Bank of England, often referred to as a depiction of the bank in ruins, in fact represents "its walls, vaults and arches freshly laid," as in being a building site. Abramson, "Bank of England," here 213.

[384] Gillian Darley, "The Grand Tour," ed. Margaret Richardson and Mary Anne Stevens, in *John Soane Architect: Master of Space and Light* (London: Royal Academy of Arts, 1999), 96–113. Soane was in Italy from 1778 to 1780.

[385] Dorothy Stroud, *Sir John Soane Architect*, 1st ed. 1984 (London: De la Mare, 1996), 35.

[386] Soane possessed an impressive library, and at least fourteen Vitruvius editions are locatable in its current online catalogue: Martin 1547; Barbaro 1556; Rusconi 1590; De Laet 1649; Rusconi 1660; Perrault 1674; Perrault 1684; Perrault 1692; Perrault 1747; Galiani 1758; Newton 1791; Stratico 1825–1830; Wilkins 1812–1817; Gwilt 1826. On Soane's reading habits, see Margaret Willies, "Building a Library: The Books of Sir John Soane," in *Reading Matters: Five Centuries of Discovering Books* (New Haven, CT: Yale University Press, 2010), 109–135.

43 Sir John Soane, Tyringham House, 1792–1801, presentation drawing of the entrance hall, exhibited at the Royal Academy in 1798

entrance hall, the built version of which was designed by June 1796, is an exercise in adapting Roman architectural language to contemporary standards of living and, as shown in the extant design development drawings for the room, Soane gave it a lot of attention. A preliminary sketch suggests a large square entrance from which a few steps lead to a transverse tribune that connects to the main hall on the opposite façade.[387] The tetrastyle configuration is already delineated and holds up an elevated cupola that would shape the external volume of the house behind the semi-circular portico. Subsequent design drawings retain the sequence of this first plan but squeeze the entrance into a rectangle with a vaulted ceiling. Here, a sensitive configuration of the tetrastyle arrangement successfully avoids a tunnel effect: the four columns, only slightly detached from the walls and supporting a shallow groin vault, form a rectangle that is perceived as a square. The resulting bay performs as a detached figure within the entrance hall, with a dramatic quality enhanced by the bold *entasis* of the Doric columns and the projecting entablatures above them. This scenic quality is enhanced by the contrast between its neutral color and the dark paint used on the remaining surfaces of the ceiling, consisting of short vaults with a complex form that link the arched doorways at either end of the room to the groin vault over the central bay. Tyringham's spectacular entrance, reminiscent of Roman antiquities, introduced a grammar and a design strategy Soane would use again at the Bank of England and elsewhere.

Moggerhanger House is a similarly theatrical setting. In the multiple design proposals Soane presented to his client, several suggest a tetrastyle entrance vestibule, including a backlit perspective rendering with prominent lintels in the foreground that shows columns placed farther away from the walls than at Tyringham. In the end the vestibule was not built as a tetrastyle, but the dining room at Moggerhanger was. We see

---

[387] Sir John Soane's Museum Collection Online at http://collections.soane.org/home, SM 42–45, February 12, 1796.

in Soane's various designs for this space a search for a precise form: some are tetrastyle, others not, and one plan shows a semi-circular niche for the fireplace at the center of the wall facing the windows. In the tetrastyle layout that was finally built, the four Ionic columns are placed quite close to the walls to avoid being too much of an encumbrance, and, along with the carefully crafted ceiling details, they mark out a central rectangle in relation to the peripheral windows, doorways, and fireplace, now on a perpendicular wall. In Soane's hand, the tetrastyle is used as an apparatus to shape our perception of the room, making memorable an otherwise banal space.

Soane's use of the tetrastyle was very different from Palladio's and from previous neo-Palladian examples in Britain. Palladio found in Vitruvius's passage describing the tetrastyle an effective technical and formal solution to respond to the architectural problems he faced in his building practice. He made the sentence travel between book and building, and the success of his work—later to become a model itself—secured a modest but enduring legacy for the tetrastyle in neoclassical architecture. Soane however, with his knowledge of Pompeian houses, treated the configuration as more of a scenographic element than a structural one, using it as a formal device to articulate the public ambition of his clients at a domestic scale.

SHIFTING TYPE

Contemporary access to archaeological research allows us to learn about the ancient Roman use of the tetrastyle *cavaedium*[388] from examples in the urban houses of Pompeii, the villas of the Bay of Naples, and from other sites across the Roman Empire.[389] But when Vitruvius's treatise reached its most influential momentum, such vestiges were unknown. The lack of archaeological evidence meant that readers had to look to textual records for more information on the tetrastyle room, and thus literary descriptions of Roman houses came to fuel architects' imaginations. The most famous of these are the letters of Pliny the Younger (61–ca. 113) to Gallus and Apollinaris that describe the author's villas near the seaside in Laurentinum—the so-called "Laurentine villa"—and in the foothills of the Apennine Mountains in Tuscany—the so-called "Tuscan villa."[390] Pierre de la Ruffinière du Prey's comprehensive history of the attempts to locate and restitute Pliny's villas over the centuries shows how such

---

388 See Pierre Gros, *Maisons, palais, villas et tombeaux*, vol. 2 of *L'architecture romaine: Du début du IIIe siècle av. J.-C. à la fin du Haut-Empire*, 2nd ed. (Paris: Picard, 2006), 27–29.

389 See Annalisa Marzano and Guy P. R. Métraux, *The Roman Villa in the Mediterranean Basin: Late Republic to Late Antiquity* (Cambridge: Cambridge University Press, 2018).

390 "Pliny's Letter to Gallus," Book 2, Epistle 17 and "Pliny's Letter to Apollinaris," Book 5, Epistle 6, in *The Letters of Pliny the Younger,* translation John Boyle, 1751, transcribed in Pierre de la Ruffinière Du Prey, ed., *The Villas of Pliny: From Antiquity to Posterity* (Chicago: University of Chicago Press, 1994), 311–319.

projects mixed information drawn from archaeological surveys and literary inquiries with a strong dose of architectural invention.[391] Pliny's unknown villas joined Vitruvius's cryptic text as a trigger for imaginative architectural responses to the tetrastyle enigma.

Du Prey's account of the story of Pedro José Marquez (1741–1820) is a case in point. Marquez was a former Jesuit from Mexico living in Rome who, in the early 1790s, joined two companions visiting an excavation by the seaside near Rome where they hoped to find the remains of the Laurentine villa.[392] Marquez is of interest here since he was a prolific and self-confident author who, in 1795, published a book discussing Roman houses in relation to Vitruvius's "doctrine."[393] In it he argues, contrary to every other author who has ever commented on Vitruvius, that the tetrastyle *cavaedium* was configured with "the four columns in a row,"[394] a disposition Marquez relates to the tetrastyle structure of temple façades, described by Vitruvius in Book III.[395] This formula did not gain much attention, but it is telling as to just how far from the source a reading can go, even when enounced by a careful reader like Marquez who was aware of the archaeological, literary and architectural sources. In a subsequent book, Marquez illustrated his interpretations of Pliny's villas without any mention of tetrastyle rooms,[396] likely a consequence of the difficulty of reconciling his awkward understanding of the tetrastyle with a precise design. Nonetheless, Marquez's enthusiastic correction of the reading of Vitruvius's sentence reveals how a scholar might filter information drawn from site visits, restitutions, readings,

---

391 Du Prey, *The Villas of Pliny*.

392 Marquez went to the Sacchetti excavation, near Castel Fusano, accompanied by the Spanish architect Silvestre Perez (1767–1825) and the French priest Charles-Louis Petit-Radel (1756–1836). Du Prey, *The Villas of Pliny*, 86.

393 Pietro Marquez, *Delle case di citta degli antichi Romani secondo la dottrina di Vitruvio* (Rome: Il Salomoni, 1795).

394 Marquez, *Delle case di citta*, 33.

395 Vitruvius, III, 3, 7.

396 Pietro Marquez, *Delle ville di Plinio il Giovane* (Rome: Salomoni, 1796).

and publications through the innovative paths of their own imagination to end up with their own prescriptive text.

The fluctuating enthusiasm for reconstructions of Pliny's villas spans centuries, from a 1615 essay by Vincenzo Scamozzi to the competition on the Laurentine villa launched by Maurice Culot in 1981,[397] a challenge that drew proposals from architects eager to establish their positions as intellectuals within the field.[398] The entries, among them projects by Léon Krier and Bernard Huet (1932–2001), are a wide-ranging and complex mix of references, sources, and architectural *partis*. Excepting the proposal of architect-archaeologist Jean-Pierre Adam, whose imaginative effort embraced analogy as a strategy to execute an authentic Roman project according to a contemporary geometry,[399] most of the compositions are characterized by a postmodern irony, which is equally present in the various proposed tetrastyle *cavaedia*. Taken together, the competition entries evoke a lost ideal of the villa as a unque place of freedom and balance, where, far from the stress of the city, the owner can commit to a life of the spirit and the intellect without neglecting more mundane concerns like conducting business, all while enjoying the benefits of nature. In most cases, the restitutions attempted to revive this ideal by establishing a link between antiquity and the present, and the sublime environments of the architectural renderings seem to suspend time as they engage with Pliny's memories.

In an earlier restitution published in 1838,[400] Louis Pierre Haudebourte (1788–1849) laments the state of the modern

---

397 See Institut Français d'Architecture, *La Laurentine et l'invention de la villa romaine* (Paris: Éditions du Moniteur, 1982).

398 Du Prey has inventoried a list of fifty-six reconstructions, including the Laurentine and Tuscan villas, ranging from Scamozzi to an archaeology essay from 1993.

399 Jean-Pierre Adam, "La ville de Pline le Jeune aux Laurentes," in *La Laurentine et l'invention de la villa romaine*, by Institut Français d'Architecture (Paris: Éditions du Moniteur, 1982), 170–175. Thirty years later he devoted a monograph to the Roman house. See Jean-Pierre Adam, *La maison romaine* (Arles: Honoré Clair, 2012).

400 Louis Pierre Haudebourte, *Le Laurentin maison de campagne de Pline le Jeune: Restituée d'après la description de Pline* (Paris: Carilian-Goeury, 1838).

world and wonders about the luxury and perfection of antiquity. He falls into a dream, and in this delusional state of mind tours the Laurentine villa with Pliny the Younger, who warmly discusses the architectural and social qualities of his house. Haudebourte's illustrations are populated with figures that invest the visit with a measurable scale similar to that of the archaeological vestiges he had visited in Pompeii.[401] This time-travel strategy was inspired by *Le palais de Scaurus* of 1819, an acclaimed account of Roman architecture by François Mazois, in which Mérovir, the son of a former king of Gaul defeated by Caesar, writes from the cosmopolitan and sophisticated capital to a friend back in Gaul of "everything extraordinary, interesting, and novel that Rome could offer him."[402] Mazois knew Pompeii well. Between 1809 and 1811 he had made use of an unprecedented permit to survey and publish archaeological sites in the Bay of Naples while gathering material for his magnum opus, *Les Ruines de Pompéi*, the first volume of which was published in 1812.[403] A second volume on private buildings and houses, published between 1821 and 1824, features two tetrastyle *cavaedia*:[404] the house of the baker and a pair of houses named after the general Championnet.[405] The house of the baker was a modest construction with a

---

401 On his knowledge of Pompeii, see Haudebourte, *Le Laurentin*, 22; and also Du Prey, *The Villas of Pliny*, 95, n. 43.

402 François Mazois, *Le Palais de Scaurus, ou description d'une maison romaine, fragment d'un voyage fait à Rome, vers la fin de la République, par Mérovir, prince des Suèves*, 1st ed. 1819 (Paris: Firmin Didot, 1822), 10.

403 See Mattusch, *Rediscovering the Ancient World*; Pietro Giovanni Guzzo, Maria Rosaria Esposito, and Nicoleta Ossanna Cavadini, eds., *Herculaneum and Pompeii: Visions of a Discovery* (Geneva: Skira, 2018). See also Nicolas Monteix, "Mazois, François" (biographical note, 2009), https://www.inha.fr/fr/ressources/publications/publications-numeriques/dictionnaire-critique-des-historiens-de-l-art/mazois-francois.html?search-keywords=mazois.

404 Mazois, *Les Ruines de Pompéi*. Mazois discusses the two tetrastyle *cavaedia* in the introductory "Essai sur les habitations des anciens Romains," 19–23. In it he reviews the variations on the *cavaedium* introduced in the Vitruvius illustrations by Fra Giocondo, Andrea Palladio, Claude Perrault, and Berardo Galiani and addresses the long debate on the ambivalent usage of the terms atrium and *cavaedium*, noting that he finds the most authoritative clarification in Varro's (116–27 BCE) Roman treatises.

405 Mazois, *Les Ruines de Pompéi*, plate XVIII, "Maison d'un boulanger"; plate XIX, "Vue de l'intérieur de la maison d'un boulanger"; plate XX, "Vue de la maison dite

44 Louis Pierre Haudebourte, restitution of a tetrastyle *cavaedium* in Pliny the Younger's Laurentine Villa, 1838

rough *cavaedium* featuring four square columns and a low ceiling.[406] Mazois's plate provides a technical drawing of the oven. The plates showing the Championnet houses—including a view of the ruins, a plan, and a cross section—represent an elegant tetrastyle *cavaedium*. Echoes of Mazois's cross section are easily found in Haudebourte's rendering of the atrium of the Laurentine villa, ranging from the proportions of the columns and plan to the peripheral lintel that defines the *compluvium* and its relation to the decorated girders. And even though Haudebourte's text mentions refined Doric columns, the illustration shows Corinthian columns with capitals identical to those in Mazois's plates.

Mazois's publications came not long after a similar project by François Piranesi (1756–1810), whose two-volume account of his father's surveys of Pompeii was published in 1804.[407] In contrast to the late-eighteenth-century illustrations of Pompeian architecture that tended to focus on decorative details at the expense of context, Piranesi's detailed work communicated a sense of the atmosphere of the ruined city to a wide European readership. In addition to several plates showing domestic *cavaedia*, there is also a synthetic reconstruction of various "Vitruvian" atria and courts.[408] The latter attests to the younger Piranesi's procedure of matching the construction details and proportions of the archaeological remains to Vitruvian precepts and combining them to create an idealized form, a process quite different from Mazois's

---

du général Championet"; plate XXI, "Plans de la même maison et d'une maison voisine"; plate XXII, "Coupe de la maison de Championet."

406 Mazois admits this results from a transformation in that the *cavaedium* "was covered by a terrace instead of a ceiling; it was even this precise disposition that probably resulted in the careful replacement of the columns with pilasters; since, in almost all other cavaedia, we have sacrificed the quality of solidness for the pleasantness of sight." Mazois, *Les Ruines de Pompéi*, 57, translated by the author.

407 Francesco Piranesi and Giuseppe Antonio Guattani, eds., *Antiquités de la Grande Grèce, aujourd'hui Royaume de Naples* (Paris: Piranesi and Leblanc, 1804).

408 Piranesi and Guattani, *Antiquités de la Grande Grèce*, plate XXII, "Plan de deux atrium *toscans* et *pluviatum* de Vitruve adaptés à diverses cours des maisons vis-à-vis celle du Chirurgien à Pompeïa"; plate XXIII, "Coupes des divers atrium designés dans la planche no. 22."

measured drawings of specific constructions. The result is a well-composed plate that is illustrative of the various forms and shapes that exist *in loco*. Together, the albums of Piranesi and Mazois are significant in that they contain the first printed images of actual Roman tetrastyle rooms, providing images that were to circulate widely.[409] Both rely on Vitruvius as a secondary source. However, the relationships between these publications and their architectural sources point in different directions: while Piranesi took Vitruvius to the archaeological site, Mazois brought the archaeological site to Vitruvius.

Meanwhile in Paris, grandiose restitutions of Roman villas were being produced as academic design exercises at the École des Beaux-Arts. The *concours d'émulation*, launched in 1818 by Antoine-Laurent-Thomas Vaudoyer (1756–1846), is a case in point.[410] For the exercise, three prizes were awarded, and in 1834 two of the winning projects—by Amable Macquet (1790–1840) and Achille Normand (1802–1860)—were included in a Grand Prix de Rome album published in 1834 by Vaudoyer and Louis-Pierre Baltard (1764–1846). Vaudoyer's brief refers explicitly to Pliny, and although he knew that the overall composition and the dimensions of the two villas are not given in the letters, the program nonetheless imposes a symmetrical design and a courtyard up to 150 meters long. Not only is the scale of the resulting projects monumental—far from the relatively modest and welcoming qualities Pliny's letters evoke—but their *partis* involve intricate enfilades of spaces that suggest the influence of Renaissance palazzi or the inaugural restitution of the Laurentine villa by Scamozzi. Another source of inspiration of these and other Beaux-Arts projects was Jean-Nicolas-Louis Durand (1760–1834). Plate 42 of his *Recueil et parallèle*,[411] dedicated to the Roman house, ignored recent archaeological research and instead reflected the or-

---

409 In the lavish Vitruvius edition of 1836, Luigi Marini reproduced the plans of the Championnet houses published by Mazois. Marini 1836.

410 See Du Prey, *The Villas of Pliny*, 167–176. See also Institut Français d'Architecture, *La Laurentine et l'invention de la villa romaine*, 116–123.

411 Jean-Nicolas-Louis Durand, *Recueil et parallèle des édifices de tout genre*,

thogonal rationale of the French academy in its presentation of a roster of Roman sources. The engraving acts as a matrix from which the reader can select a predetermined architectural solution to any program, regardless of its specificities. One of these solutions is the Vitruvian tetrastyle *cavaedium*, presented in Palladio's version. Durand also illustrated a tetrastyle space in his *Précis*[412] that is echoed in the atria of the prizewinning entries in the *concours d'émulation*.[413] Thus, despite the incorporation of archaeological knowledge of Roman houses into recent editions of Vitruvius, there is no reliable link between the Vitruvian tetrastyle sentence and these prizewinning academic tetrastyle spaces.

The 1852 restitution of the Laurentine villa published by Jules Bouchet (1799–1860) features comparative parallels between his antecedents, placing Macquet's project alongside those by Haudebourte, Marquez, Jean-François Félibien des Avaux (1656?–1733),[414] and Scamozzi.[415] Bouchet acknowledges the importance of the excavations in Pompeii and Herculaneum to his endeavor: "twenty cubic meters of dust, removed from the site of these two unfortunate cities, have all of a sudden taught more on the domestic architecture of the Ancients, have better commented on Pliny and Vitruvius, than all the ingenious theories of speculative antiquarians."[416] Bouchet's proposal for the Laurentine villa's tetrastyle atrium is close to Haudebourte's, although grander and more eloquent, with its four Doric columns and monumental statuary.[417] The

anciens et modernes: Remarquables par leur beauté, par leur grandeur ou par leur singularités et dessinés sur une même échelle (Paris: chez l'auteur, [1801]).

412 Jean-Nicolas-Louis Durand, *Précis des leçons d'architecture données à l'École Polytechnique* (Paris: Bernard et l'Auteur, n.d.), plate 11. Durand represents the entrance of Palladio's palazzo Thiene.

413 In both projects by Macquet and Normand, however, the atrium is overloaded by the complex apparatus of the rest of the composition.

414 Jean-François Félibien des Avaux, *Les plans et les descriptions des deux plus belles maisons de campagne de Pline le consul* (Paris: Florentin and P. Delaulne, 1699).

415 Jules Bouchet, *Le Laurentin, maison de campagne de Pline-le-Consul, restitué d'après sa lettre à Gallus* (Paris: l'auteur, 1852).

416 Bouchet, *Le Laurentin*, 20.

417 A Parisian tetrastyle *cavaedium* that refers at once to Mazois, Haude-

marked difference between these two archaeological reconstructions and the theoretical Beaux-Arts exercises illustrates the schism that had developed between the formalism of architectural training and the philological accuracy prized in archaeological and literary studies. Vitruvius was not immune to this split. As we have seen, nineteenth-century editions focused on reconciling the Roman author's descriptions of the private house with growing archaeological knowledge. Edited with architectural education in mind, the Choisy edition of 1909 pulls the text the other way, presenting it, line by line, as a design method for organizing a project according to Vitruvian principles. The effects of such variations of interest are also evident in other contemporary editions of Vitruvius.

One original tetrastyle space that sprung from this mixture of Durand's academic rationalism, scholarly archaeological surveys, architectural imagination, and the ubiquity of Vitruvius, is that conceived by Karl Friedrich Schinkel (1781–1841), who visited Italy on his Grand Tour between 1803 and 1805.[418] His exquisite Charlottenhof for Friedrich Wilhelm IV of Prussia (1795–1861) includes numerous Italian references, including

---

bourte, and Bouchet was a central feature of the "Pompeian" house built by the prince Napoléon-Jérôme Bonaparte (1822–1891) for his mistress Rachel at 18 Avenue Montaigne by a team of architects, sculptors, and painters. The overall architectural design is commonly attributed to Alfred-Nicolas Normand (1822–1909). Gautier praised this contemporary revival of the Pompeian residence as "a precise restitution where Vitruvius himself would not find anything to reproach." Théophile Gautier, Arsène Houssaye, and Charles Coligny, *Le palais pompéien de l'avenue Montaigne: Études sur la maison gréco-romaine, ancienne résidence du prince Napoléon* (Paris: Au Palais Pompéien, 1866), 10. The tetrastyle *cavaedium*, with the house's various functions gravitating around it, is depicted in Gustave Boulanger's (1824–1888) painting *Répétition du 'Joueur de flûte' et de 'La femme de Diomède' chez le prince Napoléon* from 1861 (see the image on the back cover of this publication). The house was demolished in 1891 after being sold and subsequently abandoned. See Pierre Saddy, *Alfred Normand, architecte, 1822–1909* (Paris: Caisse nationale des monuments historiques et des sites, 1978).

418 See Kurt W. Forster, *Schinkel: A Meander through His Life and Work* (Basel: Birkhäuser, 2017); Barry Bergdoll, *Karl Friedrich Schinkel: An Architecture for Prussia* (New York: Rizzoli, 1994). For a thorough German reference book on Schinkel, see Eva Börsch-Supan, *Karl Friedrich Schinkel, Lebenswerk: Arbeiten für König Friedrich Wilhelm III; Von Preussen und Kronprinz Friedrich Wilhelm (IV)* (Berlin: Deutscher Kunstverlag, 2011).

direct quotes from Pliny.[419] As a tourist, Schinkel devoted attention to vernacular architecture as well as the canonic monuments of antiquity.[420] The breadth and charm of his touristic experience can be seen in the romantic *Italiensehnsucht* character of the Charlottenhof. The site is organized by a series of offset axial promenades amidst suspended pergolas placed at sequential levels, leading the visitor to discover each area in movement, restaging the perspectives step-by-step. The various components of the complex—the Gardener's House and the Tea Pavilion, with the so-called Roman Bath between them—function both as autonomous constructions and parts of a larger ensemble.

Schinkel's knowledge of Roman domestic architecture makes it no surprise to find a tetrastyle *cavaedium* as the centerpiece of the Roman Bath at Charlottenhof.[421] The pavilion was designed by Schinkel between 1829 and 1833 and built under the supervision of his pupil Ludwig Persius (1803–1845).[422] The project was developed in a lengthy collaboration between the architects and the client Wilhelm IV, himself a prolific draftsman who was not shy to experiment with imaginative architectural layouts for the works he commissioned.[423] Wilhelm's preference for square plans that recall the compositional matrices of Durand[424] often led him to tetrastyle

---

419 Du Prey, *The Villas of Pliny*, 290.

420 On his Italian visits, see Benedetto Gravagnuolo, "From Schinkel to Le Corbusier: The Myth of the Mediterranean in Modern Architecture," ed. Jean-François Lejeune and Michelangelo Sabatino, in *Modern Architecture and the Mediterranean: Vernacular Dialogues and Contested Identities* (London: Routledge, 2010), 14–39.

421 Schinkel devoted more attention to vernacular architecture than to classical architecture while traveling because he knew he could rely on publications for the latter. This suggests that his references for the bath house are more likely to have come from books than from site visits.

422 See Barry Bergdoll and Hillert Ibbeken, *Karl Friedrich Schinkel, Ludwig Persius, Friedrich August Stüler: Bauten in Berlin und Potsdam* (Stuttgart: Axel Menges, 2013).

423 See Antje Adler, *Gelebte Antike: Friedrich Wilhelm IV und Charlottenhof* (Berlin: Duncker & Humblot, 2012). For an online inventory of the drawings, see Stiftung Preussische Schlösser und Gärten Berlin-Brandenburg (henceforth SPSG), Drawings of King Friedrich Wilhelm IV of Prussia (1795–1861), at https://bestandskataloge.spsg.de.

424 SPSG-GK II (12) III-1-A-52: "Palastes mit zentralem Kuppelsaal," ca. 1831.

45 Karl Friedrich Schinkel, Roman Bath at Charlottenhof, Potsdam, 1829–1833

structures. An early example is a drawing for a construction in Tollensee, dating from the early 1820s,[425] in which we can see the inception of the Roman Bath plan later delineated by Schinkel.[426] Wilhelm also drew various iterations of the plan for the Charlottenhof.[427] Such schematic orthogonal drawings are more evidence of an interest than effective architectural solutions in themselves, in that the detailing and full-scale materialization of the ideas they represent called on the expertise of the professional architects Wilhelm worked with. In the case of the Roman Bath, Schinkel's drawings add complexity and erudition to the initial tetrastyle design. Despite variations in the published and unpublished design drawings, all of them use an axial composition to emphasize the central *impluvium*. The built *cavaedium* is evocative of Pompeii, with its polychrome wall frescoes and the freestanding sculpture of a female figure, pushing the Vitruvian element of the design far into the background. However, both references are present in the complex web of relations encircling the project that link together the engagement of the client, Schinkel's fascination for Pliny's villas, his memories of his travels in Italy, and the practical effectiveness of the four columns in organizing a space on a square plan.

Thus, while Palladio moved the tetrastyle space from the *cavaedium* of the Vitruvian house to the entrance of the palazzo and the hall of the villa, at Charlottenhof Schinkel takes it from the Pompeiian *cavaedium* or atrium to the pleasing atmosphere of the bath. This scheme of a tetrastyle bathroom was repeated by Emmanuel Pontremoli (1865–1956) when he designed and built the Villa Kérylos by the Mediterranean in Beaulieu-sur-Mer between 1902 and 1908.[428] The client was

425 SPSG-GK II (12) V-2-Ac-35: "Tollens," ca. 1820–1823.

426 Staatliche Museen zu Berlin, Entwurf zur Arkadenhalle mit Atrium, SM 51.22. Online at https://www.deutsche-digitale-bibliothek.de/item/XVLHOWRBOZW4N5ABSLPGD6FTOKRNJM2W.

427 SPSG-GK II (12) II-1-Cg-95: "Entwurfsansicht der Römischen Bäder," ca. 1832.

428 See Emmanuel Pontremoli and Joseph Chamonard, *Kérylos* (Paris: Éditions des Bibliothèques Nationales de France, 1934). See also Pierre Pinon, "Vu de Kérylos:

46 Emmanuel Pontremoli, Villa Kérylos, Beaulieu-sur-Mer, 1902–1908, *balaneion*

Théodore Reinach (1860–1928), a French archaeologist and politician who specialized in ancient Greek history. Accordingly, Kérylos is Greek in inspiration, with Hellenic motifs on the walls, floors, and tiling contributing to its singular atmosphere. The bathroom epitomizes the delightful qualities of the villa.

Villa Kérylos is a large house squeezed onto a small seaside promontory amid terraces and pergolas of exuberant vegetation that visually blend the construction into the rocky coast. Its pleasant shape and use as a retreat from urban activity recall Pliny's description of his villas, even if the small size of the site precludes the practice of agriculture, making it impossible to combine *negotium* with *otium* as Pliny did. Pontremoli had sojourned in Rome between 1891 and 1895 and later joined archaeological surveys in Didyma on the Aegean Sea.[429] In 1914 he was appointed professor at the École des Beaux-Arts in Paris, and twenty years later, in 1934, he became the first architect to direct the school. That same year he published a small monograph on the Kérylos, which at the time, as Jacques Gubler has pointed out, enjoyed a quasi-mythical status as "an inaccessible, well-protected private house located some 900 kilometers outside of Paris."[430] The Kérylos reflects Vitruvius's description of the Greek house, but uses a peristyle to distribute access to the various rooms rather than an atrium.[431] In his description of the villa, Pontremoli quotes Vitruvius to justify the position of the library on the eastern façade—"sheltered from the sun"[432] —as would a good modern

Réappropriation des monuments et changement de signification," in *Architecture du rêve: Actes du 3ème colloque de la Villa Kérylos à Beaulieu-sur-Mer les 29 & 30 Octobre 1992* (Paris: Académie des Inscriptions et Belles-Lettres, 1994), 11–23, https://www.persee.fr/doc/keryl_1275-6229_1994_act_3_1_880.

429 See biographical note in Institut Français d'Architecture, Fonds Pontremoli 341 AA, https://archiwebture.citedelarchitecture.fr/fonds/FRAPN02_PONTR. See also Dominique Jarrassé, "Emmanuel Pontremoli," ed. Jean-Paul Midant, in *Dictionnaire de l'architecture du XXe siècle* (Paris: Hazan/Institut Français de Architecture, 1996), 716.

430 Jacques Gubler, *Jean Tschumi: Architecture at Full Scale* (Milan: Skira, 2008), 38. Tschumi was Pontremoli's student at the Beaux-Arts between 1923 and 1931.

431 On this feature of the Kérylos, see Gubler, *Jean Tschumi*, 41.

432 Pontremoli and Chamonard, *Kérylos*, 7.

functionalist. The villa is also famously modern in its sophisticated technological equipment, which includes electric wiring, plumbing, and heating, combined with built-in bathtubs and radiators.

In accordance with its Greek pedigree, the bathroom is named "*Balaneion*" and has the word Ναϊάδες (*Naiads*) inscribed on its wooden door.[433] It is located across the peristyle from the main part of the villa on the ground floor of the guest wing, making it feel somewhat independent. With no upper floor to support, the tetrastyle columns are a formal device rather than structural reinforcements. The central axis of the square room is emphasized by the four columns and a circular niche with a quarter-spherical dome at the head of the room, granting the composition a classical grandeur evocative of Schinkel's published plate of the Roman Bath at the Charlottenhof. But unlike Schinkel's room, an open atrium with an *impluvium* to store the collected water, Pontremoli's version is roofed over and in lieu of the *impluvium*, steps provide access to a sunken tub. The proximity of this tetrastyle bath to the *cavaedium* is intriguing, as the Vitruvian text is simultaneously present in the Greek *parti* of the plan and repressed in the imaginative reuse of the configuration as the setting for a bath.

A synchronous example of a tetrastyle bathroom can be found at Villa Karma, a luxurious house on the shore of Lake Geneva completed in 1912. Although the project is often attributed to Adolf Loos (1870–1933), the story of Villa Karma involves a more convoluted series of interventions.[434] The house reflects the taste and the expectations of its owner, the Viennese doctor Theodor Beer (1866–1919), who bought an existing house on the plot in 1903 [435] An initial expansion

---

433 Pontremoli and Chamonard, *Kérylos*, 31–33.

434 See Jacques Gubler, "'Sur l'album photographique de la villa Karma,' lettre à A. M. Vogt," ed. Katharina Medici-Mall, in *Fünf Punkte in der Architekturgeschichte: Festschrift für Adolf Max Vogt* (Basel: Birkhäuser, 1985), 214–229.

435 Vera J. Behal, "Die Villa Karma und ihre Architekten Lavanchy, Loos, Ehrlich," in *Adolf Loos* (Vienna: Graphische Sammlung Albertina, 1989), 135–

by the local architect Henri Lavanchy (1836–1914) extended the house from its original core, adding three new façades and defining the subtle relationship between inside and outside that is key to the house's *Stimmung*. Loos was commissioned in 1905 to design the interior and the gardens, but, after devoting a great deal of attention to various rooms, was fired with the work already underway. The Croatian architect Hugo Ehrlich (1879–1936) replaced him as on-site architect in 1908 and took Loos' input into account as he saw the project through to completion.[436] Each room is a refined blend of fixtures and materials that creates an atmosphere conducive to the activity it was destined for, from music room to library, from bedroom to bathroom.

The bathroom is a narrow compartment on an upper floor of the extension framed by long blind walls, one of which produces an abstract blank space on the façade. From the door, one's attention is drawn to the light diffused from a north-facing window on the distant opposite wall. The room's floors and walls are made of the same white-veined black marble as the sinks, shelves, and bathtub embedded into them, forming a continuous surface whose lush depth is exaggerated by contrast with the white-plastered barrel-vaulted ceiling. Four Doric marble columns supporting an arch indicate the presence of the bathtub a few steps lower than the rest of the room. The drama of this tetrastyle configuration distinguishes the upper from the lower level and turns the pleasurable experience of bathing into a choreographed procession.

Only the four columns link this sensuous bathroom to the Vitruvian passage on tetrastyle *cavaedia*. It owes its existence to a dynamic of displacement through which a formal description of the atrium of the Roman house became a reference that

---

158; Benedetto Gravagnuolo, *Adolf Loos: Theory and Works* (Milan/Vienna: Idea Books/Löcker Verlag, 1982), 106–112.

436 Gubler provides the transcription of a letter from Ehrlich to the Lausanne architect Henri-Robert Von der Mühll (1898–1980) in which Ehrlich provides a detailed account of the project's development and claims authorship for his work on the Villa, including the bathroom.

shaped modern bathroom designs. And even in the bathroom of a compact home, the classical columns continue to convey luxury and grandeur. Charlottenhof, Kérylos, and Karma are separated by time and context, as are the reconstructions and recreations of Pliny's villas. The formal connections between them and the persistence of the tetrastyle configuration, rather than providing evidence of practices of emulation, are reminders of the shared space of formal imagination. By the nineteenth and early twentieth centuries, Vitruvius had become ubiquitous, as were images of Roman antiquity and the Pompeiian models. As the type began to be used without considering its precise origin, the tetrastyle became a mnemonic or reminiscent form that could be adapted to serve various contexts. The tetrastyle of Book VI was no longer a *cavaedium*, or even an atrium, an entrance, a hall, or a bathroom, but an unconscious reference to use when needed, unconnected to the purpose of the original sentence.

VITRUVIUS
BY ACCIDENT

Schönleinstraβe metro station in Berlin, built in 1927, has two symmetrical tetrastyle halls located on an intermediate level between the platform and the street. Like the other stations on the U8 line, it is clad in a grid of color-glazed 30 × 30 centimeter terracotta tiles. The structural elements of the halls and platforms are laid out accordingly, with rows of three, four, or more columns aligned to a grid. With this strict geometry and no decorative elements, the U8 stations are in keeping with the austerity of earlier Berlin metro stations designed by Alfred Grenander (1863–1931) and after him Peter Behrens (1868–1940).[437] Schönleinstraβe was built as a standard cut-and-cover station with a single island platform. The areas leading to the tracks derive their architectural character from the glossy tiles and the colored artificial light they reflect. The tetrastyle halls—a convenient solution to the combined requirements of platform size, station length, and subway access points[438] —are only unintentionally affiliated with Vitruvius, as is the use of modular building components.

Another tetrastyle, designed by Johann Lukas von Hildebrandt (1668–1745) and built between 1717 and 1723, can be found at Vienna's Upper Belvedere. In 1732, when the upper

---

437 A tetrastyle room by Peter Behrens can be found in the music salon for the third *Deutsche Kunstgewerbeausstellung* in Dresden in 1906. See Fritz Hoeber, *Peter Behrens* (Munich: Verlag Müller u. Rentsch, 1913), 46–52.

438 See Christoph Brachmann, *Licht und Farbe im Berliner Untergrund: U-Bahnhöfe der klassischen Moderne* (Berlin: Gebr. Mann, 2003).

VITRUVIUS BY ACCIDENT

213

47 Berlin Schönleinstraße U8 subway station, 1927

floor required additional support, four *atlantes* were added at ground level, turning the Sala Terena into a baroque tetrastyle hall.[439] The strategy seems to confirm that the tetrastyle is an intuitive structural solution, one that seems quite obvious in its ability to assure the building's structural soundness while preserving the formal layout of spaces. Like Schönleinstraβe metro, the Belvedere hall is not a deliberate reference to Vitruvius or to any architectural theory, but rather the result of a conjunction of technical requirements, proper dimensioning, and a good deal of pragmatism. It is only by accident that they belong to the inventory of tetrastyle halls going back to Vitruvius's sentence.

Another subtle, unspoken reference to Vitruvius can be found in Brazil. Following the 1964 military coup, the architect João Vilanova Artigas (1915–1985) was arrested for political reasons.[440] From exile in Uruguay between 1965 and 1967, he designed a house in São Paulo for Elza Berquó, a project that reflects his disenchantment with the inability of architecture to effect social change in Brazil.[441] The main feature of the Berquó House is an inner courtyard with four columns made of tree trunks supporting a large concrete roof slab. This conjunction of rough wood and reinforced concrete sparks an obvious formal clash between nature and technical progress, amplified by the resemblance of the trees—laid out on a square plan—to the proto-columns of Marc-Antoine Laugier's (1713–1769) mythical primitive hut.[442] The central

---

439 See Peter Stephan, *Das Obere Belvedere in Wien: Architektonisches Konzept und Ikonographie; Das Schloss des Prinzen Eugen als Abbild seines Selbstverständnisses* (Vienna: Böhlau, 2010).

440 Artigas's acclaimed University of São Paulo School of Architecture design was from 1962, and construction was completed in 1968.

441 Marcio Cotrim, *Vilanova Artigas: Casas paulistas* (São Paulo: Romano Guerra, 2017), 163–169.

442 The famous engraving of the primitive hut, by Charles-Dominique-Joseph Eisen, was published in Marc Antoine Laugier, *Essai sur l'Architecture*, 2nd ed., 1755. Laugier despaired that the image distracted readers from his argument. For a detailed account of the life and adventures of Laugier's book, see Fabio Restrepo Hernández, "Ceci est mon testament: Marc-Antoine Laugier" (PhD diss., Universidad Politécnica de Catalunya, Escuela Técnica Superior de Arquitectura de Barcelona, 2010). On the way

48 Vilanova Artigas, Berquó House, São Paulo, 1965–1967

opening in the roof gives the space the compluvium of a proper Vitruvian *cavaedium*. Such permeability between inside and outside became a trademark of postwar architecture in São Paulo, where brutalism met the tropics. Writing on the project, Artigas claimed to have beeen ironic: "I made this concrete structure supported on tree trunks to say, at that time, that all this technique of reinforced concrete, which makes this magnificent architecture we are all familiar with, is no more than an irreparable foolishness in the face of the political conditions under which we then lived."[443] Artigas was confident that modern architecture could bring about social progress by means of technological development. His architectural language, with its raw concrete beams, slabs, and columns, materializes the physical labor put into building, a pathos that supports the ethical goal of modern architecture to improve social conditions. In this way, Artigas and other Brazilian architects used concrete to free a path for Brazilian modernism amidst cultural precepts from Europe and the United States.[444] Nonetheless, Artigas acknowledged that the Berquó courtyard is a reference to the Spanish patio, a close neighbor of the Roman atrium Vitruvius describes, and it fulfills a similar function as a distributor, linking peripheral spaces to the center of the house. But in the hands of Artigas, the *cavaedium* is far from the space carved out from within a built mass typical of the atria of Roman houses and grand Renaissance villas. Instead, it is made fluid by means of intersecting floating concrete walls and transparent sliding doors; and the unlikely meeting of trees and concrete challenges the sense of structural soundness praised in the Vitruvian sentence. Rather than an achievement of statics, the structure is a metaphor of political frailty.

Eisen's image become a reference within architectural discourse, see Pedro Ignazio Alonso, "Shoot the Artist," in *Disparen sobre el artista/Acrónimo* (Providencia, Santiago de Chile: Ediciones Arq, 2016), 6–11.

443 João Vilanova Artigas, "Casa Elza Berquó," in *Vilanova Artigas*, by Marcelo Ferraz (São Paulo: Instituto Lina Bo e P. M. Bardi/Fundação Vilanova Artigas, 1997), 138–141, here 138.

444 A synthetic explanation of this argument can be found in Adrian Forty, *Concrete and Culture: A Material History* (London: Reaktion Books, 2012), 125–129.

Artigas's experiment with the contradictions of his tree trunks suggests the ironic quality of postmodernism, but whereas postmodern irony is triggered by a play of architectural forms and language, the irony of the Berquó House is structural. Postmodernism's flirtation with historical references led to a number of less accidental Vitruvian tetrastyle spaces than Artigas's. Among them are examples by the American architect Thomas Gordon Smith, the youngest contributor to the Strada Novissima at the 1980 Venice Biennale exhibition, *The Presence of the Past*, held just before architectural postmodernism reached peak frenzy.[445] Two years earlier, Smith had completed a pair of houses in Livermore, California, which he named Laurentine and Tuscan after Pliny, anticipating Culot's Laurentine competition of 1981. These houses—that do not include tetrastyle spaces—are rather conventional suburban middle-class American homes except that they explode with color and postmodern irony, of which their epithets are just the beginning.[446] Heinrich Klotz (1935–1999) visited them in September 1980 while collecting materials for the new Deutsches Architekturmuseum in Frankfurt and its inaugural exhibition *Die Revision der Moderne*, which in 1984 further enshrined postmodernism in contemporary architectural culture.[447] His recorded notes describe the way "Smith uses classical motifs and combines them with modern needs. A garage is simply turned into a portico, the garage door has a column, the pediment an acroterium." Klotz was aware of the risky game Smith was playing: "the houses jumble meanings together, setting them in dangerous contrast and taking them to the edge of tolerability."[448]

---

445 Szacka, *Exhibiting the Postmodern*, 169–170.

446 Heinrich Klotz, *Die Revision der Moderne: Postmoderne Architektur 1960–1980* (Munich: Prestel, 1984), 263–278.

447 Oliver Elser, ed., "Die Klotz-Tapes: Das Making-of der Postmoderne/The Klotz Tapes: The Making of Postmodernism," *Arch+ features* 47, no. 26 (2014): 115–121.

448 Elser, "Die Klotz-Tapes," 115, 119.

In 1988, before moving to Indiana to teach, Smith published a treatise on classical architecture,[449] the beginning of the work that eventually led to the publication of his own edition of Vitruvius in 2003.[450] Smith's Vitruvius is based on Morris Hicky Morgan's translation but retains only the books having "relevance to contemporary practice," meaning he edited out subjects that were "historically important but lack application to architectural practice today."[451] His comments on Vitruvius range from strategies to adopt when designing classical compositions with contemporary means—such as the best way to model capitals to respond to the requirements of digital laser-cutting technologies—to advice on accurately applying Vitruvian concepts when proportioning the various elements of a composition. This pragmatic approach is highlighted in the annotated illustrations that facilitate the reader's understanding of the text as a model for their own designs, a strategy confirmed by the final element of the book, a presentation of Smith's Vitruvian House, built in Indiana in 1989.[452] It is certainly not accidental that Smith uses the term *oecus* to refer to the house's square-plan tetrastyle living room, knowing that Vitruvius prescribes a two-square rectangular proportion for four-columned *oeci*.[453] His liberal and literal quotes from historical sources make his Vitruvian intentions clear.

Some other postmodern examples of quasi-Vitruvian tetrastyles are less deliberate. One is the acclaimed Casa Tonini in Ticino built between 1972 and 1974 by Bruno Reichlin and Fabio Reinhart, Swiss pupils of Aldo Rossi (1931–1997).[454] The house is a contemporary interpretation of the Palladian

---

449 Thomas Gordon Smith, *Classical Architecture: Rule and Invention* (Layton, UT: Gibbs M. Smith, 1988).

450 Gordon Smith 2003.

451 Gordon Smith 2003, 10.

452 Gordon Smith 2003, 51–57.

453 "Dining rooms ought to be twice as long as they are wide. ... Corinthian and four-columned *oeci* ... should have the same ratio of width and length as the *symmetriae* for dining rooms." Vitruvius VI, 8, quoted from Gordon Smith 2003, 191. See above the section "Proportional Deadlock" and Marini's 1836 illustration of a square *oecus*, plate no. CV.

454 Martin Steinmann, ed., *Tendenzen: Neuere Architektur im Tessin/Tenden-*

49 Thomas Gordon Smith, Vitruvian House, Indiana, 1989–1991

villa, a type popular among the Ticinese bourgeoisie in the late nineteenth and early twentieth centuries.[455] From a nine-square plan, the architects developed a spatial composition of imbricated cubic volumes following a mathematical sequence: a square within a square, within a square. The core of the house is a tetrastyle space, with the four piers establishing a grid marked in the floor tiling and a ceiling open to the galleries of the upper floors in lieu of a *compluvium*.

Another postmodern cousin to Vitruvius is the house Charles Moore (1925–1993) built in 1962 in Orinda, California, near Berkeley.[456] It is square in plan with a pitched wooden roof. The interior space is characterized by two square *aediculae*, each defined by four cylindrical columns of recycled wood that support contrasting white lintels with light shafts above them. The smaller tetrastyle *aedicula* encloses a cinematic sunken bathtub, recalling Schinkel and Pontremoli,[457] while the larger one defines a living area that, in Moore's words, is meant to "ensure that something in this small structure would be grand."[458] The references are not to the *cavaedium* but to the mythical primitive hut and the Vitruvian account of how details of wooden construction shaped the classical temple, as well as to forms like the *ciborium* and the *baldachin*—both elemental structures with spiritual connotations.[459] Again in the architect's words, the "aedicula provided a way of accommodating this general need for a symbolic center in the

---

cies: *Recent Architecture in Ticino/Tendenze: architettura recente nel Ticino*, 1st ed. 1977 (Zurich: gta Verlag, 2010).

455 See the catalogue of the contemporary exhibition on Swiss Palladian villas at the Institute for the History and Theory of Architecture (gta) at ETH Zurich, where Reichlin and Reinhardt were assistant professors: Christina Reble, ed., *Die Präsenz Palladios in der Schweizer Architektur* (Zurich: gta Verlag, 1976).

456 Elser, "Die Klotz-Tapes," 116–117.

457 See "Shifting Type" in the section above.

458 Charles Moore, Gerald Allen, and Donlyn Lyndon, *The Place of Houses*, 1st ed. 1974 (Berkeley: University of California Press, 2000), 60–61.

459 Sylvia Lavin used an equivalent device in the installation of the exhibition *Architecture Itself and Other Postmodernist Myths*, held at the Canadian Centre for Architecture in 2018.

midst of the specific demands of the household."[460] The same tetrastyle device was used again by Moore, Turnbull, and their associates to nest the floating chambers in the Sea Ranch Condominium units, built by the Pacific Ocean in 1965.[461]

It comes as a surprise to find a tetrastyle entrance in Le Corbusier's (1887–1965) Villa Stein-de Monzie, in Garches, designed from 1926 to 1927 and completed by the end of 1928.[462] The villa is known for its ideal proportions,[463] a mathematical quality achieved by means of the *plan libre*. By basing his famous structural system on a grid of concrete columns, Le Corbusier could lay out the plan independently of the façade, setting partition walls, ramps, and staircases in a dynamic scenery that engages the moving user in a thrilling *promenade architecturale*. The structural grid lends a rhythmic beat to this physical experience, as the independent columns are perceived in relation to the free-floating wall surfaces and voids within the building envelope. The four columns of the entrance hall are set apart from the rest of the structural grid so that the visitor first perceives a stable tetrastyle space from which depart a prominent staircase and various disparate elements.

The 2:1:2:1:2 proportional rhythm of the Villa Stein's structural plan led Colin Rowe to remark on its resemblance to Palladio's villa La Malcontenta, a building and an architect for which and whom Le Corbusier had professed admiration.[464] Nonetheless, as Joseph Quetglas later pointed out, the original tetrastyle source for the Villa Stein lies back in

---

460 Moore, Allen, and Lyndon, *The Place of Houses*, 51.

461 This mythological form of the tetrastyle, which Moore associates with Mayan or Hindu temples, can be found in the central hearts of Mycenae megarons.

462 Tim Benton, *The Villas of Le Corbusier: 1920–1930* (New Haven, CT: Yale University Press, 1987), 165–185.

463 Colin Rowe, "The Mathematics of the Ideal Villa," in *The Mathematics of the Ideal Villa and Other Essays*, 1st ed. 1947 (Cambridge, MA: MIT Press, 1976), 1–28.

464 On this relation, see also Stanislaus von Moos, *Le Corbusier: Elements of a Synthesis*, 2nd ed. (Rotterdam: 010 Publishers, 2009), 92–96. On Le Corbusier's visit to La Malcontenta in 1934, see Antoni Foscari *Tumult and Order: Malcontenta 1924–1939*, trans. Lucinda Byatt (Zurich: Lars Müller, 2012), 139–152.

50 Le Corbusier and Pierre Jeanneret, Villa Stein-de Monzie, Garches, 1926–1928

VITRUVIUS BY ACCIDENT

Pompeii.[465] In 1911, before adopting his pseudonym, Charles-Edouard Jeanneret spent five days in Pompeii as part of his *Voyage d'Orient*, during which he measured and sketched the tetrastyle *cavaedium* of the House of the Silver Wedding.[466] A few years later, in 1922, Le Corbusier traveled to Vicenza in the company of his client Raoul La Roche (1889–1965) and visited Palladio's works, including the Palazzo Barbarano da Porto where he drew a quick sketch of the tetrastyle entrance.[467] The following year, he published his sketches of Pompeii in *Vers une architecture*, accompanied by a description of the House of the Silver Wedding and the power of its four cylindrical columns: "Again a small vestibule that clears the street from your mind. And suddenly you are in the cavaedium (atrium); four columns in the center (four cylinders) rise in one go toward the shadow of the roof, a sensation of strength and witness to potent means."[468]

When Le Corbusier designed this tetrastyle entrance, both Palladio and Pompeii were fresh in his memory. Although he certainly knew Vitruvius, he seldom quoted the Roman author. The only Vitruvian title in the modern architect's library was a Japanese gift with a subtitle that massaged his ego: "From Vitruvius to Le Corbusier."[469] It is thus unlikely that he was

---

465 Josep Quetglas, "Las cuatro columnas: Palladio y Le Corbusier," in *Massilia, Centre d'Investigacions Estètiquesm San Cugat del Vallès*, 2003, 102–109.

466 Giuliano Gresleri, ed., *Le Corbusier, Charles-Edouard Jeanneret, Voyage d'Orient: Carnets* (Milan: Electa/Fondation Le Corbusier, 2002), 126–127, Carnet 4. For a detailed account of the Pompeii sojourn, see Alfonso Mattia Berritto, *Pompei 1911: Le Corbusier e l'origine della casa* (Naples: Clean, 2011).

467 Kurt W. Forster, "Album La Roche," ed. Guido Beltramini and Howard Burns, in *Palladio* (London: Royal Academy of Arts, 2009), 400–401. For a facsimile of the album, see Stanislaus von Moos, ed., *Album La Roche* ([Paris]: Gallimard, 1996).

468 Le Corbusier, *Toward an Architecture*, trans. John Goodman (Los Angeles: Getty Research Institute, 2007), 218–219; Le Corbusier, *Vers une architecture*, 1st ed. 1923 (Paris: Flammarion, 1995), 148–149. In 1929 he also included the Pompeii sketches in the first volume of his *Œuvre complete:* Willy Boesiger and Oscar Stonorov, eds., *Le Corbusier: Œuvre Complète, 1910–29* (Zurich: H. Girsberger & Cie, 1930), 19.

469 Arnaud Dercelles, "Catalogue de la bibliothèque personelle de Le Corbusier," in *Le Corbusier et le livre* (Barcelona: Col-legi d'Arquitectes de Catalunya, [2005]). The only Vitruvius listed in Dercelles is a title signed by the author that we were not able to locate in other libraries: Kenjy Imai, *Architecture & Humanity: From Vitruvius to Le Corbusier* (Tokyo, 1954). Von Moos quotes a 1951 lecture by Rudolf Wittkower in Milan,

thinking about Vitruvius's tetrastyle sentence when drafting the entrance hall for the Villa Stein.[470] The Corbusian sources were real buildings: one made before Vitruvius's book and the other after it.

Echoes of the Vitruvian tetrastyle form had thus reached modern architecture in two ways: indirectly via Palladio, who had pulled it from the book to the building; and directly from the remains of the built references that were also Vitruvius's source. So it is that even when an architect avoids the lost sentence in Vitruvius's cryptic text, some of the architectural ideas contained in its passages can resurface in the most unexpected places.

"De Divina Proportione," addressing proportion as a historical topic that "originated with Vitruvius and ended with Le Corbusier." Moos, *Le Corbusier*, 315. Some years later the same trajectory was used as the title of a French anthology of architectural texts: Gérard Uniack, *De Vitruve à Le Corbusier: Textes d'architectes* (Paris: Dunod, 1968).

470 This was done by March 1927. See drawings FLC 10517 and 10518, published in Benton, *Villas of Le Corbusier*, 182.

EPILOGUE

Happy-Go-Lucky

This systematic survey of Vitruvius publications has considered their book forms as material objects rather than as texts. To see what links might be established between the physical copies and the architecture of their time, I have taken the tetrastyle sentence as a case in point and assessed its representation in the published Vitruvian versions alongside an eclectic collection of built tetrastyle spaces. The result is a foggy picture, a chimera, that suggests that the discourse embodied in books does not run parallel to architectural practice, but rather that the two are perennially permeable, their relationship zigzagging and oscillating between desired connotations and accidental references. The hope is that acknowledging this insouciance can be useful to understanding architectural books as physical objects in relation to history, theory, and architecture itself.

To possess a physical copy of Vitruvius, regardless of whether one reads it or not, is to possess an idea evocative of architecture's cultural background, of its long-standing sources, and of the value of order and proportion. Regardless of the abuse heaped on the author for his perceived limitations, such as his impenetrable Latin and the long-forgotten concepts his book describes, it is exactly these puzzling characteristics that give readers license to innovate. The quasi-magical status of the object—that does not even possess an original title—presents a unique opportunity for appropriation. But rather than inspiring fetishism, each reprinting reinstates the book as a brand-new object. Vitruvius, always anachronistic and thereby always timely, became a useful instrument for architects and intellectuals, provided they had sufficient imagination to translate its structure into operative concepts. And, as we have seen, they had a wealth of imagination.

The malleable nature of Vitruvian theory is in part a result of changes to the form in which it is physically expressed. For example, Giocondo's early-sixteenth-century transformation of Vitruvius from a large table book into a handy portable edition made it accessible to a wider clientele in a wider range of places—freed from libraries and scholarly cloisters, it could be read in the open air. The content of each edition is shaped by the hierarchical organization of the component parts, from Latin source to translation, from editorial comments to illustration captions, from footnotes to printers' marks, from the navigation system to the structure of cross-references. Each page is part of a network that steers architectural concepts along paths linking to various times and places, granting it a rich, complex texture. The reverberations of typographic information that resulted recall El Lissitzky's (1890–1941) "topography of typography."

The illustrations are a key component of this content, and focusing on them leads to a consideration of the book's physical qualities. Be they woodcuts in Giocondo and Cesariano, engravings by Leclerc in Perrault, sharp Greek Revival images in Wilkins, or offset-printed renderings of archaeological reconstitutions by Noble Howe, the various solutions illustrators found to the challenge of the tetrastyle sentence of Book VI demonstrate the intrinsic open nature of the text and the many ways in which various agendas can shape Vitruvius's words. Today, the most physically impressive aspect of the Vitruviana is the sheer volume and scope of publication: in addition to the editions discussed here, even as you read this the book continues to be republished somewhere in the world. And even though accurate text editions are increasingly available in digital formats, more and more conventional copies of the book are being printed than ever before, in numbers that dwarf the countless photocopies made in the late twentieth century.

The way each edition relates to the building culture of its time allows a closer look at the complex knitting of theory and practice. If during the Renaissance the rediscovery of antiquity and the corresponding desire to understand archaeological remains drove readers to Vitruvius, in the eighteenth and nineteenth centuries the archaeological remains themselves—especially at Pompeii and Herculaneum—returned the favor to shed new light on Vitruvius's text. While Barbaro's editions supplied Palladian illustrations to facilitate the fashioning of architecture *all'antica*, Choisy set up a systematic reading process meant to encourage contemporary architecture to follow a Vitruvian design method of proportion and composition. Just prior to World War II, Stürzenacker enriched his 1938 German translation with images of the architecture of the Third Reich; in 1965 André Dalmas used model contemporary buildings to illustrate the ongoing application of Vitruvian principles and to demonstrate the genealogical value of postwar architectural trends. Thus a continuum of quotes and cross-references link the built environment and the architectural treatise, alongside similarly wide ranges of variation in the sizes of buildings and books, techniques used for construction and printing, and in the compositional acrobatics needed to unite multiple voices and discursive layers within coherent objects. Such liveliness and diversity explain Vitruvius's ongoing relevance to past, present, and future building practices.

The primary legacy of Vitruvianism rests in the architectural orders, with a sense of the anthropomorphic symmetry of human and divine architecture a close second. These are significant themes that I might have used, in my own analytical yet perhaps enigmatic book, to approach and assess the publishing history of Vitruvius editions. Others are the education of architects, the primitive hut, the synthetic triad of architectural qualities—*firmitas*, *utilitas*, *venustas*—and the virtues of mathematics as a means to determine building proportions. I instead chose a more accidental lens: the tetrastyle room. And in the end, my hope is that this narrow topic grants a new insight into Vitruvius's readership and the core relation between theory and practice. This may either be productive or futile but, in fact, it almost leads to the conclusion that there may be no relationship whatsoever. Architectural practice seems doomed to an earthly realm, with the inevitable need for com-

51 Pompeii, House of the Silver Wedding, excavation, autumn 1892, photograph published in August Mau, *Pompeii: Its Life and Art*, 1899

promise jeopardizing the perfect application of theoretical formulations. However, the tetrastyle room also suggests the opposite. Architects do know theory, practicing and experimenting with and moving between the two with great ease and freedom. Subconscious references, latent ideas, accidental quotes, circumstantial constraints all conspire to weave an endless network of connections between the book and the building.

VITRUVIANA
1486-2016

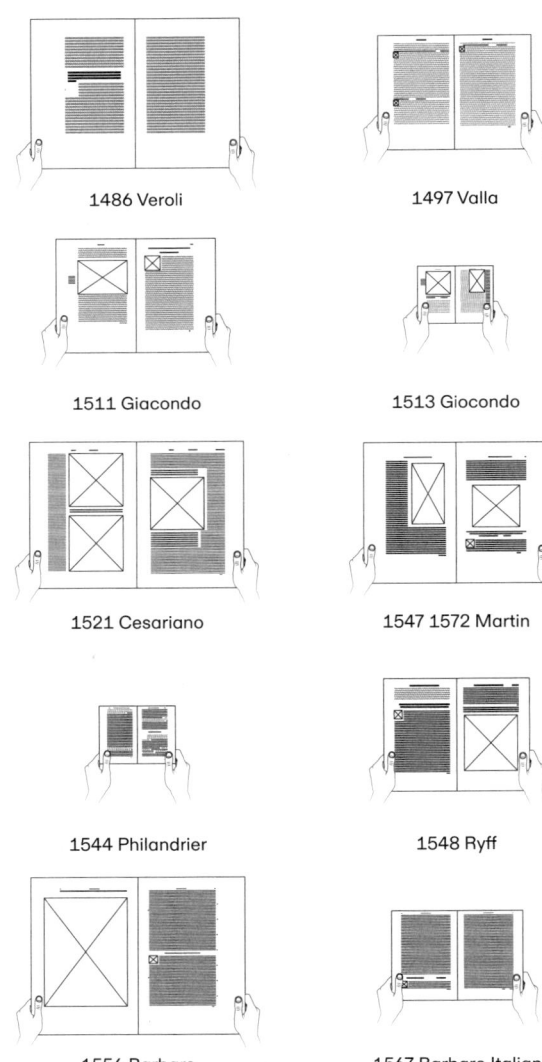

1486 Veroli

1497 Valla

1511 Giocondo

1513 Giocondo

1521 Cesariano

1547 1572 Martin

1544 Philandrier

1548 Ryff

1556 Barbaro

1567 Barbaro Italian

52 Panorama of Vitruvius Layouts

VITRUVIANA 1486-2016

1567 Barbaro Latin

1586 Philandrier

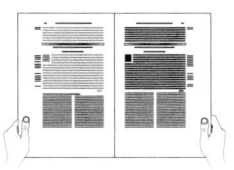

1673 Perrault

1674 Perrault

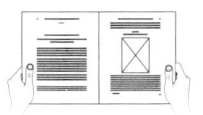

1758 Galiani

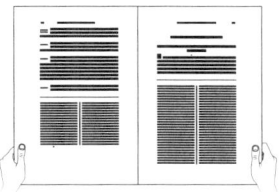

1791 Newton

1796 Rode

1800 Rode

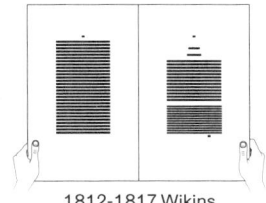

1802 Orsini

1812-1817 Wikins

* reprint with minor changes
± partial edition
▯ only illustrations
% proemia
ab. abridged
ed. edition
trans. translation
comm. commentary
illus. illustration

Sulpitius 1486 Joannes Sulpitius Verulanus [Giovanni Sulpizio da Veroli or Verolensis], ed., *L. Victruuii Pollionis de architectura libri decem* (Rome: n.p.)

Cattaneo 1496 [Francesco Cattaneo], ed., *L. Vitruuii Pollionis de architectura libri decem* (Florence: n.p.)

Bevilaqua 1497 *L. Vitruuii Pollionis de architectura libri decem* (Venice: Simon Papiensis dictus Beuilaqua)

Giocondo 1511 Giovanni Giocondo, ed. and illus., *M. Vitruuius per Iocundum solito castigatior factus cum figuris et tabula ut iam legi et intelligi possit* (Venice: Ioannis de Tridino alias Tacuino)

Giocondo 1513 Giovanni Giocondo, ed. and illus., *Vitruuius iterum et Frontinus a' Iocundo reuisi repurgatique quantum ex collatione licuit* (Florence: Philippus de Giunta)

Cesariano 1521 Cesare Cesariano, trans., illus., and comm., *Di Lucio Vitruvio Pollione de architectura libri dece traducti de latino in vulgare affigurati* (Como: Gotardus da Ponte)

Giocondo 1522 * Giovanni Giocondo, ed. and illus., *M. Vitruuii de architectura libri decem nuper maxima diligentia castigati atq; excusi* (Florence: Philippus de Giunta)

Giocondo 1523 Giovanni Giocondo, ed., *M. Vitruuii de architectura libri decem, summa diligentia recogniti, atq; excusi. Cum nonnullis figuris sub hoc signo ▯ positis, nunq antea impræssis* ([Lyon]: Guillaume Huyon])

Durantino 1524 Francesco Lutio Durantino, ed., *M·L·Vitruuio Pollione de architectura traducto di latino in vulgare dal vero exemplare con le figure a li soi loci con mirãdo ordine insignito* (Venice: Ioannes Antonio & Piero fratelli da Sabio)

Durantino 1535 Francesco Lutio Durantino, ed., *M·L·Vitruuio Pollione di Architettura dal vero esemplare latino nella volgar lingua tradotto: e con le figure a suoi luoghi con mirãdo ordine insignito* (Venice: Nicolò di Aristotele detto Zoppino)

Caporali 1536 ± I–V Giovanni Battista Caporali, ed., *Architettura: Con il suo cõmento et figure Vetruvio in volgar lingua raportato per ·M·Gianbatista Caporali di Perugia* (Perugia: Iano Bigazzini)

Ryff 1543 Walther Hermann Ryff, ed., *M. Vitruuii, uiri suae professionis peritissimi, de architectura libri decem, ad Augustum Cæsarem accuratiss. conscripti: & nunc primum in Germania qua potuit diligentia excusi, atq; hinc inde schematibus exornati* (Argentorati [Strasbourg]: Officina Knoblochiana, Georgius Machaeropioeus [Georg Messerschmidt])

Philandrier 1544 Guillaume Philandrier, comm., *Gulielmi Philandri Castilionii Galli ciuis Ro. in decem libros M. Vitruuii Pollionis de Architectura Annotationes* (Rome: Ioannes Andreas Dossena Thaurinensis)

Philandrier 1545 Guillaume Philandrier, comm., *Gulielmi Philandri Castilionii Galli ciuis Ro. in decem libros M. Vitruuii Pollionis de architectura annotationes* (Paris: Michaëlis Fezandat)

Martin 1547 Jean Martin, trans., Jean Goujon, illus., *Architecture ou Art de bien bastir, de Marc Vitruue Pollion Autheur Romain antique* (Paris: Jacques Gazeau)

Ryff 1548 Walther Hermann Ryff, trans., *Vitruuius Teutsch, nemlichen des aller namhafftigisten und hocherfarnesten, Römischen Architecti, und Kunstreichen Werck[-] oder Bawmeisters, Marci Vitruuii Pollionis, Zehen Bücher von der Architectur und künstlichem Bawen* (Nuremberg: Johan Petreius)

Ryff 1550 Walther Hermann Ryff, ed., Guillaume Philandrier, comm., *M. Vitruuii Pollionis, uiri suae professionis peritissimi, de architectura libri.X* (Argentorati [Strasbourg]: Officina Knoblochiana, Georgius Machaeropioeus [Georg Messerschmidt])

Philandrier 1552 Guillaume Philandrier, comm., *M. Vitruuii Pollionis de architectura libri decem ad Caesarem Augustum, omnibus omnium editionibus longè emendatiores, collatis ueteribus exemplis* (Lyon: Ioannes Tornaesius [Jean de Tournes])

Barbaro 1556 Daniele Barbaro, trans. and comm., [Andrea Palladio, illus.], *I dieci libri dell'architettura di M. Vitruvio* (Venice: Francesco Marcolini)

Gardet 1556–1559 ab. Jean Gardet, ed., Dominique Bertin, illus., *Epitome ou Extrait abrégé des dix livres d'architecture de Marc Vitruve Pollion* (Toulouse: Guyon Boudeville)

Philandrier 1557 Guillaume Philandrier, comm., *In M. Vitruuium de architectura annotationes Guilielmi Philandri* (Venice: Ex officina Stellæ)

Gardet 1565 ab. * Jan Gardet, ed., Dominique Bertin, illus., *Epitome ou Extrait abrégé des dix livres d'architecture de Marc Vitruve Pollion* (Paris: Gabriel Buon)

Gardet 1567 ab. * Jan Gardet, ed., Dominique Bertin, illus., *Epitome ou Extrait abrégé des dix livres d'architecture de Marc Vitruve Pollion* (Paris: Gabriel Buon)

Barbaro 1567 [Latin] Daniele Barbaro, ed. and comm., [Andrea Palladio, illus.], *M. Vitruuii Pollionis de architectura libri decem* (Venice: Franciscus Franciscius Senensis & Ioannes Crugher Germanus)

Barbaro 1567 [Italian] Daniele Barbaro, trans. and comm., [Andrea Palladio, illus.], *I dieci libri dell'architettura di M. Vitruvio* (Venice: Franciscus Franciscius Senensis & Ioannes Crugher Germanus)

Gardet 1568 ab. * Jan Gardet, ed., Dominique Bertin, illus., *Epitome ou Extrait abrégé des dix livres d'architecture de Marc Vitruve Pollion* (Paris: Gabriel Buon)

Martin 1572 Jean Martin, trans., Jean Goujon, illus., *Architecture ou Art de bien bastir, de Marc Vitruve Pollion Autheur Romain antique* (Paris: Hierosme de Marnef & Guillaume Cauellat)

Ryff 1575 Walther Hermann Ryff, trans., *Vitruuius: Des allernamhafftigisten vnnd hocherfarnesten römischen Architecti vnnd kunstreichen Werck- oder Bawmeysters, Marci Vitruuii Pollionis, zehen Bücher von der Architectur vnd künstlichem Bawen* (Basel: Sebastian Henricpetri)

Urrea 1582 Miguel de Urrea, trans., *M. Vitruuio Pollion de architectura, dividido en diez libros* (Alcalá de Henares: Juan Gracián)

Ryff 1582 * Walther Hermann Ryff, trans., *Bawkunst, oder, Architectur aller fürnemsten, notwendigsten, angehörigen mathematischen vnd mechanischen Künsten, eygentlicher Bericht vnd verständtliche Vnderrichtung, zu rechtem Verstandt der Lehr Vitruuii in drey fürnemme Bücher abgetheilet* (Basel: Sebastian Henricpetri)

Barbaro 1584 * Daniele Barbaro, trans. and comm., [Andrea Palladio, illus.], *I dieci libri dell'architettura di M. Vitruvio* (Venice: Franciscus Franciscius Senensis)

Philandrier 1586 * Guillaume Philandrier, comm., *M. Vitruuii Pollionis de architectura libri decem* (Lyon: Ioannes Tornaesius [Jean de Tournes])

Rusconi 1590 ☐ Giovanni Antonio Rusconi, illus., *Della architettura* (Venice: Gioliti)

Gardet 1597 ab. * Jean Gardet, ed., and Dominique Bertin, illus., *Abrégé des dix livres d'architecture de M. Vitruve Pollion* (Paris: Antoine Du Breuil)

Ryff 1614 * Walther Hermann Ryff, trans., *Vitruuius: Des aller namhafftigisten vnnd hocherfahrnesten, römischen Architecti, vnnd kunstreichen Werck- oder Bawmeisters, Marci Vitruuii Pollionis, zehen Bücher von der Architectur vnd künstlichem Bawen* (Basel: Sebastian Henricpetri)

Martin 1618 * Jean Martin, trans., *Architecture ou Art de bien bastir, de Marc Vitruve Pollion* (Geneva: Jean de Tournes)

Martin 1628 * Jean Martin, trans., *Architecture ou Art de bien bastir, de Marc Vitruve Pollion* (Geneva: Jean de Tournes)

Barbaro 1629 * Daniele Barbaro, trans. and comm., [Andrea Palladio, illus.], *I dieci libri dell'architettvra di M. Vitruvio* (Venice: Alessandro de' Vecchi)

Barbaro 1641 * Daniele Barbaro, trans. and comm., [Andrea Palladio, illus.], *L'architettura di Vitruvio libri dieci* (Venice: Turrini)

De Laet 1649 Joannes de Laet, ed., Daniele Barbaro and Guillaume Philandrier, comm., *M. Vitruvii Pollionis de architectura libri decem* (Amsterdam: Louis Elzevir)

Rusconi 1660 ◻ Giovanni Antonio Rusconi, illus., *I dieci libri d'architettura* (Venice: Nicolini)

Perrault 1673 Claude Perrault, trans., comm., and illus., *Les dix livres d'architecture de Vitruve, corrigez et traduits nouvellement en François, avec des Notes & des Figures* (Paris: Jean Baptiste Coignard)

Perrault 1674 ab. Claude Perrault, *Abrégé des dix livres d'architecture de Vitruve* (Paris: Jean Baptiste Coignard)

Perrault 1681 ab. Claude Perrault, *Architecture générale de Vitruve* (Amsterdam: Huguetans)

Perrault 1684 Claude Perrault, trans., comm., and illus., *Les dix livres d'architecture de Vitruve corrigez et traduits nouvellement en François, avec des Notes & des Figures* (Paris: Jean Baptiste Coignard)

Perrault 1692 ab. Claude Perrault, *An Abridgment of the Architecture of Vitruvius: Containing a System of the Whole Works of That Author* (London: Abel Swall and T. Child)

Perrault 1703 ab. Claude Perrault; Abel Boyer, trans., *The Theory and Practice of Architecture, or Vitruvius and Vignola Abridg'd* (London: Richard Wellington)

Perrault 1711 ab. Claude Perrault; Carlo Cataneo, trans., Daniele Barbaro, commentary, *Compendio dell'architettura generale di Vitruvio* (Venice: Girolamo Albrizzi)

Perrault 1729 ab.* Claude Perrault, *The Theory and Practice of Architecture, or Vitruvius and Vignola Abridg'd* (London: Richard Wellington)

1747 Perrault ab.* Claude Perrault; Carlo Cattaneo, trans., Daniele Barbaro comm., *L'architettura generale di Vitruvio* (Venice: Giambatista Albrizzi)

1757 Perrault ab. Claude Perrault; M. Müller, trans., *Des grossen und weltberühmten Vitruvii Architectura* (Nürnberg, Würzburg and Prague: Paul Lochner und Meyer)

Galiani 1758 Berardo Galiani, trans., comm., and illus., *L'architettura di M. Vitruvio Pollione* (Naples: Simoniana)

Perrault 1761 ab. Claude Perrault; Joseph Castañeda, trans., *Compendio de los diez libros de Arquitectura de Vitruvio* (Madrid: Gabriel Ramirez)

Perrault 1768 ab.* Claude Perrault, *Abrégé des dix livres d'architecture de Vitruve* (Paris: Jean Baptiste Coignard; Basel: Im Hof)

Newton 1771 ± I-V William Newton, trans. and illus., *The Architecture of M. Vitruvius Pollio* (London: J. Dodsley)

Ortiz y Sanz 1787 José Francisco Ortiz y Sanz, trans., comm., and illus., *Los diez libros de architectura de M. Vitruvio Polión* (Madrid: Imprenta Real)

Perrault 1789 ab. Claude Perrault; Fedor Karzhavin, trans., Сокращенный Витрувій, или совершенный архитекторъ | *Sokrashchennyi Vitruvii ili sovershennyi arkhitektor* (Moscow: Университетская типографія Н. Новикова | Universitetskaia Tipografia N. Novikova [Nikolay Novikov])

Perrault 1790-1797 Claude Perrault, ed.; Vasilii Bazhenov and Fedor Karzhavin, trans., Марка Витрувія Полліона объ архитектуръ | *Marka Vitruviia Polliona ob arkhitektur* (St. Petersburg: Императорская Академія наукъ | Imperatorskaia Akademiia Naukie [Imperial Academy of Sciences])

Galiani 1790 Berardo Galiani, trans., comm., and illus., *L'architettura di Marco Vitruvio Pollione* (Siena: Luigi e Benedetto Bindi; Naples: Fratelli Terres)

Newton 1791 William Newton, trans. and illus., *The Architecture of M. Vitruvius Pollio* (London: James Newton)

Perrault 1794 ab. Claude Perrault, *L'architettura generale di Vitruvio* (Venice: Antonio Zatta)

Rode 1796 August Rode, trans., *Des Marcus Vitruvius Pollio Baukunst* (Leipzig: Georg Joachim Göschen)

Rode 1800 August Rode, ed., *Marci Vitruvii Pollionis de architectura libri decem* (Berlin: Augustus Mylius)

Rode 1801 August Rode, illus., *Formae ad explicandos M. Vitruvii Pollionis decem libros de architectura* | *Kupfer zu Vitruvs zehn Büchern von der Baukunst* (Berlin: Augustus Mylius)

Orsini 1802 Baldassarre Orsini, *Dell'architettura di M. Vitruvio Pollione libri diece* (Perugia: Carlo Baduel)

Bipontina 1807 *M. Vitruvii Pollionis de architectura libri decem* (Argentorati [Strasbourg]: Societas Bipontina)

Schneider 1807-1808 Johann Gottlob Schneider, ed., *Marci Vitruvii Pollionis de architectura libri decem* (Leipzig: Georg Joachim Göschen)

Wilkins 1812/13-1817 William Wilkins, trans., *The Civil Architecture of Vitruvius: Comprising Those Books of the Author Which Relate to the Public and Private Edifices of the Ancients* (London: Longman, Hurst, Rees, Orme, and Brown)

Moreau de Bioul 1816 Jean-Michel de Moreau de Bioul, trans., *L'architecture de Vitruve* (Brussels: Adolphe Stapleaux)

Stratico 1825-1830 Giovanni Poleni and Simone Stratigo, eds., *M. Vitruvii Pollionis architectura* (Udine: Fratres Mattiuzzi)

Gwilt 1826 Joseph Gwilt, trans., *The Architecture of Marcus Vitruvius Pollio in Ten Books* (London: Priestley and Weale)

Amati 1829-1830 Carlo Amati, ed., *Dell'architettura di Marco Vitruvio Pollione libri dieci* (Milano: Pirola)

Viviani 1830-1833 Quirico Viviani, trans., *L'architettura di Vitruvio* (Udine: Mattiuzzi)

Galiani 1832 Berardo Galiani, trans. and comm., *Dell'architettura libri dieci di M. Vitruvio Pollione* (Milan: Alessandro Dozio)

Tauchnitz 1836 Carl Tauchnitz, *Marci Vitruvii Pollionis de architectura libri decem* (Leipzig: Carl Tauchnitz)

Marini 1836 Luigi Marini, ed., *Vitruvii de architectura libri decem* (Rome: Luigi Marini)

Marini 1836-1837 Luigi Marini, trans. and comm., *L'architettura di Vitruvio* (Rome: Luigi Marini)

Tardieu-Coussin 1837 Claude Perrault, trans., Louis-Eugène-Thomas Tardieu and Louis Ambroise Coussin, eds., *Les dix livres d'architecture de Vitruve, avec les notes de Perrault* (Paris: Eugène Tardieu/Ambroise Coussin)

Raczyński 1840 Edward Raczyński, trans., *Marka Witruwiusza Polliona o budownictwie ksiąg dziesięć* (Wrocław: Zygmunt Schletter)

Galiani 1844 Berardo Galiani, trans. and comm., *Dell'architettura libri dieci di M. Vitruvio Pollione* (Milan: Pirotta)

Perrault/Nisard 1846 Claude Perrault, trans., Désiré Nisard, ed., *Celse, Vitruve, Censorin (œuvres complètes)* (Paris: J. J. Dubochet, Le Chevalier et Cie.)

Maufras 1847 Charles-Louis Maufras, trans., *L'architecture de Vitruve* (Paris: C. L. F.Panckoucke)

Perrault/Nisard 1852 * Claude Perrault, trans.; Désiré Nisard, ed., *Celse, Vitruve, Censorin (œuvres complètes)* (Paris: Dubochet, Le Chevalier et Cie.)

Galiani/Schneider 1854 Berardo Galiani, trans. and comm., Johann Gottlob Schneider, ed., *Marci Vitruuii Pollionis de architectura libri decem / Dell'architettura libri dieci di M. Vitruvio Pollione* (Venice: G. Antonelli)

Lorentzen 1857 Karl Lorentzen, *Marci Vitruuii Pollionis de architectura libri decem* (Gotha: Hugo Scheube)

Perrault/Nisard 1857 * Claude Perrault, trans., Désiré Nisard, ed., *Celse, Vitruve, Censorin (œuvres complètes)* (Paris: Firmin Didot Frères, Fils et Cie.)

Perrault/Tardieu-Coussin 1859 * Claude Perrault, trans., Eugène Tardieu and Ambroise Coussin, eds., *Les dix livres d'architecture de Vitruve, avec les notes de Perrault* (Paris: A. Morel/Carillan-Goeury)

Gwilt 1860 * Joseph Gwilt, trans., *The Architecture of Marcus Vitruvius Pollio in Ten Books* (London: John Weale)

Reber 1865 Franz von Reber, trans. and comm., *Des Vitruvius zehn Bücher über Architektur* (Stuttgart: Krais & Hoffmann)

Perrault/Nisard 1866 Claude Perrault, trans., Désiré Nisard, ed., *Celse, Vitruve, Censorin (œuvres complètes)* (Paris: Firmin Didot Frères, Fils et Cie.)

Rose 1867 Valentin Rose and Hermann Müller-Strübing, eds., *Vitruuii de architectura libri decem* (Leipzig: B. G. Teubner)

Tauchnitz 1869 Carl Tauchnitz, *Marci Vitruvii Pollionis de architectura libri decem* (Leipzig: Otto Holtze)

Gwilt 1874 Joseph Gwilt, trans., *The Architecture of Marcus Vitruvius Pollio in Ten Books* (London: Lockwood & Co.)

Perrault/Nisard 1877 Claude Perrault, trans., Désiré Nisard, ed., *Celse, Vitruve, Censorin (œuvres complètes)* (Paris: Firmin Didot Frères, Fils et Cie.)

Reber 1885 * Franz von Reber, trans. and comm., *Des Vitruvius zehn Bücher über Architektur* (Stuttgart: Krais & Hoffmann)

Tauchnitz 1892 * [Carl Tauchnitz], *Marci Vitruuii Pollionis de architectura libri decem* (Leipzig: Otto Holtze)

Fuchs 1898 Béla Fuchs, trans., Jusztin Bódiss, ed., *Marcus Vitruvius Pollio: Tiz könyve az építészetről* (Budapest: A Magyar Mérnök- és Építész-Egylet [Hungarian Association of Engineers and Architects])

Rose 1899 Valentin Rose, *Vitruuii de architectura libri decem* (Leipzig: B. G. Teubner)

Gwilt 1909 * Joseph Gwilt, trans., *The Architecture of Marcus Vitruvius Pollio in Ten Books* (London: Lockwood & Co.)

Choisy 1909 Auguste Choisy, ed., trans., comm., and illus., *Vitruve* (Paris: Lahure)

Reber 1912 Franz von Reber, trans. and comm., *Des Vitruvius zehn Bücher über Architektur* (Berlin-Schöneberg: Langenscheidt)

Krohn 1912 Friedrich Krohn, ed., *Vitruuii de architectura libri decem* (Leipzig: B. G. Teubner)

Prestel 1912-1914 Jakob Prestel, trans. and comm., *Zehn Bücher über Architektur des Marcus Vitruvius Pollio* (Strasbourg: Heitz & Mündel)

Morgan 1914 Morris Hicky Morgan [and Albert A. Howard], trans., Herbert Langford Warren, illus., *Vitruvius: The Ten Books on Architecture* (Cambridge, MA: Harvard University Press)

Mialaret 1914 J. H. A. Mialaret, trans. and comm., *Vitruvius's tien boeken over de bouwkunst* (Amsterdam: L. J. Veen; Maastricht: F. Schmitz)

Ebhardt 1918 ab. Bodo Ebhardt, *Die Zehn Bücher der Architektur des Vitruv und ihre Herausgeber seit 1484* (Berlin: Burgverlag)

Morgan 1926 Morris Hicky Morgan [and Albert A. Howard], trans., Herbert Langford Warren, illus., *Vitruvius: The Ten Books on Architecture* (Cambridge, MA: Harvard University Press; London: Humphrey Milford/Oxford University Press)

Granger 1931-1934 Frank Granger, ed. and trans., *Vitruvius on Architecture* (New York: G. P. Putnam's Sons; London: Heinemann)

Fleres 1933 Ugo Fleres, trans. and ed., *Vitruvio: Dell'architettura* (Villasanta, Milan: Notari)

Mishulin 1936 Aleksandr Vasilevich Mishulin, trans., Марк Витрувий Поллион: Об архитектуре десять книг | *Mark Vitruvii Pollion: Ob arkhitekture desiat knig* (Leningrad: Sotsekgiz [State Socio-economic Publishing House])

Petrovsky 1936 Fyodor Aleksandrovich Petrovsky, trans., Витрувий: Десять книг об архитектуре | *Vitruvii Desiat knig ob arkhitekture* (Moscow: Всесоюзная Академия Архитектуры | Vsesoiuznaia Akademiia Arkhitektury [All-Union Academy of Architecture])

Stürzenacker 1938 Erich Stürzenacker, ed., *Marcus Vitruvius Pollio: Über die Baukunst* (Essen: Bildgut)

Zubov 1938 Vasilii Pavlovich Zubov, ed. and trans., Aleksandr Ivanovich Venediktov and Fyodor A. Petrovsky, trans. [Daniele Barbaro, comm.], Десять книг об архитектуре Витрувия с комментарием Даниеле Барбаро | *Desiat knig ob arkhitekture Vitruviia s kommentariem Daniele Barbaro* (Moscow: Всесоюзная Академия Архитектуры | Vsesoiuznaia Akademiia Arkhitektury [All-Union Academy of Architecture])

Perrault 1943 ab. Claude Perrault; Giuseppe Guenzati, ed., *Vitruvio: I dieci librdell'architettura* (Casale Monferrato: Migliette)

Morita 1943 Keiichi Morita, trans., ウィトルーウィウス建築書 | *Witorūwiusu kenchikusho* [Vitruvii de Architectura] (Tokyo: 生活社 | Seikatsusha)

Granger 1944* Frank Granger, ed. and trans., *Vitruvius on Architecture* (New York: G. P. Putnam's Sons; London: Heinemann)

Pokorný 1944 ± V Jaroslav Pokorný, trans., *Vitruvius: Antické divadlo* [Vitruvius: Ancient Theatre] (Prague: Ústav pro učebné pomůcky průmyslových a odborných škol [Institute for Educational Tools in Industrial and Vocational Schools])

Perrault 1946 Claude Perrault, trans., *Les dix livres d'architecture de Vitruve* (Paris: Éditions du Raisin)

Fleres 1947* Ugo Fleres, trans. and ed., *Vitruvio: Dell'architectura* ([Milan]: Garzanti)

Otoupalík 1953 Alois Otoupalík, trans., *Vitruvius: Deset knih o architektuře* (Prague: Státní nakladatelství krásné literatury, hudby a umění (SNKLHU) [State Publishing House of Literature, Music, and Art])

Granger 1955-1956* Frank Granger, ed. and trans., *Vitruvius on Architecture* (London: Heinemann; Cambridge, MA: Harvard University Press)

Blánquez 1955 Augustín Blánquez, trans., *Marco Lucio Vitruvio: Los diez libros de arquitectura* (Barcelona: Iberia)

Kumaniecki 1956 Kazimierz Kumaniecki, trans., Piotr Biegański, ed., *Witruwiusz: O architekturze ksiąg dziesięć* (Warsaw: Państwowe Wydawnictwo Naukowe (PWN) [National Scientific Publishers])

Prestel 1959 * Jakob Prestel, trans., *Marcus Vitruvius Pollio: Zehn Bücher über Architektur* (Baden-Baden: Heitz)

Morgan 1960 Morris Hicky Morgan, trans., Herbert Langford Warren, ed. and illus., *Vitruvius: The Ten Books on Architecture* (New York: Dover)

Ferri 1960 ± I-VII Silvio Ferri, trans. and comm., *Vitruvio: architettura (dai libri I-VII)* (Rome: Fratelli Palombi)

Granger 1961-1962 * Frank Granger, ed. and trans., *Vitruvius on Architecture* (London: Heinemann; Cambridge, MA: Harvard University Press)

Ebhardt 1962 ab. Bodo Ebhardt, ed., *Vitruvius: Die Zehn Bücher der Architektur des Vitruv und ihre Herausgeber seit 1484* (Ossining, NY: William Salloch)

Cantacuzino 1964 George Matei Cantacuzino, trans., *Vitruviu: Despre arhitectura* (Bucharest: Academia Română [Romanian Academy])

Fensterbusch 1964 Curt Fensterbusch, ed., trans., and comm., *Vitruuii de architectura libri decem | Vitruv: Zehn Bücher über Architektur* (Berlin: Akademie)

Martin 1964 Jean Martin, trans., Jean Goujon, illus., *Architecture, ou, Art de bien bastir* (Farnborough, UK/Ridgewood, NJ: Gregg Press)

Perrault/Dalmas 1965 Claude Perrault, trans., André Dalmas, ed., *Vitruve: Les dix livres d'architecture* (Paris: André Balland/Les Libraires Associés)

Perrault/Dalmas 1967 Claude Perrault, trans., André Dalmas, ed., *Vitruve: Les dix livres d'architecture* (Paris: André Balland/Les Libraires Associés)

Cesariano 1968 Cesare Cesariano, trans., comm., and illus., *De architectura* (Bronx, NY: Benjamin Blom)

Rusconi 1968 ◻ Antonio Rusconi, illus., *Dell'architettura* (Farnborough: Gregg Press)

Budé Collection 1969 ± IX Jean Soubiran, ed., trans., and comm., *Vitruve: De l'architecture* (Limoges: Les Belles Lettres)

Morita 1969 Keiichi Morita, trans., ウィトルーウィウス建築書 I *Witorūwiusu kenchikusho* [Vitruvii de Architectura] (Tokyo: 東海大学出版会 [Tokai University Press])

Cesariano 1969 Cesare Cesariano, trans., comm., and illus., *Vitruvius de Architectura: Nachdruck der kommentierten ersten italienischen Ausgabe* (Munich: Fink)

Blánquez 1970 * Augustín Blánquez, trans., *Marco Lucio Vitruvio: Los diez libros de arquitectura* (Barcelona: Iberia)

Granger 1970 * Frank Granger, ed. and trans., *Vitruvius on Architecture* (London: Heinemann; Cambridge, MA: Harvard University Press)

Choisy 1971 Auguste Choisy, ed., *Vitruve* (Paris: De Nobele)

Ryff 1973 Walther Hermann Ryff, trans., Erik Forssman, comm., *Zehen Bücher von der Architektur* (Hildesheim: Olms)

Andreu 1973 Carmen Andreu, trans., *Marcus L. Vitruvius: De architectura* (Madrid: Union Explosivos Rio Tinto/Ediciones de Arte y Bibliofilia)

Budé Collection 1973 ± VIII Louis Callebat, ed., trans., and comm., *Vitruve: De l'architecture–Livre VIII* (Paris: Les Belles Lettres)

Prestel 1974 Jakob Prestel, trans., *Marcus Vitruvius Pollio: Zehn Bücher über Architektur* (Baden-Baden: Valentin Koerner)

Ortiz y Sanz 1974 Joseph Francisco Ortiz y Sanz, trans., comm., and illus., *Los diez libros de architectura de M. Vitruvio Polión* (Oviedo: Colegios Oficiales de Aparejadores y Arquitectos Técnicos)

Cherubini 1975 Laura Cherubini, trans., *Vitruvius Pollio* (Pisa: Giardini)

Calvo 1975 Marco Fabio Calvo, trans., Vincenzo Fontana and Paolo Morachiello, eds., *Vitruvio e Raffaello: Il "De architectura" di Vitruvio nella traduzione inedita di Fabio Calvo ravennate* (Rome: Officina)

Fensterbusch 1976 * Curt Fensterbusch, ed., trans., and comm., *Vitruuii de architectura libri decem | Vitruv: Zehn Bücher über Architektur* (Darmstadt: Wissenschaftliche Buchgesellschaft)

Urrea 1978 Miguel de Urrea, trans., *M. Vitruuio Pollion: De architectura* ([Valencia: Albatros)

Florian 1978 Giovanni Florian, ed., *Vitruvio Pollione: Dell'architettura* (Pisa: Giardini)

Morita 1979 * Keiichi Morita, trans., ウィトルーウィウス建築書 | *Witorūwiusu kenchikusho* [Vitruvii de Architectura] (Tokyo: 東海大学出版会 [Tokai University Press])

Perrault 1979 Claude Perrault, ed., *Les dix livres d'architecture de Vitruve* (Brussels: Pierre Mardaga)

Otoupalík 1979 Alois Otoupalík, trans., *Vitruvius: Deset knih o architektuře* (Prague: Svoboda)

Blánquez 1980 * Agustín Blánquez, trans., *Marco Lucio Vitruvio: Los diez libros de arquitectura* (Barcelona: Iberia)

Fensterbusch 1981 Curt Fensterbusch, ed., trans., and comm., *Vitruuii de architectura libri decem | Vitruv: Zehn Bücher über Architektur* (Darmstadt: Wissenschaftliche Buchgesellschaft)

Cesariano 1981 Cesare Cesariano, trans., Arnaldo Bruschi, Adriano Carugo, and Francesco Paolo Fiore, eds., *De Architectura traslato commentato e affigurato da Cesare Cesariano 1521* (Milan: Il Polifilo)

Perrault 1981 ab. Claude Perrault; Joseph Castañeda, trans., Joaquín Bérchez, ed., *Compendio de los diez libros de arquitectura de Vitruvio* (Murcia: Comisión de Cultura del Colegio Oficial de Aparejadores y Arquitectos Técnicos)

Blánquez 1982 * Agustín Blánquez, trans., *Marco Lucio Vitruvio: Los diez libros de arquitectura* (Barcelona: Iberia)

Prestel 1983 Jakob Prestel, trans., *Marcus Vitruvius Pollio: Zehn Bücher über Architektur* (Baden-Baden: Valentin Koerner)

Granger 1983 * Frank Granger, ed. and trans., *Vitruvius on Architecture* (Cambridge, MA: Harvard University Press)

Martini 1985 Francesco di Giorgio Martini, trans., Gustina Scaglia, ed., *Il "Vitruvio Magliabechiano"* (Florence Gonnelli)

Caporali 1985 ± I–V Giovanni Battista Caporali, ed., *Marco Vitruuio Pollione: De architectura libri I–V* (Perugia: Volumnia)

Blánquez 1985 * Agustín Blánquez, trans., *Marco Lucio Vitruvio: Los diez libros de arquitectura* (Barcelona: Iberia)

Gao 1986 Gao Lütai, trans., 维特鲁威 «建筑十书» | *Weiteluwei: Jianzhu shi shu* (Beijing: 中国建筑工业出版社 | Zhongguo jianzhu gongye chubanshe)

Budé Collection 1986 ± X Louis Callebat, ed. and trans., Philippe Fleury, comm., *Vitruve: De l'architecture–Livre X* (Paris: Les Belles Lettres)

Perrault/Dalmas 1986 Claude Perrault, trans., André Dalmas, ed., *Vitruve: Les dix livres d'architecture* (Paris: Errance)

Fensterbusch 1987 * Curt Fensterbusch, ed., trans., and comm., *Vitruuii de architectura libri decem | Vitruv: Zehn Bücher über Architektur. Vitruv* (Darmstadt: Wissenschaftliche Buchgesellschaft)

Ortiz y Sanz 1987 José Francisco Ortiz y Sanz, trans. and comm., *Marco Vitruvio Polión: Los diez libros de arquitectura* (Madrid: Akal)

Ortiz y Sanz 1987 José Francisco Ortiz y Sanz, trans. and comm., *Marco Vitrubio: Los diez libros de arquitectura* (Barcelona: Alta Fulla)

Barbaro 1987 Daniele Barbaro, trans. and comm., [Andrea Palladio, illus.], Manfredo Tafuri and Manuela Morresi, eds.,*Vitruvio: I dieci libri dell'architettura* (Milan: Il Polifilo)

Rode 1987 August Rode, trans., Beat Wyss and Georg Germann eds., *Vitruv: Baukunst* (Zurich/Munich: Artemis)

Prestel 1987 Jakob Prestel, *Marcus Vitruvius Pollio: Zehn Bücher über Architektur* (Baden-Baden: Valentin Koerner)

Amati 1988 Carlo Amati; Gabriele Morolli, ed., *L'architettura di Vitruvio nella versione di Carlo Amati (1829–1830)* (Florence: Alinea)

Perrault 1988 Claude Perrault, ed., *Les dix livres d'architecture de Vitruve* (Brussels: Pierre Mardaga)

Granger 1989 * Frank Granger, ed. and trans., *Vitruvius on Architecture* (Cambridge, MA: Harvard University Press)

Artigas 1989 Esther Artigas, trans., Antoni Castro, ed., *M. Vitruvi d'arquitectura* ([Barcelona]: Agrupació de Fabricants de Ciment de Catalunya)

Ortiz y Sanz 1989 José Francisco Ortiz y Sanz, trans. and comm., *Architectura de M. Vitruvio Polión* (Lugo: Alvarellos)

Budé Collection 1990 ± I Phillipe Fleury, ed., trans., and comm., *Vitruve: De l'architecture–Livre I* (Paris: Les Belles Lettres)

Budé Collection 1990 ± III Pierre Gros, ed., trans., and comm., *Vitruve: De l'architecture–Livre III* (Paris: Les Belles Lettres)

Mylonas 1990 % Pavlos Mylonas, trans., Βιτρουβίου τὰ δέκα προοίμια: Δείγματα γραφῆς γιὰ τὴν ἑλληνικὴ μετάφραση τοῦ λατινικοῦ συγγράμματος: *De architectura | Vitrouviou ta deka prooimia, deigmata grafis gia tin elliniki metafrasi tou latinikou syngrammatos:* De architectura, in volume 4 of Φίλια Ἔπη εἰς Γεώργιον Ἐ. Μυλωνᾶν | Filia Epi eis Georgion E. Mylonan (Athens: Αρχαιολογικὴ Εταιρεία | Archaiologiki Etaireia [Archaeological Society])

Güven 1990 Suna Güven, trans., *Vitruvius: Mimarlık üzerine on kitap* (Ankara: Şevki Vanlı Mimarlık Vakfı Yayınları)

Blánquez 1991 Augustín Blánquez, trans., *Marco Lucio Vitruvio: Los diez libros de arquitectura* (Barcelona: Iberia)

Fensterbusch 1991 Curt Fensterbusch, ed., trans., and comm., *Vitruuii de architectura libri decem | Vitruv: Zehn Bücher über Architektur* (Darmstadt: Wissenschaftliche Buchgesellschaft)

Ortiz y Sanz 1992 * José Francisco Ortiz y Sanz, trans. and comm., *Marco Vitruvio Polión: Los diez libros de arquitectura* (Madrid: Akal)

Budé Collection 1992 ± IV Pierre Gros, ed., trans., and comm., *Vitruve: De l'architecture–Livre 4* (Paris: Les Belles Lettres)

Güven 1993 * Suna Güven, trans., *Vitruvius: Mimarlık üzerine on kitap* (Ankara: Şevki Vanlı Mimarlık Vakfı)

Ortiz y Sanz 1993 José Francisco Ortiz y Sanz, trans. and comm., *Marco Vitrubio: Los diez libros de arquitectura* (Barcelona: Alta Fulla)

Migotto 1993 Luciano Migotto, trans., *Marcus Vitruvius Pollione: De architectura; Libri X* (Pordenone: Studio Tesi)

Barbaro 1994 * Daniele Barbaro, [Andrea Palladio, illus.], Manfredo Tafuri and Manuela Morresi, eds., *Vitruvio: I dieci libri dell'architettura* (Milan: Il Polifilo)

Amati 1994 Carlo Amati, Gabriele Morolli, ed., *L'architettura di Vitruvio nella versione di Carlo Amati (1829–1830)* (Florence: Alinea)

Granger 1995-1996 * Frank Granger, ed. and trans., *Vitruvius on Architecture* (Cambridge, MA: Harvard University Press)

Domingo 1995 José Luis Oliver Domingo, trans., *Marco Lucio Vitruvio Polión: Los diez libros de arquitectura* (Madrid: Alianza)

Rode 1995 August Rode, trans., Beat Wyss and Georg Germann, eds., *Vitruv: Baukunst* (Basel: Birkhäuser)

Budé Collection 1995 ± VII Bernard Liou and Michel Zuinghedau, ed. and trans., Marie-Thérèse Cam, comm., *Vitruve: De l'architecture–Livre VII* (Paris: Les Belles Lettres)

Perrault 1995 Claude Perrault, ed., *Les dix livres d'architecture de Vitruve* ([Paris]: Bibliothèque de l'Image)

Perrault 1996 * Claude Perrault, ed., *Les dix livres d'architecture de Vitruve corrigés et traduits en 1684 par Claude Perrault* (Liège: Mardaga)

Dalmas 1996 André Dalmas, *Pour mieux lire Vitruve: Les dix livres d'architecture* (Paris: Le Nouveau Commerce)

Rusconi 1996 ☐ Giovanni Antonio Rusconi, illus., Anna Bedon, ed., *Della architettura* (Vicenza: CISA Andrea Palladio)

Fensterbusch 1996 * Curt Fensterbusch, ed., trans., and comm., *Vitruuii de architectura libri decem* | *Vitruv: Zehn Bücher über Architektur* (Darmstadt: Premius Verlag)

Blánquez 1997 * Augustín Blánquez, trans., *Marco Lucio Vitruvio: Los diez libros de arquitectura* (Barcelona: Iberia)

Barbaro 1997 Daniele Barbaro, [Andrea Palladio, illus.], Manfredo Tafuri and Manuela Morresi, eds., *Vitruvio: I dieci libri dell'architettura* (Milan: Il Polifilo)

Gros/Corso/Romano 1997 Pierre Gros, ed., Antonio Corso and Elisa Romano, trans., *Vitruvio: De architectura* (Turin: Einaudi)

Lefas 1997-2009 Pavlos Lefas, trans., Βιτρούβιου περί αρχιτεκτονικής | *Vitrouviou peri architektonikis* | *Vitruvii de architectura* (Athens: Plethron)

Zerefos 1998 Stelios Zerefos, trans., *Vitruvius*: Δέκα Βιβλία | *Deka Vivlia* (Thessaloniki: Παρατηρητής | Paratiritis)

Perrault/Rua 1998 Claude Perrault, ed., Maria Helena Rua, trans., *Os dez livros de arquitectura de Vitrúvio* (Lisbon: Departamento de Engenharia Civil do Instituto Superior Técnico)

Granger 1998 * Frank Granger, ed. and trans., *Vitruvius on Architecture* (Cambridge, MA: Harvard University Press)

Güven 1998 * Suna Güven, trans., *Vitruvius. Mimarlık üzerine on kitap* (Ankara: Şevki Vanlı Mimarlık Vakfı)

Bossalino 1998 Franca Bossalino, *Marco Vitruvio Pollione: De architectura libri X* (Rome: Kappa)

Migotto 1998 ± VI ab. Luciano Migotto, trans., *Vitruvio: Case d'aria e terra acqua e fuoco* (Pordenone: Edizioni Biblioteca dell'Immagine)

Perrault/Dalmas 1999 Claude Perrault, trans., André Dalmas, ed., *Vitruve: Les dix livres d'architecture* (Paris: Errance)

Ortiz y Sanz 1999 José Francisco Ortiz y Sanz, trans. and comm., *Los diez libros de architectura de M. Vitruvio Polión* (Toledo: Antonio Pareja)

Budé Collection 1999 ± II Louis Callebat ed., trans., and comm., *Vitruve: De l'architecture, livre 2* (Paris: Les Belles Lettres)

Rowland 1999 Ingrid Drake Rowland, trans., Thomas Noble Howe, comm. and illus., *Vitruvius: Ten Books on Architecture* (Cambridge: Cambridge University Press)

Barbaro 1999 Daniele Barbaro, trans. and comm., *I dieci libri dell'architettura di M. Vitruvio* (Rome: Bardi)

Lagonegro 1999 Marco Aurélio Lagonegro, trans., *Vitrúvio: Da arquitetura* (São Paulo: HUCITEC)

Kumaniecki 1999 Kazimierz Kumaniecki, trans., Anna Sadurska, *Witruwiusz: O architekturze ksiąg dziesięć* (Warsaw: Prószyński i S-ka)

Blánquez 2000 * Augustín Blánquez, trans., *Marco Lucio Vitruvio: Los diez libros de architectura* (Barcelona: Iberia)

Iruretagoiena 2000 Xanti Iruretagoiena, trans., Eduardo Artamendi, ed., *Vitruvio: Arkitekturaz hamar liburuak* (Bilbao: Klasikoak)

Brochet 2000 Dominique Brochet, trans., *Vitruve: Les dix livres d'architecture* (Paris: Errance)

Philandrier 2000-2011 Guillaume Philandrier; Frédérique Lemerle, ed., trans., and comm., *Les Annotations sur L'Architecture de Vitruve* (Paris: Garnier)

Gao 2001 Gao Lütai, trans., 维特鲁威《建筑十书》| *Weiteluwei: Jianzhu shi shu* | *Vitruvius: The Ten Books on Architecture* (Beijing: 知识产权出版社 | Zhishi chanquan chubanshe)

Ortiz y Sanz 2001 * José Francisco Ortiz y Sanz, trans. and comm., *Marco Vitruvio Polión: Los diez libros de arquitectura* (Madrid: Akal)

Rode 2001 August Rode, trans., Beat Wyss and Georg Germann, eds., *Vitruv: Baukunst* (Basel: Birkhäuser)

Otoupalík 2001 Alois Otoupalík, trans., *Marcus Vitruvius Pollio: Deset knih o architektuře* (Prague: Arista)

Budé Collection 2002 ± I, III, IV, VII-X * Jean Soubiran, Louis Callebat, Phillipe Fleury, Pierre Gros, Bernard Liou, Michel Zuinghedau, Marie-Thérèse Cam, *Vitruve: De l'architecture* (Paris: Les Belles Lettres)

Granger 2002 * Frank Granger, ed. and trans., *Vitruvius on Architecture* (Cambridge, MA: Harvard University Press)

Martini 2002 Francesco di Giorgio Martini, trans., Marco Biffi, ed., *La traduzione del De architectura di Vitruvio dal ms. II.I.141 della Biblioteca nazionale centrale di Firenze* (Pisa: Scuola Normale Superiore)

Ferri 2002 ± I-VII Silvio Ferri, trans. and comm., *Vitruvio: Architettura (dai libri I-VII)* (Milan: BUR)

Cesariano 2002 ± II-IV Cesare Cesariano, trans. and illus., Alessandro Rovetta, ed., *Vitruvio: De architectura, libri II-IV; I materiali, i templi, gli ordini* (Milano: V&P Università)

Bossalino 2002 Franca Bossalino and Vilma Nazzi, trans., *Marco Vitruvio Pollione: De architectura libri X* (Rome: Kappa)

Lagonegro 2002 Marco Aurélio Lagonegro, trans. and comm., *Vitrúvio: Da arquitetura* (São Paulo: HUCITEC/Annablume)

Petrovsky 2003 Fyodor Aleksandrovich Petrovsky, trans., Витрувий: Десять книг об архитектуре | *Vitruvii: Desiat knig ob arkhitekture* (Moscow: Едиториал УРСС | Editorial URSS)

Martini 2003 Francesco di Giorgio Martini, trans., Massimo Mussini, ed. and comm., *Francesco di Giorgio e Vitruvio: Le traduzioni del "De architectura" nei codici Zichy, Spencer 129 e Magliabechiano II.I.141* (Florence: Leo S. Olschki)

Gordon Smith 2003 ± I, III-VI Thomas Gordon Smith, ed., *Vitruvius on Architecture* (New York: Monacelli Press)

Sulpitius 2003 Joannes Sulpitius Verulanus, Ingrid Drake Rowland, ed., Giovanni Battista da Sangallo, comm. and illus., *Vitruvius: Ten Books on Architecture: The Corsini Incunabulum* (Rome: Edizione dell'Elefante)

Ortiz y Sanz 2003 José Francisco Ortiz y Sanz, trans. and comm., *Los diez libros de archîtectura de M. Vitruvio Polión* (Vitoria-Gasteiz: Old Book Factory)

Budé Collection 2004 ± VI Louis Callebat, ed., trans. and comm., *Vitruve: De l'architecture–Livre VI* (Paris: Les Belles Lettres)

Sgarbi 2004 Claudio Sgarbi, ed., *Vitruvio ferrarese: De architectura* (Modena: Franco Cosimo Panini)

Reber 2004 Franz von Reber, trans. and comm., *Vitruv: Zehn Bücher über Architektur; De architectura libri decem* (Wiesbaden: Marixverlag)

Gao 2004 Gao Lütai, trans., 维特鲁威《建筑十书》| *Weiteluwei: Jianzhu shi shu* | *Vitruvius: The Ten Books on Architecture* (Beijing: 知识产权出版社 | Zhishi chanquan chubanshe)

Güven 2005 * Suna Güven, *Vitruvius: Mimarlık üzerine on kitap* (Ankara: Şevki Vanlı Mimarlık Vakfı)

Petrovsky 2005 Fyodor Aleksandrovich Petrovsky, trans., Витрувий: Десять книг об архитектуре | *Vitruvii: Desiat knig ob arkhitekture* (Moscow: КомКнига | KomKniga)

Galiani 2005 Berardo Galiani, trans. and comm., *L'architettura di Marco Vitruvio Pollione* (Rome: Dedalo)

Brochet 2006 Dominique Brochet, trans., *Vitruve: Les dix livres d'architecture* (Paris: Errance)

Petrovsky 2006 Fyodor Aleksandrovich Petrovsky, trans., Витрувий: Десять книг об архитектуре | *Vitruvii: Desiat knig ob arkhitekture* (Moscow: Архитектура-С | Arkhitektura-S)

Maciel 2006 Manuel Justino Maciel, trans., *Vitrúvio: Tratado de arquitectura* (Lisbon: IST Press)

Barbaro 2006 Daniele Barbaro, trans. and comm., Carunchio Tancredi, ed., *I dieci libri dell'architettura di M. Vitruvio* (Rome: Bardi)

Perrault 2007 ab. * Claude Perrault, Joseph Castañeda, trans., *Compendio de los diez libros de arquitectura de Vitruvio* (Mairena de Aljarafe: Extramuros)

Blánquez 2007 * Agustín Blánquez, trans., *Marco Lucio Vitruvio: Los diez libros de arquitectura* (Barcelona: Iberia)

Rowland 2007 * Ingrid Drake Rowland, trans., Thomas Noble Howe, comm. and illus., *Ten Books on Architecture* (Cambridge: Cambridge University Press)

Maciel 2007 Manuel Justino Maciel, *Vitrúvio: Tratado de arquitetura* (São Paulo: Martins Fontes)

Migotto 2008 Luciano Migotto, *Marco Vitruvio Pollione: De architectura libri X : Testo latino a fronte* (Pordenone: Studio Tesi)

Cano 2008 ± I-V Francisco Manzanero Cano, trans. and comm., *Vitruvio: Arquitectura, libros I-V* (Madrid: Gredos)

Fensterbusch 2008 * Curt Fensterbusch, ed., trans., and comm., *Vitruv: Zehn Bücher über Architektur* (Darmstadt: Wissenschaftliche Buchgesellschaft)

Ortiz y Sanz 2008 * José Francisco Ortiz y Sanz, trans. and comm., *Marco Vitruvio Polión: Los diez libros de arquitectura* (Barcelona: Linkgua)

Ferri 2008 ± I-VII Silvio Ferri, trans. and comm., *Vitruvio: Architettura: (dai libri I-VII)* (Milan: BUR)

Gulyás 2008 *Tíz könyv az építészetről*, trans. Dénes Gulyás (Budapest: Kossuth)

Gulyás 2009 *Tíz könyv az építészetről*, trans. Dénes Gulyás (Szeged: Quintus)

Perrault 2009 ab. * Claude Perrault; Joseph Castañeda, trans., *Compendio de los diez libros de arquitectura de Vitruvio* (Valladolid: Maxtor)

Maciel 2009 * Manuel Justino Maciel, *Vitrúvio: Tratado de arquitectura* (Lisbon: IST Press)

Reber 2009 Franz von Reber, trans. and comm., *Vitruv: Zehn Bücher über Architektur; De architectura libri decem* (Wiesbaden: Marixverlag)

Budé Collection 2009 ± V Catherine Saliou, ed. and trans., *Vitruve: De l'architecture–Livre V* (Paris: Les Belles Lettres)

Schofield 2009 Richard Schofield, trans., *Vitruvius: On Architecture* (London: Penguin)

Otoupalík 2009 Alois Otoupalík, trans., *Deset knih o architektuře* (Prague: Arista, Maitrea, TeMi)

Giraldo 2010 Asdrúbal Valencia Giraldo, ed., *Marco Lucio Vitruvio Polión: Los diez libros de la arquitectura (Selección)* (Medellín: Universidad de Antioquia)

Krohn 2010 Fritz Krohn, ed., *Vitruvii de architectura libri decem* (Berlin: De Gruyter)

Ortiz y Sanz 2010 José Francisco Ortiz y Sanz, trans. and comm., *Marco Vitruvio Polión: Los diez libros de arquitectura* (Barcelona: Linkgua)

Petrovsky 2011 * Fyodor Aleksandrovich Petrovsky, trans., Витрувий: Десять книг об архитектуре | *Vitruvii: Desiat knig ob arkhitekture* (Moscow: URSS, 2011)

Perrault 2012 Claude Perrault, *Les dix livres d'architecture de Vitruve* (Rungis: Maxtor)

Petrovsky 2012 * Fyodor Aleksandrovich Petrovsky, trans., Витрувий: Десять книг об архитектуре | *Vitruvii: Desiat knig ob arkhitekture* (Moscow: Либроком | Librokom)

Chen 2012 Chen Ping and Ingrid Drake Rowland, trans., Thomas Noble Howe, comm. and illus., 维特鲁威 «建筑十书» | Weiteluwei: Jianzhu shi shu | Vitruvius: Ten Books on Architecture (Beijing: 北京大学出版社 Beijing daxue chubanshe [Peking University Press])

Reber 2012 Franz von Reber, trans. and comm., *Vitruv: Zehn Bücher über Architektur; De architectura libri decem* (Wiesbaden: Marixverlag)

Fensterbusch 2013 * Curt Fensterbusch, ed., trans., and comm., *Vitruv: Zehn Bücher über Architektur* (Darmstadt: Wissenschaftliche Buchgesellschaft)

Gao 2013 * Gao Lütai, trans., 维特鲁威 «建筑十书» | *Weiteluwei: Jianzhu shi shu | Vitruvius: The Ten Books on Architecture* (Beijing: 知识产权出版社 | Zhishi chanquan chubanshe)

Ortiz y Sanz 2014 * José Francisco Ortiz y Sanz, trans. and comm., *Marco Vitruvio Polión: Los diez libros de arquitectura* (Barcelona: Linkgua)

Granger 2014 * Frank Granger, ed. and trans., *Vitruvius on Architecture* (Cambridge, MA: Harvard University Press)

Petrovsky 2015 * Fyodor Aleksandrovich Petrovsky, trans., Витрувий: Десять книг об архитектуре | *Vitruvii: Desiat knig ob arkhitekture* (Moscow: Ленанд)

Gros 2015 Pierre Gros, ed., trans., and comm., *Vitruve: De l'architecture; De architectura* (Paris: Les Belles Lettres)

Maciel 2015 * Manuel Justino Maciel, *Vitrúvio: Tratado de arquitectura* (Lisbon: IST Press)

Reber 2015 Franz von Reber, ed., *Vitruv: Zehn Bücher über Architektur; De architectura libri decem* (Wiesbaden: Marixverlag)

Morgan 2016 Morris Hicky Morgan, trans., Herbert Langford Warren and A. M. Nelson Robinson, illus., *The Ten Books on Architecture* (New Delhi: Kaveri Book)

Isager 2016 Jacob Isager, trans., *Vitruv: Om arkitektur* (Odense: Syddansk Universitetsforlag)

This chronology aims to be a complete list of the printed editions of Vitruvius, but it is certainly incomplete. Maintaining homogeneous criteria across five centuries of printing culture proved difficult, and we oscillated between being faithful to the spelling and nuances of each edition and providing clarity for a contemporary reader. For instance, in classical Latin there is no distinction between the modern "Latin" letters V and U or between I and J. The practice we have opted for here is to write V as the upper-case variant and u for the lower-case rendering, as seems to be a convention in many of the works cited here. For the sake of legibility, we have dispensed with the use of j as the second component of a double vowel, so that any instances of Vitruuij, for example, have been converted to Vitruuii. Many of the early works present their titles in capitals, and we have converted these to sentence-style capitalization (with the exception of the titles of English and German translations). In general, we have attempted to preserve fluctuations in spelling throughout the chronology, while offering the greatest possible consistency in the way the entries are presented.

Another challenging task was to properly credit the book "authors" as editors (ed.), translators (trans.), commentators (comm.), and/or illustrators (illus.), knowing the roles were often blurred and may have been performed by authors left unacknowledged in the colophons. In many cases translations were "recycled" from previous editions, and we were not always able to trace all the subtleties of individual authorial involvement within the scope of this work. Hence our solution was to keep the key reference while trying to present the main authorship of the edition and its position within the Vitruviana. For instance, when a later edition adopted illustrations from an earlier edition—or mixed together illustrations from various editions—we have set the question of authorship aside. For the Latin editions we privileged the attribution "ed.," whereas for translations, despite the large amount of editorial work involved, we have not credited the translator as editor. The same applies for commentaries: in cases where the editorial work is more relevant than the commentaries, we have simplified the role to that of editor.

Reprints are another subtle distinction. The importance of a reprint and the effort involved in producing one were quite different in the twentieth and sixteenth centuries. We aimed to identify complete reprints, and to consider an edition produced under a different publisher as a new version even if it is similar to previous iterations.

This Vitruviana was collated by André Tavares and edited with the assistance of Simon Cowper.

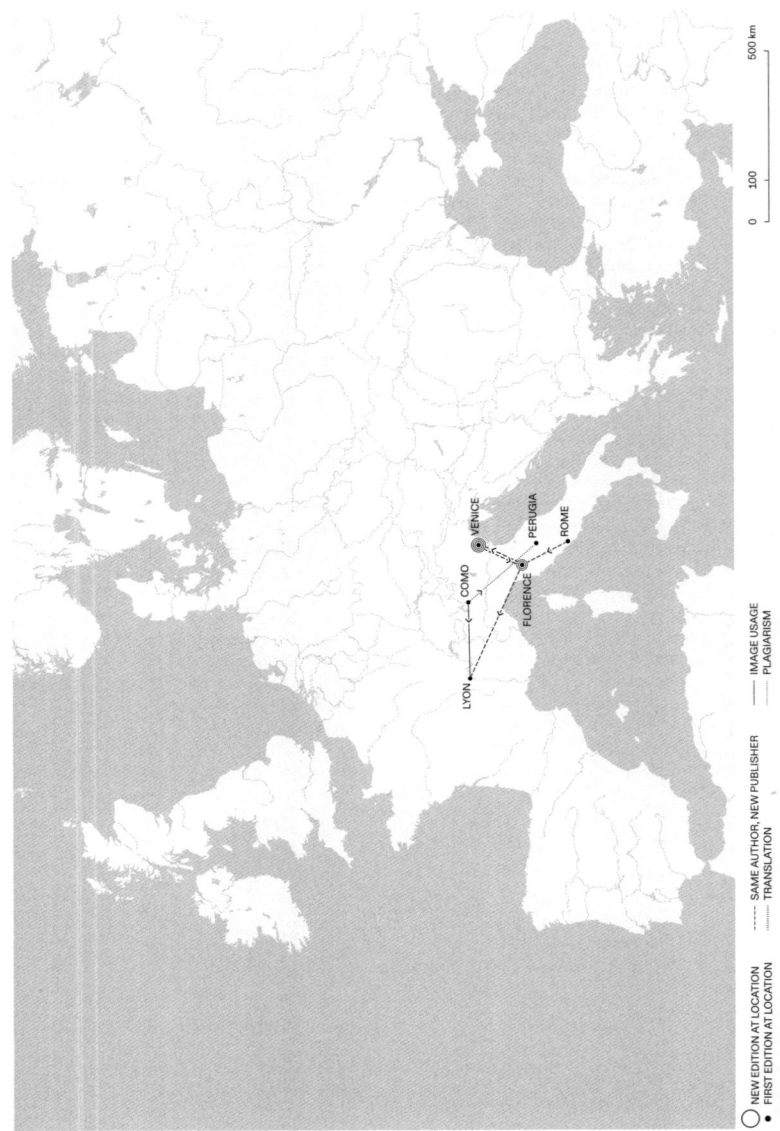

53 Setting Authority, 1486–1536

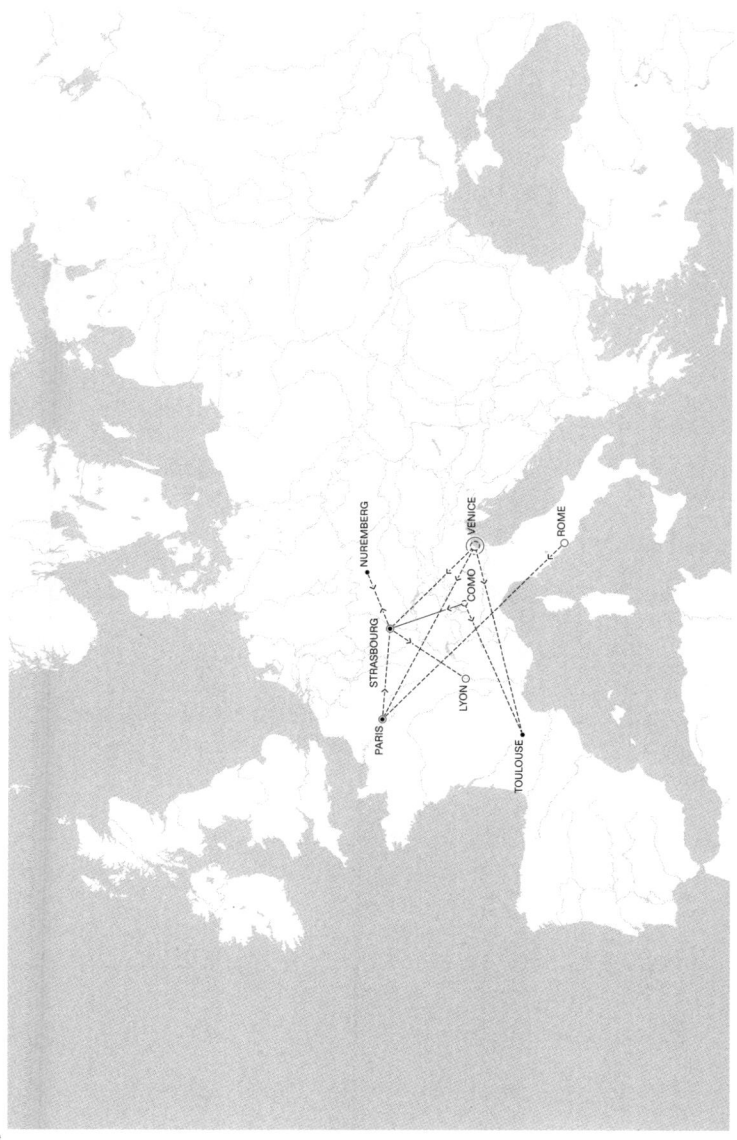

54 Crossing Regional Boundaries, 1526–1556

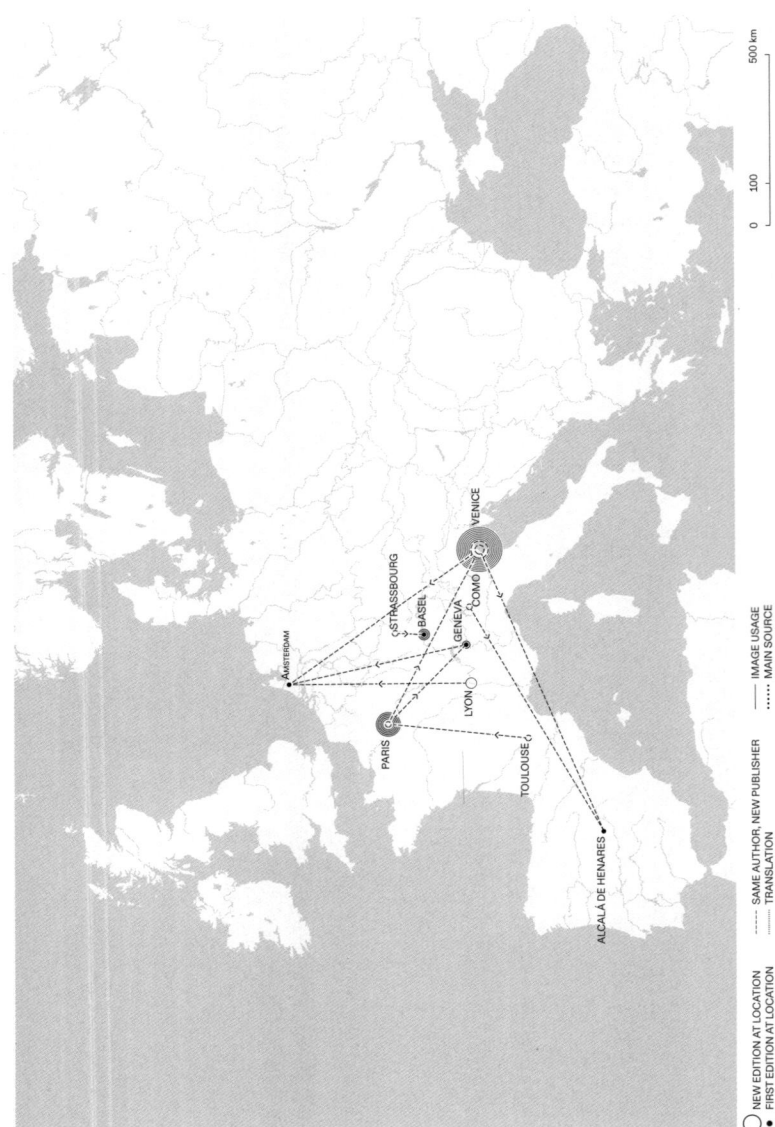

55 The Age of Orders, 1556–1649

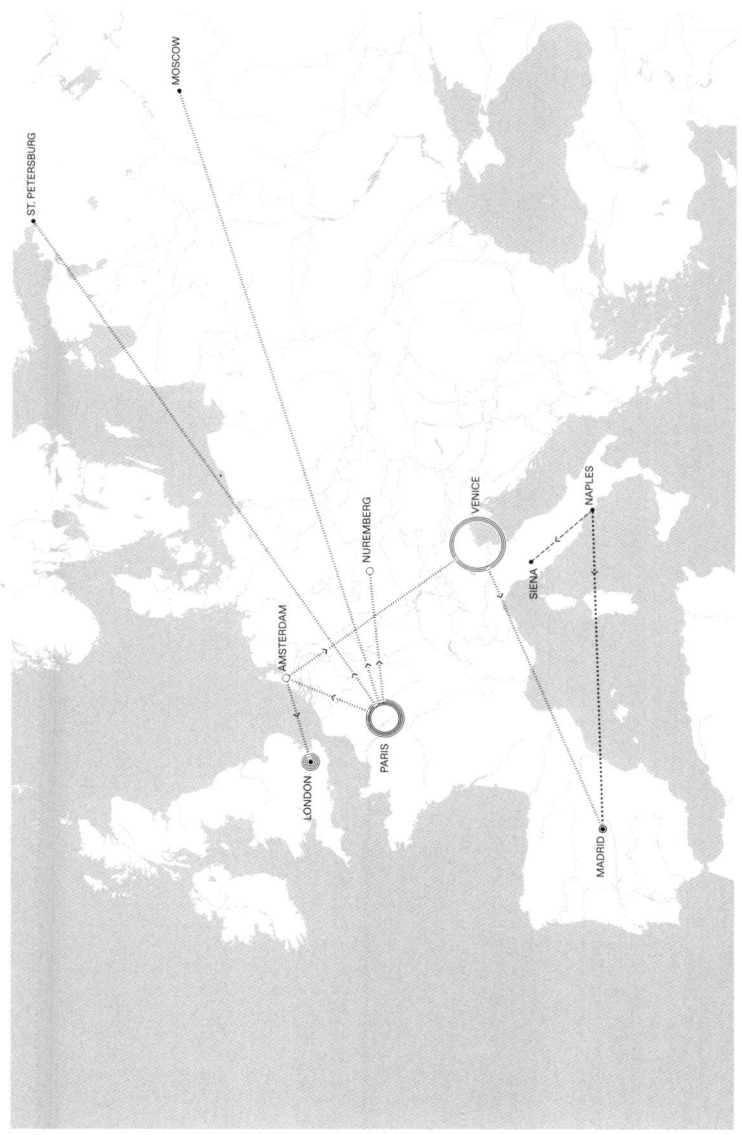

56 Grounding Theory, 1673–1791

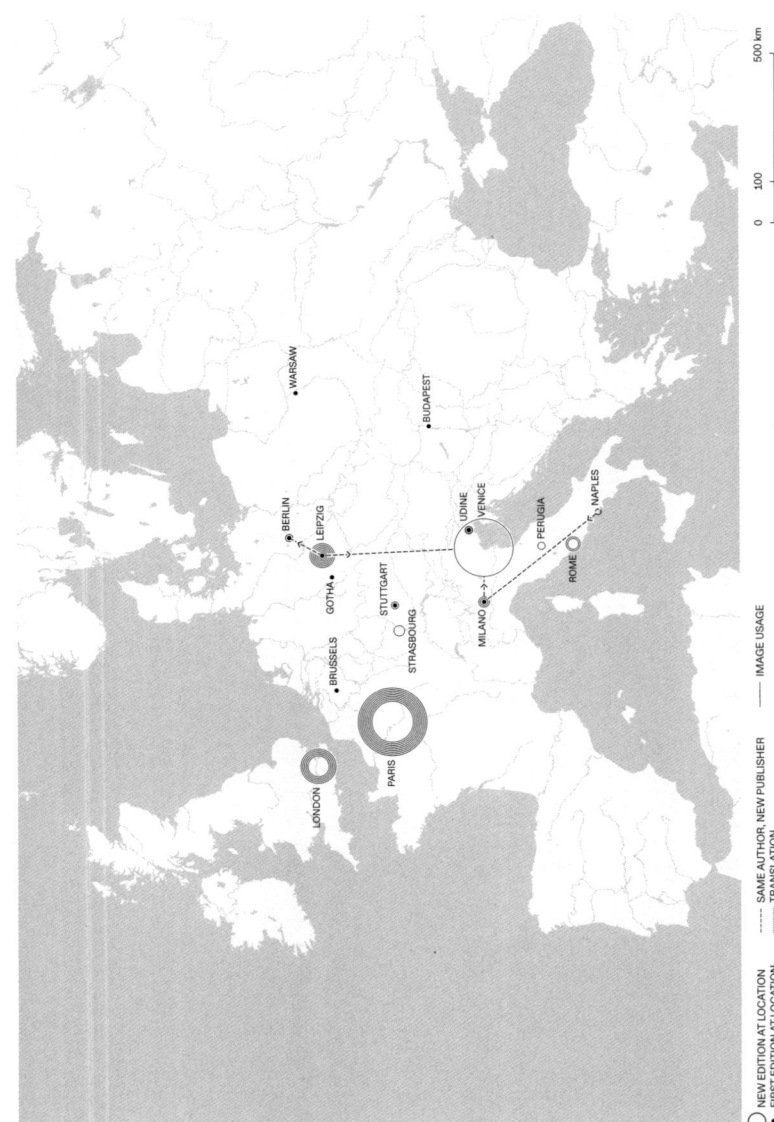

57 Diffuse Knowledge, 1796–1909

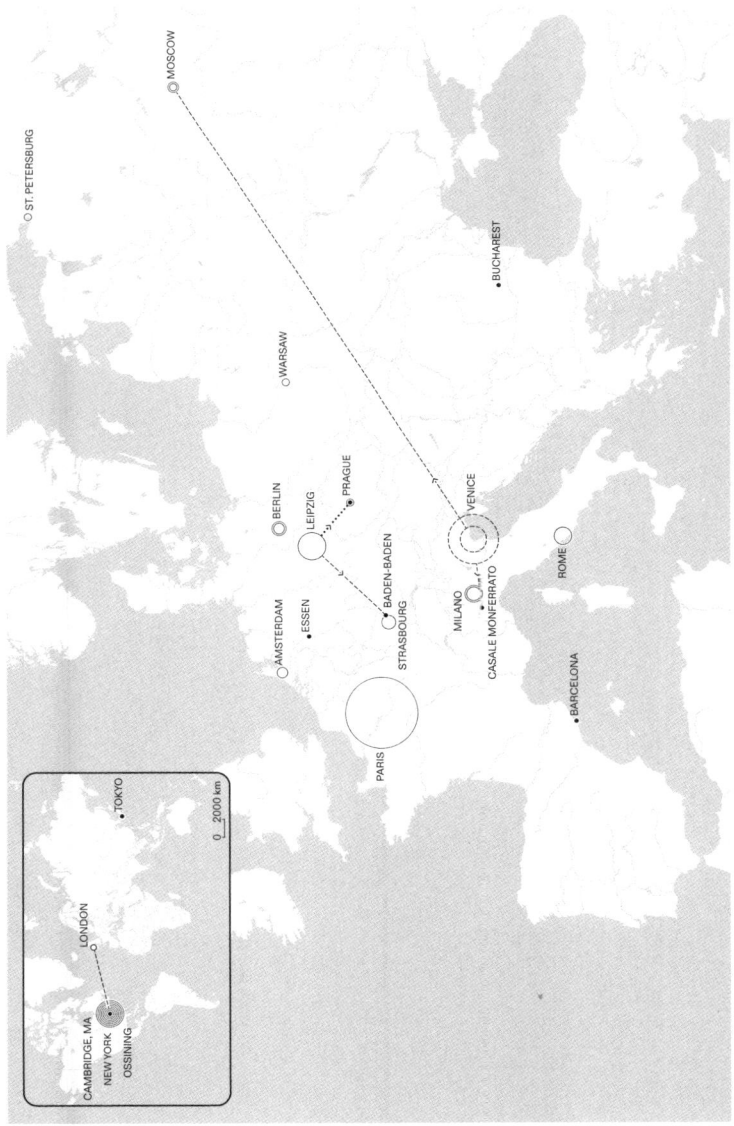

58 An Author of the Twentieth Century, 1914–1964

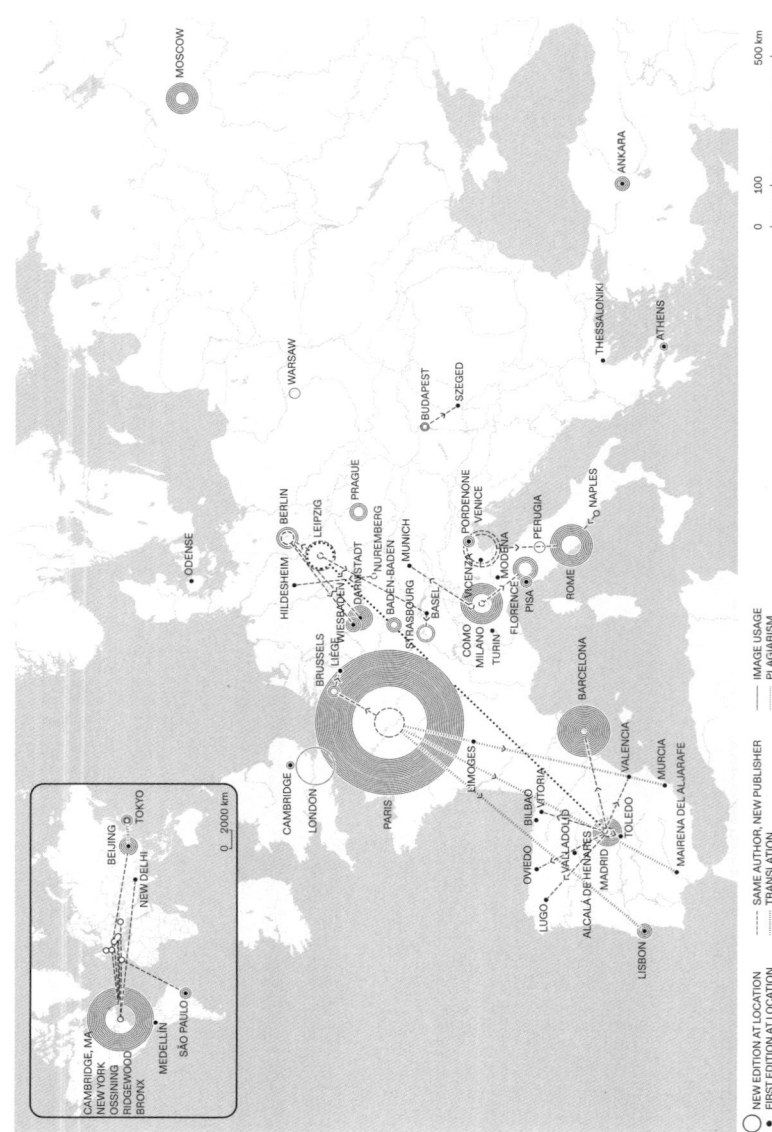

59 Vitruvius Academicus, 1964–2016

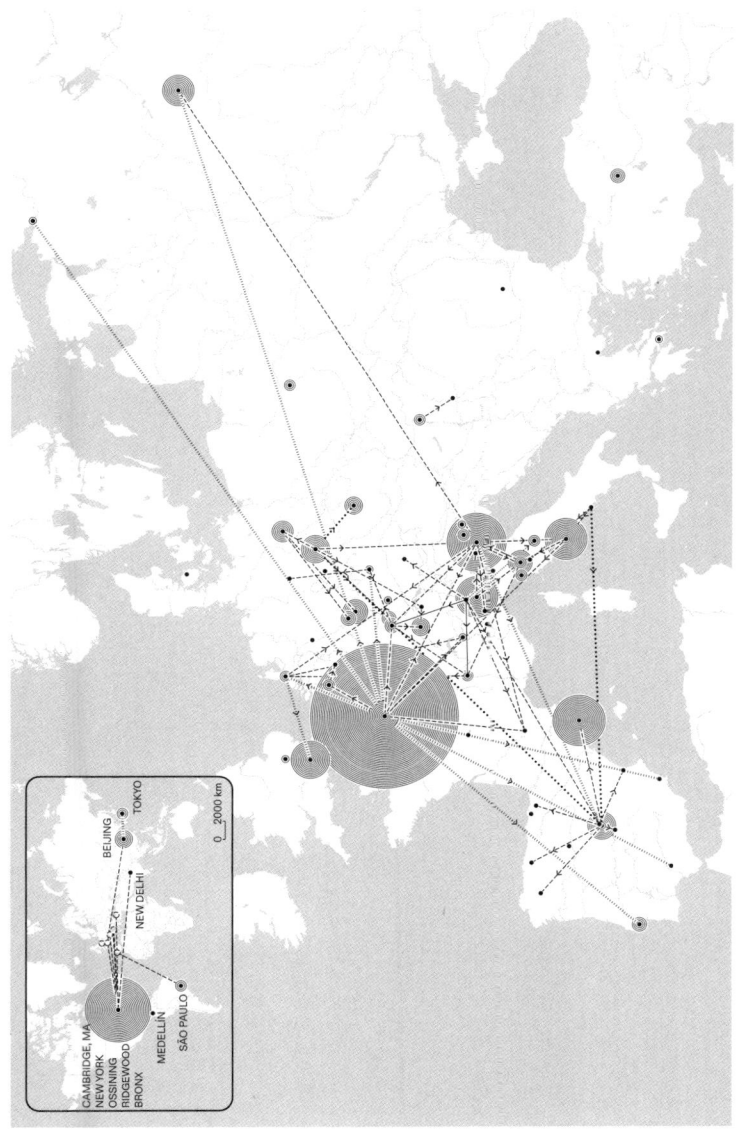

60 Vitruviana, 1486–2016

ANNEX

BIBLIOGRAPHY

Abramson, Daniel. "Bank of England." Edited by Margaret Richardson and Mary Anne Stevens. In *John Soane Architect: Master of Space and Light*, 208–251. London: Royal Academy of Arts, 1999.

Abramson, Daniel. *Building the Bank of England: Money, Architecture, Society, 1694–1942*. New Haven, CT: Yale University Press, 2005.

Adam, Jean-Pierre. *La maison romaine*. Arles: Honoré Clair, 2012.

Adam, Jean-Pierre. "La ville de Pline le Jeune aux Laurentes." In *La Laurentine et l'invention de la villa romaine*, by Institut Français d'Architecture, 170–175. Paris: Éditions du Moniteur, 1982.

Adler, Antje. *Gelebte Antike: Friedrich Wilhelm IV und Charlottenhof*. Berlin: Duncker & Humblot, 2012.

Alberti, Leon Battista, ed. *Da arte edificatória*. Translated by Arnaldo Espírito Santo. Lisbon: Fundação Calouste Gulbenkian, 2011.

Alberti, Leon Battista. *L'architecture et art de bien bastir*. Paris: Jaques Kerver, 1553.

Alberti, Leon Battista. *On the Art of Building in Ten Books*. Translated by Joseph Rykwert, Neil Leach, and Robert Tavernor. Cambridge, MA: MIT Press, 1988.

Alonso, Pedro Ignazio. "Shoot the Artist." In *Disparen sobre el artista/Acrónimo*, 6–11. Providencia, Santiago de Chile: Ediciones Arq, 2016.

Alves, José da Felicidade. *Introdução ao estudo da obra de Francisco de Holanda*. Lisbon: Livros Horizonte, 1984.

Anderson, Christy. *Inigo Jones and the Classical Tradition*. New York: Cambridge University Press, 2007.

Angerhofer, Paul J., Mary Ann Addy Maxwell, and Robert L. Maxwell. *In aedibus Aldi: The Legacy of Aldus Manutius and His Press*. Provo, UT: Friends of the Harold B. Lee Library-Brigham Young University, 1995.

Artigas, João Vilanova. "Casa Elza Berquó." In *Vilanova Artigas*, by Marcelo Ferraz, 138–141. São Paulo: Instituto Lina Bo e P. M. Bardi/Fundação Vilanova Artigas, 1997.

Barbier, Frédéric. "L'industrialisation des techniques." In *Histoire de l'édition française: Le temps des éditeurs; Du romantisme à la Belle Époque*, by Roger Chartier and Henri-Jean Martin, 51–66. 1st ed. 1985. Vol. 3. Paris: Fayard/Cercle de la Librairie, 1990.

Barozzio da Vignola, Iacomo. *Regola delli cinqve ordini d'architettvra*. Rome, [1562].

Barthes, Roland. "Les planches de l'encyclopédie." In *Le degré zéro de l'écriture: Suivi de nouveaux essais critiques*, Repr. 1972, 89–104. Paris: Éditions du Seuil, 1964.

Barthes, Roland. "The Plates of the Encyclopedia." Translated by Richard Howard. In *New Critical Essays*. New York: Hill and Wang, 1980.

Bedon, Anna. "Giovan Antonio Rusconi: Illustratore di Vitruvio, artista, ingegnere, architetto." In *Della architettura di Gio: Antonio Rusconi*. Vicenza: Centro Internazionale di Architettura Andrea Palladio, 1996.

Behal, Vera J. "Die Villa Karma und ihre Architekten Lavanchy, Loos, Ehrlich." In *Adolf Loos*, 135–158. Vienna: Graphische Sammlung Albertina, 1989.

Belluzzi, Amedeo, and Kurt W. Forster. "Palazzo Te." In *Giulio Romano*, 317–335. Milan: Electa, 1989.

Beltramini, Guido. "La nuova língua dell'architettura nei decenni di Aldo." In *Aldo Manuzio: Il renascimento di Venezia*, 29–41. Venice: Marsilio, 2016.

Beltramini, Guido. "Palazzo Barbarano." Edited by Guido Beltramini and Howard Burns. In *Palladio*, 208–215. Vol. 6. London: Royal Academy of Arts, 2009.

Beltramini, Guido. "Study for the Plan of Palazzo Barbarano (Alternative B) 1568–1569." Edited by Guido Beltramini and Howard Burns. In *Palladio*, 213–221.

Vol. 6. London: Royal Academy of Arts, 2009.

Beltramini, Guido, and Howard Burns, eds. "Andrea Palladio 1508–1580." In *Palladio*. Vol. 6. London: Royal Academy of Arts, 2009.

Beltramini, Guido, and Davide Gasparotto, eds. *Aldo Manuzio: Il rinascimento di Venezia*. Venice: Marsilio, 2016.

Beltramini, Maria. "Palladio e il *Sesto Libro* di Sebastiano Serlio." Edited by Franco Barbieri. In *Palladio 1508–2008: Il simposio del cinquecentenario*, 187–188. Venice: Marsilio, 2008.

Benelli, Francesco. "Secondo Fra Giocondo: Antonio da Sangallo il Giovane e l'edizione di Fra Giocondo del 1513 del Metropolitan Museum of Art di New York." In *Giovanni Giocondo, umanista, architetto e antiquario*, 53–68. Venice: Marsilio, 2014.

Benton, Tim. *The Villas of Le Corbusier: 1920–1930*. New Haven, CT: Yale University Press, 1987.

Bergdoll, Barry. *Karl Friedrich Schinkel: An Architecture for Prussia*. New York: Rizzoli, 1994.

Bergdoll, Barry, and Hillert Ibbeken. *Karl Friedrich Schinkel, Ludwig Persius, Friedrich August Stüler: Bauten in Berlin und Potsdam*. Stuttgart: Axel Menges, 2013.

Berritto, Alfonso Mattia. *Pompei 1911: Le Corbusier e l'origine della casa*. Naples: Clean, 2011.

Biffi, Marco. *La traduzione del De architectura di Vitruvio dal ms. II.I.141 della Biblioteca Nazionale Centrale di Firenze*. Pisa: Scuola Normale Superiore, 2002.

Bilou, Francisco. "Miguel de Arruda, entre Évora e Estremoz: Novos documentos (1532–1562)." *Boletim do Arquivo Distrital de Évora*, no. 3 (September 2015): 53–57.

Blondel, François. *Cours d'architecture enseigné dans l'Academie royale d'architecture*. Paris: Lambert Roulland, 1675–1683.

B uom, Joannem. *Quinque columnarum exacta descriptio atque deliniatio, cum symmetrica earum distributione*. Zurich: C. Froschouerum, 1550.

Boesiger, Willy, and Oscar Stonorov, eds. *Le Corbusier: Œuvre Complète, 1910–29*. Zurich: H. Girsberger & Cie, 1930.

Bois, Yve-Alain. "Montage and Architecture." *Assemblage: A Critical Journal of Architecture and Design Culture*, no. 10 (December 1989): 110–131.

Borman, Tracy. *King's Mistress, Queen's Servant: The Life and Times of Henrietta Howard*. London: Vintage Books, 2010.

Börsch-Supan, Eva. *Karl Friedrich Schinkel, Lebenswerk: Arbeiten für König Friedrich Wilhelm III; Von Preussen und Kronprinz Friedrich Wilhelm (IV)*. Berlin: Deutscher Kunstverlag, 2011.

Bouchet, Jules. *Le Laurentin, maison de campagne de Pline-le-Consul, restitué d'après sa lettre à Gallus*. Paris: l'auteur, 1852.

Brochmann, Christoph. *Licht und Farbe im Berliner Untergrund: U-Bahnhöfe der klassischen Moderne*. Berlin: Gebr. Mann, 2003.

Burns, Howard, ed. *Andrea Palladio, 1508–1580: The Portico and the Farmyard*. [London]: Arts Council of Great Britain, 1975.

Burns, Howard. "Giulio Romano and the Palazzo Thiene." Edited by Guido Beltramini and Howard Burns. In *Palladio*, 40–43. London: Royal Academy of Arts, 2009.

Burns, Howard. "I progetti vicentini di Giulio Romano." In *Giulio Romano*, 502–505. Milan: Electa, 1989.

Callebat, Louis, and Philippe Fleury, eds *Dictionnaire des termes techniques du De architectura de Vitruve*. Hildesheim: Olms-Weidmann, 1995.

Callebat, Louis, Philippe Fleury, Pierre Bouet, and Michel Zuinghedau, eds. *Vitruve: De architectura; Concordance. Documentation bibliographique,* lexicale et grammaticale. 2 vols. Hildesheim: Olms-Weidmann, 1984.

Campbell, Colen. *Vitruvius Britannicus; or, The British Architect: Containing the Plans, Elevations and Sections of the Regular Buildings, Both Publick and Private in Great Britain, with Variety of New Designs, in 200 Large Folio Plates, Engraven by the Vest Hands, and Drawn Either from the Buildings Themselves or the Original Designs of the Architects*. London, 1717.

Carpo, Mario. *Architecture in the Age of Printing: Orality, Writing, Typography, and Printed Images in the History of Architectural Theory*. 1st Italian ed. 1998. Translated by Sarah Benson. Cambridge, MA: MIT Press, 2001.

Carpo, Mario. "Préface à la traduction francaise." Translated by Ginette Morel. In *L'architecture a l'âge de l'imprimerie: Culture orale, culture écrite, livre et reproduction mécanique de l'image dans l'histoire des théories architecturales*. Paris: La Villette, 2008.

Carpo, Mario. "The Making of the Typographical Architect." Edited by Vaughan Hart and Peter Hicks. In *Paper Palaces: The Rise of the Renaissance Architectural Treatise*, 158–169. New Haven, CT: Yale University Press, 1998.

Casotti, Maria Walcher. "Giacomo Barozzi da Vignola: Regola delli cinque ordini d'architettura." Edited by Elena Bassi, Sandro Benedetti, Renato Bonelli, Licisco Magagnato, Paola Marini, Tommaso Scalesse, Camillo Semenzato, and Maria Walcher Casotti. In *Trattati: Pietro Cataneo, Giacomo Barozzi da Vignola; Con l'aggiunta degli scritti di architettura di Alvise Cornaro, Francesco Giorgi, Claudio Tolomei, Giangiorgio Trissino, Giorgio Vasari*, 499–577. Milan: Polifilo, 1985.

Cellauro, Louis. "Notice on Daniele Barbaro." Edited by Frédérique Lemerle and Yves Pauwels. In *Architectura: Architecture, textes et images (XVIe–XVIIe siècles)*, online. Tours: Centre d'Études Supérieures de la Renaissance, Université François-Rabelais, 2010. http://architectura.cesr.univ-tours.fr/Traite/Notice/Barbaro1556.asp?param=en.

Cellauro, Louis. "Palladio e le illustrazioni delle edizioni del 1556 e del 1567 di Vitruvio." *Saggi e memorie di storia dell'arte*, no. 22 (1998): 55–128.

Cerceau, Jacques Androuet. *Livre d'architectvre contenant les plans & dessaings de cinquante bastimens tous differens*. Paris: Benoît Prévost, 1559.

Cerceau, Jacques Androuet. *Second livre d'architectvre contenant plusieurs et diverses ordonnances de cheminees, lucarnes, portes, fonteines*. Paris: André Wechel, 1561.

Chartier, Roger. *La main de l'auteur et l'esprit de l'imprimeur XVIe–XVIIIe siècle*. Paris: Gallimard, 2015.

Chartier, Roger. *The Business of Enlightenment: A Publishing History of the Encyclopédie 1775–1800*. Cambridge, MA: Belknap Press of Harvard University Press, 1979.

Choay, Françoise. *La règle et le modèle: Sur la théorie de l'architecture et de l'urbanisme*. 1st ed. 1980. Paris: Seuil, 1996.

Ciapponi, Lucia. "Fra Giocondo da Verona and His Edition of Vitruvius." *Journal of the Warburg and Courtauld Institutes* 47 (1984): 72–90. https://doi.org/10.2307/751439.

Ciucci, Giorgio. *Gli architetti e il Fascismo: Architettura e città 1922–1933*. Turin: Enaudi, 1989.

Clark, Katerina. *Moscow, the Fourth Rome: Cosmopolitanism, and the Evolution of Soviet Culture, 1931–1941*. Cambridge, MA: Harvard University Press, 2011.

Clemons, G. Scott, and H. George Fletcher. *Aldus Manutius: A Legacy More Lasting than Bronze*. New York: Grolier Club, 2015.

Cohen, Jean-Louis. "Retro-grad ou les impasses du réalisme 'socialiste' en URSS." In *Les années 30: L'architecture et les arts de l'espace entre industrie et nostalgie*, 163–179. Paris: Éditions du Patrimoine, 1997.

Construction Moderne. "Bibliographie." 26, no. 31 (April 29, 1911): 371–372.

Corbusier, Le. *Toward an Architecture.* Translated by John Goodman. Los Angeles: Getty Research Institute, 2007.

Corbusier, Le. *Vers une architecture.* 1st ed. 1923. Paris: Flammarion, 1995.

Cotrim, Marcio. *Vilanova Artigas: Casas paulistas.* São Paulo: Romano Guerra, 2017.

Craig, Maurice. "James Fergusson." Edited by John Summerson. In *Concerning Architecture: Essays on Architectural Writers and Writing Presented to Nikolaus Pevsner,* 140–152. London: Allen Lane the Penguin Press, 1968.

Daiki, Amanai. "The Founding of Bunriha Kenchiku Kai: 'Art' and 'Expression' in Early Japanese Architectural Circle, 1988–1920." *Aesthetics,* no. 13 (2009): 235–248.

Darley, Gillian. "The Grand Tour." Edited by Margaret Richardson and Mary Anne Stevens. In *John Soane Architect: Master of Space and Light,* 96–113. London: Royal Academy of Arts, 1999.

Dartein, Fernand. "Notice sur la vie et les travaux de M. Auguste Choisy." *Annales des ponts et chaussées* 3 (May 1910): 7–46.

Dercelles, Arnaud. "Catalogue de la bibliothèque personelle de Le Corbusier." In *Le Corbusier et le livre.* Barcelona: Col·legi d'Arquitectes de Catalunya, [2005].

Deswarte, Sylvie. "Franscisco de Holanda, teórico entre o renascimento e o maneirismo." Edited by Vítor Serrão. In *História da Arte em Portugal,* 10–29. O Maneirismo, vol. 7. Lisbon: Alfa, 1986.

Deswarte-Rosa, Sylvie, ed. *Sebastiano Serlio a Lyon: Architecture et Imprimerie, Volume 1; Le traité d'architecture de Sebastiano Serlio. Une grande entreprise éditoriale au XVIe siècle.* Lyon: Mémoire Active, 2004.

Dias, Ana Carvalho, and Renata Faria Barbosa. "O primitivo sistema hidráulico do 'convento novo': Contributo dos trabalhos de arqueologia no Convento de Cristo, Tomar." *Monumentos,* no. 37 (November 2009): 162–171.

Diderot and d'Alembert. *Éncyclopédie, ou dictionnaire raisonné des sciences, des arts et des métiers.* 28 vols. Paris: Briasson, David, Le Breton, Durand, 1751.

Dosio, Giovanni Antonio. *Vrbis Romæ ædificiorvm illustrivm qvæ svpersvnt reliqviæ.* [Rome], 1569.

Du Prey, Pierre de la Ruffinière, ed. *The Villas of Pliny: From Antiquity to Posterity.* Chicago: University of Chicago Press, 1994.

Durand, Jean-Nicolas-Louis. *Précis des leçons d'architecture données à l'École Polytechnique.* Paris: Bernard et l'Auteur, n.d.

Durand, Jean-Nicolas-Louis. *Recueil et parallèle des édifices de tout genre, anciens et modernes: Remarquables par leur beauté, par leur grandeur ou par leur singularités et dessinés sur une même échelle.* Paris: chez l'auteur, [1801].

Eisenthal, Esther. "John Webb's Reconstruction of the Ancient House." *Architectural History* 28 (1985): 7–18, 20–31. https://doi.org/10.2307/1568524.

Elser, Oliver, ed. "Die Klotz-Tapes: Das Making-of der Postmoderne/The Klotz Tapes: The Making of Postmodernism." *Arch+ features* 47, no. 26 (2014): 115–121.

Essaïan, Élisabeth. *Le Prix de Rome: Le "Grand Tour" des architectes soviétiques sous Mussolini.* Paris: Éditions B2, 2012.

Fane-Saunders, Peter. *Pliny the Elder and the Emergence of Renaissance Architecture.* New York: Cambridge University Press, 2016.

Félibien des Avaux, Jean-François. *Les plans et les descriptions des deux plus belles maisons de campagne de Pline le consul.* Paris: Florentin and P. Delaulne, 1699.

Feng, Jiren. *Chinese Architecture and Metaphor: Song Culture in the Yingzao Fashi Building Manual.* Honolulu:

University of Hawai'i Press; Hong Kong University Press, 2012.

Filarete, Antonio Piero Averlino. *Filarete's Treatise on Architecture*. Translated by John R. Spencer. New Haven, CT: Yale University Press, 1965.

Filarete, Antonio Piero Averlino. *Tractat über die Baukunst: Nebst seinen Büchern von der Zeichenkunst und den Bauten der Medici*. Vienna: Graeser, 1896.

Fiore, Francesco Paolo, ed. *Sebastiano Serlio, architettura civile: Libri sesto settimo e ottavo nei manoscritti di Monaco e Vienna*. Milan: Polifilo, 1996.

Fleming, John. *Robert Adam and his Circle in Edinburgh & Rome*. London: John Murray, 1962.

Forster, Kurt W. "Album La Roche." Edited by Guido Beltramini and Howard Burns. In *Palladio*, 400–401. London: Royal Academy of Arts, 2009.

Forster, Kurt W. *Schinkel: A Meander through His Life and Work*. Basel: Birkhäuser, 2017.

Forty, Adrian. *Concrete and Culture: A Material History*. London: Reaktion Books, 2012.

Foscari, Antoni. *Tumult and Order: Malcontenta 1924–1939*. Translated by Lucinda Byatt. Zurich: Lars Müller, 2012.

Foscari, Antonio. *Andrea Palladio: Unbuilt Venice*. Zurich: Lars Müller, 2010.

Fowler, Lawrence Hall, and Elizabeth Baer, eds. *The Fowler Architectural Collection of the Johns Hopkins University*. Baltimore: Evergreen House Foundation, 1961.

Garcez Teixeira, F. A. *A antiga Sinagoga de Tomar*. Lisbon: Tipografia do Comércio, 1925.

Gautier, Théophile, Arsène Houssaye, and Charles Coligny. *Le palais pompéien de l'avenue Montaigne: Études sur la maison gréco-romaine, ancienne résidence du prince Napoléon*. Paris: Au Palais Pompéien, 1866.

Gerbino, Anthony. "Blondel, Colbert et l'origine de l'Académie royale d'architecture." Edited by Jean-Philippe Garric, Frédérique Lemerle, and Yves Pauwels. In *Architecture et théorie: L'héritage de la Renaissance*, online ed. 20–25. Paris: Institut National d'Histoire de l'Art, 2010. https://books.openedition.org/inha/3394.

Germann, Georg. *Vitruve et le vitruvianisme: Introduction à l'histoire de la théorie architecturale*. 1st ed. 1987. Translated by Jacques Gubler. Lausanne: Presses Polytechniques et Universitaires Romandes, 2016.

Gombrich, Ernst. "Leonardo in the History of Science." Edited by Richard Woodfield. In *Ernst Gombrich, Reflections on the History of Art: Views and Reviews*, 68–73. Los Angeles: University of California Press, 1987.

Gómez, F. Pizarro, and P. Mogollón Cano-Cortés, eds. *Los diez libros de arquitectura de Marco Vitruvio Polión según la traducción castellana de Lázaro de Velasco*. Cáceres: Ciclón, 1999.

Grapaldi, Francisci Marii. *De partibus aedium libellus: Cum addita mentis emendatissimus*. 1st ed. 1494. [Parma]: [F. Ugoletto], [1501].

Gravagnuolo, Benedetto. *Adolf Loos: Theory and Works*. Milan/Vienna: Idea Books/Löcker Verlag, 1982.

Gravagnuolo, Benedetto. "From Schinkel to Le Corbusier: The Myth of the Mediterranean in Modern Architecture." Edited by Jean-François Lejeune and Michelangelo Sabatino. In *Modern Architecture and the Mediterranean: Vernacular Dialogues and Contested Identities*, 14–39. London: Routledge, 2010.

Gresleri, Giuliano, ed. *Le Corbusier, Charles-Edouard Jeanneret, Voyage d'Orient: Carnets*. Milan: Electa/Fondation Le Corbusier, 2002.

Gros, Pierre. "Giocondo: Lectures de Vitruve." Edited by Pierre Gros and Pier Nicola Pagliara. In *Giovanni Giocondo, umanista, architetto e antiquario*, 11–19. Venice: Marsilio, 2014.

Gros, Pierre. "Les illustrations du De architectura de Vitruve: Histoire d'un malentendu." In *Vitruve et la tradition des traités d'architecture: Fabrica et ratio-*

cinatio, 1st ed. 1996, 363–388. Rome: Publications de l'École française de Rome, 2006. https://books.openedition.org/efr/2515.

Gros, Pierre. "Les lectures vitruviennes du XVIe siècle et quelques-unes de leurs conséquences à l'âge classique: L'exemple de la domus." In *Architecture et théorie: L'héritage de la Renaissance*, 1–21. Paris: Institut National d'Histoire de l'Art, 2012. https://books.openedition.org/inha/3436.

Gros, Pierre. *Maisons, palais, villas et tombeaux*. Vol. 2 of *L'architecture romaine: Du début du IIIe siècle av. J.-C. à la fin du Haut-Empire*. 2nd ed. Paris: Picard, 2006.

Gubler, Jacques. "'Sur l'album photographique de la villa Karma,' lettre à A. M. Vogt." Edited by Katharina Medici-Mall. In *Fünf Punkte in der Architekturgeschichte: Festschrift für Adolf Max Vogt*, 214–229. Basel: Birkhäuser, 1985.

Gubler, Jacques. *Jean Tschumi: Architecture at Full Scale*. Milan: Skira, 2008.

Guillaume, Jean, ed. *Jacques Androuet du Cerceau: 'Un des plus grands architectes qui se soient jamais trouvés en France'*. Paris: Picard/Cité de l'architecture & du patrimoine, 2010.

Guzzo, Pietro Giovanni, Maria Rosaria Esposito, and Nicoleta Ossanna Cavadini, eds. *Herculaneum and Pompeii: Visions of a Discovery*. Geneva: Skira, 2018.

Harris, Eileen, and Nicholas Savage. *British Architectural Books and Writers 1556–1785*. Cambridge: Cambridge University Press, 1990.

Hart, Vaughan. "'Paper Palaces' from Alberti to Scamozzi." Edited by Vaughan Hart and Peter Hicks. In *Paper Palaces: The Rise of the Renaissance Architectural Treatise*, 1–29. New Haven, CT: Yale University Press, 1998.

Haudebourt, Louis Pierre. *Le Laurentin maison de campagne de Pline le Jeune: Restituée d'après la description de Pline*. Paris: Carilian-Goeury, 1838.

Hernández, Fabio Restrepo. "Ceci est mon testament: Marc-Antoine Laugier." PhD diss., Universidad Politécnica de Catalunya, Escuela Técnica Superior de Arquitectura de Barcelona, 2010.

Hoeber, Fritz. *Peter Behrens*. Munich: Verlag Müller u. Rentsch, 1913.

Institut Français d'Architecture. *La Laurentine et l'invention de la villa romaine*. Paris: Éditions du Moniteur, 1982.

Jachmann, Julian. *Die Architekturbücher des Walter Hermann Ryff: Vitruvrezeption im Kontext mathematischer Wissenschaften*. Stuttgart: ibidem, 2006.

Jacquet, Benoît. "Between Tradition and Modernity: The Two Sides of Japanese Pre-war Architecture." Edited by Susanne Kohte, Hubertus Adam, and Daniel Hubert. In *Encounters and Positions: Architecture in Japan*, 226–237. Basel: Birkhäuser, 2017.

Jacquet, Benoît, and Nicolas Fiévé. *Vers une modernité architecturale et paysagère: Modèles et savoirs partagés entre le Japon et le monde occidental*. Paris: Éditions Collège de France, 2013.

Jarrard, Alice. "Review: Metodo ed ordini nella teoria architettonica del primi moderni; Alberti, Raffaello, Serlio e Camillo by Mario Carpo. La maschera e il modello: Teoria architettonica ed evangelismo nell'extraordinario libro di Sebastiano Serlio by Mario Carpo." *Journal of the Society of Architectural Historians* 55, no. 1 (March 1996): 103–105.

Jarrassé, Dominique. "Emmanuel Pontremoli." Edited by Jean-Paul Midant. In *Dictionnaire de l'architecture du XXe siècle*, 716. Paris: Hazan/Institut Français de Architecture, 1996.

Johns, Adrian. *Piracy: The Intellectual Property Wars from Gutenberg to Gates*. Chicago: University of Chicago Press, 2009.

Khan-Magomedov, Selim O. *Pioneers of Soviet Architecture*. 1st ed. 1983.

Edited by Catherine Cooke. Translated by Alexander Lieven. London: Thames; Hudson, 1997.

Kinross, Robin. *Modern Typography: An Essay in Critical History*. 1st ed. 1992, 2nd revised ed. 2004. London: Hyphen Press, 2010.

Klotz, Heinrich. *Die Revision der Moderne: Postmoderne Architektur 1960–1980*. Munich: Prestel, 1984.

Kohte, Susanne, Hubertus Adam, and Daniel Hubert, eds. *Encounters and Positions: Architecture in Japan*. Basel: Birkhäuser, 2017.

Krinsky, Carol Herselle. "Seventy-eight Vitruvius Manuscripts." Online edition. *Journal of the Warburg and Courtauld Institutes* 30 (1967): 36–70. https://doi.org/10.2307/750736.

Kruft, Hanno-Walter. *A History of Architectural Theory from Vitruvius to the Present*. 1st German ed. 1985. New York: Princeton Architectural Press, 1994.

Krüger, Mário. "As leituras da arte edificatória." Translated by Arnaldo Espírito Santo. In *Da arte edificatória*, by Leon Battista Alberti, 17–129. Lisbon: Fundação Calouste Gulbenkian, 2011.

Kubler, George. *Portuguese Plain Architecture: Between Spices and Diamonds, 1521–1706*. Middletown, CT: Wesleyan University Press, 1972.

Kurlansky, Mark. *Paper: Paging Through History*. New York: W. W. Norton, 2016.

L'architettura di Giovanni Muzio. Milan: Abitare Segesta Cataloghi, 1994.

Laugier, Marc Antoine. *Essai sur l'Architecture*. 2nd ed. 1755.

Le projet de Vitruve: Objet, destinataires et réception du De architectura. Rome: École Française de Rome, 1994.

Leitão, Henrique. "Sobre as 'obras perdidas' de Pedro Nunes." Edited by Henrique Leitão and Lígia Azevedo Martins. In *Pedro Nunes, 1502–1578: Novas terras, novos mares e o que mays he; Novo ceo e novas estrellas*, 45–66. Lisbon: Biblioteca Nacional, 2002.

Lemerle, Frédérique. "Philandrier et le texte de Vitruve." *Mélanges de l'école française de Rome* 106, no. 2 (1994): 517–529.

Lemerle, Frédérique. "Une édition de l'Abrégé." Edited by Frédérique Lemerle and Yves Pauwels. In *Architectura: Architecture, textes et images (XVIe–XVIIe siècles)*, online. Tours: Centre d'Études Supérieures de la Renaissance, Université François-Rabelais, 2011. http://architectura.cesr.univ-tours.fr/Traite/Notice/PerraultCl1681.asp?param=.

Lemerle, Frédérique. "Vitruve Editions Martin: Traduction de Vitruve 1547." Edited by Frédérique Lemerle and Yves Pauwels. In *Architectura: Architecture, textes et images (XVIe–XVIIe siècles)*, online ed. Tours: Centre d'Études Supérieures de la Renaissance, Université François-Rabelais, 2013. http://architectura.cesr.univ-tours.fr/Traite/Notice/ENSBA_LES1785.asp?param=.

Lemerle, Frédérique. "Vitruve: De Tournes's editions, 1552." Edited by Frédérique Lemerle and Yves Pauwels. In *Architectura: Architecture, textes et images (XVIe–XVIIe siècles)*, online ed. Tours: Centre d'Études Supérieures de la Renaissance, Université François-Rabelais, 2013. http://architectura.cesr.univ-tours.fr/Traite/Notice/Phil1552.asp?param=en.

Lemerle, Frédérique, and Yves Pauwels, eds. *Architectura: Architecture, textes et images (XVIe–XVIIe siècles)*. Online ed. Tours: Centre d'Études Supérieures de la Renaissance, Université François-Rabelais, 2013. http://architectura.cesr.univ-tours.fr/Traite/index.asp?param=en.

Lester, Toby. *Da Vinci's Ghost: The Untold Story of the World's Most Famous Drawing*. London: Profile Books, 2011.

Liscombe, R. W. *William Wilkins 1778–1839*. Cambridge: Cambridge University Press, 1980.

Llewellyn, Nigel. "'Hungry and Desperate for Knowledge': Diego de Sagredo's Spanish Point of View." Edited by Vaughan Hart and Peter Hicks. In *Paper Palaces: The Rise of the Renaissance*

Architectural Treatise, 122–139. New Haven, CT: Yale University Press, 1998.

Lowry, Martin. *The World of Aldus Manutius: Business and Scholarship in Renaissance Venice*. Oxford: Blackwell, 1979.

Maciel, M. Justino. "O livro quinto do *De Architectura* de Vitrúvio." In *Miscellanea em Homenagem ao Professor Bairrão Oleiro*, 285–329. Vol. V. Lisbon: Colibri, 1996.

Maciel, M. Justino. "Os *Prooemia* vitruvianos." In *Estudos de arte e história: Homenagem a Artur Nobre de Gusmão*, 345–371. Lisbon: Vega, 1995.

Maffei, Sonia. "Il progetto di una 'concordanza storica vitruviana': Un approccio metodologico per il trattamento informatico di varianti testuali." In *Le projet de Vitruve: Objet, destinataires er réception du* De architectura, 231–245. Rome: Ecole Française de Rome, Palais Farnèse, 1994.

Mallgrave, Harry Francis. "Introduction." In *Northern European Books: Sixteenth to Early Nineteenth Centuries*. 4 vols., 1–61. The Mark J. Millard Architectural Collection, vol. 3. Washington, DC: National Gallery of Art, 1998. https://www.nga.gov/content/dam/ngaweb/research/publications/pdfs/mark-j-millard-northern-european-books.pdf.

Mandoul, Thierry. *Entre raison et utopie: L'histoire de l'architecture d'Auguste Choisy*. Wavre: Mardaga, 2008.

Manutius. *Libri de re rustica*. Venice: Aldo Manuzio; Andrea Torresano, 1514.

Marías, Fernando. "Medidas del Romano." Edited by Frédérique Lemerle and Yves Pauwels. In *Architectura: Architecture, textes et images (XVIe–XVIIe siècles)*, online ed. Tours: Centre d'Études Supérieures de la Renaissance, Université François-Rabelais, 2012. http://architectura.cesr.univ-tours.fr/Traite/Notice/Sagredo1526.asp?param=en.

Marías, Fernando. "Trattatistica teorica e Vitruvianesimo nella architettura spagnola del cinquecento." Edited by A. Chastel and J. Guillaume. In *Les traités d'architecture de la Renaissance*, 279, 307–315. Paris: Picard, 1988.

Marías, Fernando, and Felipe Pereda, eds. *Medidas del romano, Diego de Sagredo: Toledo 1526*. 2 vols. Toledo: Pareja, 2000.

Marquez, Pietro. *Delle case di citta deg'i antichi Romani secondo la dottrina di Vitruvio*. Rome: Il Salomoni, 1795.

Marquez, Pietro. *Delle ville di Plinio il Giovane*. Rome: Salomoni, 1796.

Martin, Jean, trans. *Hypnerotomachie, ou, discours du songe de Poliphile: Deduisant comme amour le combat à l'occasion de Polia*. Paris: Jaques Kerver, 1546.

Marzano, Annalisa, and Guy P. R. Métraux. *The Roman Villa in the Mediterranean Basin: Late Republic to Late Antiquity*. Cambridge: Cambridge University Press, 2018.

Mattusch, Carol C., ed. *Rediscovering the Ancient World*. Washington, DC: National Gallery of Art, 2013.

Mau, August. *Pompeii: Its Life and Art*. New York: Macmillan, 1899.

Mazois, François. *Le Palais de Scaurus, ou description d'une maison romaine, fragment d'un voyage fait à Rome, vers la fin de la République, par Mérovir, prince des Suèves*. 1st ed. 1819. Paris: Firmin Didot, 1822.

Mazois, François. *Les Ruines de Pompéi: Seconde partie; Édifices privés. Précédé d'un essai sur les habitations des anciens Romains*. Paris: Firmin Didot, 1821–1824.

McEwen, Indra Kagis. "On Claude Perrault: Modernising Vitruvius." Edited by Vaughan Hart and Peter Hicks. In *Paper Palaces: The Rise of the Renaissance Architectural Treatise*, 320–337. New Haven, CT: Yale University Press, 1998.

McEwen, Indra Kagis. *Vitruvius: Writing the Body of Architecture*. Cambridge, MA: MIT Press, 2003.

Medvedkova, Olga. "L'édition des livres d'architecture en français dans l'Angleterre du XVIIIe siècle." Edited by

Daniel Rabreau and Dominique Massounie. In *Claude Nicolas Ledoux et le livre d'architecture en français, Étienne Louis Boullée: L'utopie et la poésie de l'art*, 72–85. Paris: Editions du Patrimoine, 2006.

Medvedkova, Olga. "Un *Abrégé* moderne ou Vitruve selon la méthode." In *La construction savante: Les avatars de la littérature technique*, 43–53. Paris: Picard, 2008.

Middleton, Robin. "Introduction." In *The Ruins of the Most Beautiful Monuments of Greece*, by Julien-David Le Roy, 1–199. 1st ed. 1758. Los Angeles: Getty Research Institute, 2004.

Middleton, Robin, Gerald Beasley, and Nicholas Savage. *British Books: Seventeenth through Nineteenth Centuries*. 4 vols. The Mark J. Millard Architectural Collection, vol. 2. Washington, DC: National Gallery of Art, 1998. https://www.nga.gov/content/dam/ngaweb/research/publications/pdfs/mark-j-millard-british-books.pdf.

Millette, Daniel. "Vitruve: Editions Gardet/Bertin, 1556/1559." Edited by Frédérique Lemerle and Yves Pauwels. In *Architectura: Architecture, textes et images (XVIe–XVIIe siècles)*, online ed. Tours: Centre d'Études Supérieures de la Renaissance, Université François-Rabelais, 2012. http://architectura.cesr.univ-tours.fr/traite/Notice/GardetBertin1559.asp?param=en.

Millette, Daniel. "Vitruvius and the French Landscape of Ruins: On Jean Gardet and Dominique Bertin's 1559 Annotations of *De Architectura*." McGill-Queens University Press. Edited by Alberto Pérez-Gómez and Stephen Parcell. *CHORA: Intervals in the Philosophy of Architecture* 5 (2007): 259–284.

Mitrovic, Branko. "Studying Renaissance Architectural Theory in the Age of Stalinism." *I Tatti Studies in the Italian Renaissance* 12 (2009): 233–263. https://www.jstor.org/stable/27809576?seq=1#metadata_info_tab_contents.

Monteix, Nicolas. "Mazois, François" (biographical note, 2009). https://www.inha.fr/fr/ressources/publications/publications-numeriques/dictionnaire-critique-des-historiens-de-l-art/mazois-francois.html?search-keywords=mazois.

Moore, Charles, Gerald Allen, and Donlyn Lyndon. *The Place of Houses*. 1st ed. 1974. Berkeley: University of California Press, 2000.

Moos, Stanislaus von, ed. *Album La Roche*. [Paris]: Gallimard, 1996.

Moos, Stanislaus von. *Le Corbusier: Elements of a Synthesis*. 2nd ed. Rotterdam: 010 Publishers, 2009.

Moreira, Rafael. "A arquitectura do Renascimento no sul de Portugal: A encomenda régia entre o moderno e o romano." PhD diss. Faculdade de Ciências Sociais e Humanas da Universidade Nova de Lisboa, Lisbon, 1991.

Moreira, Rafael. "Arquitectura: Renascimento e classicismo." In *História da Arte Portuguesa*, 302–375. Do "Modo" Gótico ao Maneirismo, vol. 1. Lisbon: Círculo de Leitores, 1995.

Moreira, Rafael. "Reflexos albertianos no Renascimento Português: A descriptio urbis romae, o matemático Francisco de Melo e um mapa virtual de Portugal em 1531." Edited by Mário Krüger. In *Na génese das racionalidades modernas II: Em torno de Alberti e do Humanismo*, 427–442. Coimbra: Imprensa da Universidade de Coimbra, 2015. http://dx.doi.org/10.14195/978-989-26-1015-3_22.

Moreira, Rafael. "Um tratado português de arquitectura do século XVI (1576–1579)." Edited by Helder Carita and Renata Araújo. In *Universo Urbanístico Português: 1455–1822*, 353–398. Lisbon: Comissão Nacional para as Comemorações dos Descobrimentos Portugueses, 1998.

Morresi, Manuela. "Treatises and the Architecture of Venice in the Fifteenth and Sixteenth Centuries." Edited by Vaughan Hart and Peter Hicks. In *Paper Palaces: The Rise of the Renaissance Architectural Treatise*, 262–280. New Haven, CT: Yale University Press, 1998.

Morris, Robert. *Lectures on Architecture, Consisting of Rules Founded upon Harmonick and Arithmetical Proportions in Building*. 1st ed. 1734–1736 part II. London: R. Sayer, 1759.

Moses, John. "The Builders of Marble Hill." Talk to the Marble Hill Society, March 3, 2013. https://friendsofmarblehill.org.uk/article/the-builders-of-marble-hill/.

Mussini, Massimo. *Francesco di Giorgio e Vitruvio: Le traduzioni del De architectura nei codici Zichy, Spencer 129 e Magliabechiano II.I.141*. 2 vols. [Florence]: Leo S. Olschki, 2003.

Mylonas, Paul M. "The Affinity between Greek and Roman Cultures, as Revealed through a Research Translation of Vitruvius into Greek, and Commentary." In *Research Reports and Record of Activities, Washington, National Gallery of Art Center 6*, 71–72. May 1985.

Nohl, Hermann. *Index Vitruvianus*. Facsimile reprints of Leipzig: Teubner, 1876. Darmstadt: Wissenschaftliche Buchgesellschaft, 1965 and 1983.

Oechslin, Werner. *Palladianesimo: Teoria e prassi*. Translated by Elena Filippi. Verona: Arsenale, 2006.

Oechslin, Werner. *Palladianismus: Andrea Palladio; Kontinuität von Werk und Wirkung*. Zurich: gta Verlag, 2008.

Orsini, Baldassarre. *Della geometria e prospettiva pratica*. 2 vols. Rome: Benedetto Franzesi, 1771–1772.

Orsini, Baldassarre. *Dizionario universale d'architettura e dizionario Vitruviano*. Perugia: Carlo Baduel e Figli, 1801.

Pagliara, Pier Nicola. "Fra Giocondo e l'edizione del De architectura del 1511." Edited by Pierre Gros and Pier Nicola Pagliara. In *Giovanni Giocondo, umanista, architetto e antiquario*, 21–52. Venice: Marsilio, 2014.

Pagliara, Pier Nicola. "L'attività edilizia di Antonio da Sangallo il Giovane." *Controspazio*, no. 7 (July 1972): 19–47.

Pagliara, Pier Nicola. "Vitruvio da testo a canone." Edited by Salvatore Settis. In *Memoria dell'antico nell'arte italiana: Dalla tradizione all'archeologia*. 3 vols. Turin: Giulio Enaudi, 1986.

Palladio, Andrea. *I quattro libri dell'architettura di Andrea Palladio*. Venice: Dominico de' Franceschi, 1570.

Palladio, Andrea. *Tchetyre knigi ob arkhitekroure*. Edited by A. Gabritchevky. Translated by Ivan Joltovski. Moscow: Akademii Arkhitektoury, 1937.

Palladio, Andrea. *The Four Books on Architecture*. 1st ed. 1997. Translated by Robert Tavernor and Richard Schofield. Cambridge, MA: MIT Press, 2002.

Parslow, Christopher Charles. *Rediscovering Antiquity: Karl Weber and the Excavation of Herculaneum, Pompeii and Stabiae*. Cambridge: Cambridge University Press, 1995.

Pellechia, Linda. "Architects Read Vitruvius: Renaissance Interpretations of the Atrium of the Ancient House." *Journal of the Society of Architectural Historians* 51, no. 4 (December 1992): 377–416. https://doi.org/10.2307/990736.

Pereira, Paulo. "O 'Convento Novo' (1529–1551)." *Monumentos*, no. 37 (November 2019): 100–119.

Perrault, Claude. *Mémoires pour servir à l'histoire naturelle des animaux*. Paris: Imprimerie Royale, 1671.

Perrault, Claude. *Ordonnance des cinq espèces de colonnes selon la méthode des anciens*. Paris: Jean Baptiste Coignard, 1683.

Pevsner, Nikolaus. "James Fergusson." In *Some Architectural Writers of the Nineteenth Century*, 238–251. Oxford: Clarendon Press, 1972.

Philandrier, Guillaume. *Les annotations sur l'architecture de Vitruve: Livres I à IV*. Frédérique Lemerle ed. Paris: Classiques Garnier, 2000.

Philandrier, Guillaume. *Les annotations sur l'architecture de Vitruve: Livres V à VII*. Frédérique Lemerle ed. Paris: Classiques Garnier, 2011.

Picon, Antoine. *Claude Perrault, 1613–1688 ou la curiosité d'un classique*. Paris: Picard, 1988.

Pinon, Pierre. "Vu de Kérylos: Réappropriation des monuments et changement de signification." In *Architecture du rêve: Actes du 3ème colloque de la Villa Kérylos à Beaulieu-sur-Mer les 29 & 30 Octobre 1992*, 11–23. Paris: Académie des Inscriptions et Belles-Lettres, 1994. https://www.persee.fr/doc/keryl_1275-6229_1994_act_3_1_880.

Piranesi, Francesco, and Giuseppe Antonio Guattani, eds. *Antiquités de la Grande Grèce, aujourd'hui Royaume de Naples*. Paris: Piranesi and Leblanc, 1804.

Podzemskaia, Nadia. "Publication of Renaissance Architectural Treatises in the Soviet Union in the 1930s: Alexander Gabrichevsky's Contribution to the Theory and History of Architecture." *Journal of Art Historiography*, no. 14 (June 2016): 1–14.

Poleni, Giovanni. *Exercitationes Vitruvianae Primae*. Padua: Ioannem Manfrè and Franciscum Pitteri, 1739.

Pollak, Martha D. *Italian & Spanish Books: Fifteenth through Nineteenth Centuries*. 4 vols. The Mark J. Millard Architectural Collection, vol. 4. Washington, DC: National Gallery of Art, 2000. https://www.nga.gov/content/dam/ngaweb/research/publications/pdfs/mark-j-millard-vol-iv.pdf.

Pontremoli, Emmanuel, and Joseph Chamonard. *Kérylos*. Paris: Éditions des Bibliothèques Nationales de France, 1934.

Pope, Alexander. "'Epistle IV, to Richard Boyle, Earl of Burlington: Of the Use of Riches.' In *Moral Essays*, 1731." In *Poetical Works of Pope*. Vol. 2. Edinburgh: Nichol, 1856. https://www.gutenberg.org/files/9601/9601-h/9601-h.htm#link2H_4_0005.

Prestes, António. "Auto de Avé Maria." In *Teatro de autores portugueses do séc. XVI: Base de dados textual*. Lisbon: Centro de Estudos de Teatro, 2000. http://www.cet-e-quinhentos.com/obras.

Prinz, Wolfram. "La 'sala di quattro colonne' nell'opera di Palladio." *Bollettino del Centro Internazionale di Studi di Architettura Andrea Palladio di Vicenza*, no. 11 (1969): 371–387.

Promis, Carlo. *Trattato di architettura civile e militare di Francesco di Giorgio Martini*. Turin: Chirio & Mina, 1841.

Quetglas, Josep. "Las cuatro columnas: Palladio y Le Corbusier." In *Massilia, Centre d'Investigacions Estètiquesm San Cugat del Vallès*, 102–109. 2003.

Reble, Christina, ed. *Die Präsenz Palladios in der Schweizer Architektur*. Zurich: gta Verlag, 1976.

Rhodes, Dennis E. *A Catalogue of Incunabula in All the Libraries of Oxford University outside the Bodleian*. Oxford: Clarendon Press, 1982.

Richardson, Margaret. "Tyringham." Edited by Margaret Richardson and Mary Anne Stevens. In *John Soane Architect: Master of Space and Light*, 128–141. London: Royal Academy of Arts, 1999.

Richardson, Margaret, and Mary Anne Stevens, eds. *John Soane Architect: Master of Space and Light*. London: Royal Academy of Arts, 1999.

Rode, Auguste. *Leben des Herrn Friedrich Wilhelm von Erdmannsdorff*. Reprint of Dessau: H. Jänzer, 1801. Wörlitz: Kettmann, 1994.

[Rodrigues, António]. "Tratado de arquitectura." Ms. [1575/1576] in Biblioteca Nacional de Portugal, cod. 3675; ms. 1579 in Biblioteca Municipal do Porto.

Roettgen, Steffi. "German Painters in Naples and Their Contribution to the Revival of Antiquity 1760–1799." Edited by Carol C. Mattusch. In *Rediscovering the Ancient World on the Bay of Naples, 1710–1890*, 123–140. Washington, DC: National Gallery of Art, 2013.

Roriczer, Matthäus. *Geometria Deutsch*. [Nuremberg]: [Peter Wagner], 1489.

Rosenfeld, Myra Nan. *Serlio on Domestic Architecture*. 1st ed. 1978. Mineola, NY: Dover, 1996.

Rowe, Colin. "The Mathematics of the Ideal Villa." In *The Mathematics of the Ideal Villa and Other Essays*, 1st ed. 1947, 1–28. Cambridge, MA: MIT Press, 1976.

Rowland, Ingrid D. "Vitruvian Scholarship to Vitruvian Practice." *Memoirs of the American Academy in Rome* 50 (2005): 15–40. https://www.jstor.org/stable/4238827.

Royal Institute of British Architects. *Early Printed Books, 1478–1840: Catalogue of the British Architectural Library Early Imprints Collection*. 4 vols. London: Bowker-Saur, 1994–2003.

Rykwert, Joseph. ""Introduction"." In *On the Art of Building in Ten Books*, by Leon Battista Alberti, xviii–xix. Cambridge, MA: MIT Press, 1991.

Sá, Maria Ealo de. *El arquitecto Juan de Castillo: El construtor del mundo*. Santander: Colégio Oficial de Arquitectos de Cantabria, 2009.

Saddy, Pierre. *Alfred Normand, architecte, 1822–1909*. Paris: Caisse nationale des monuments historiques et des sites, 1978.

Sagredo, Diego de. *Medidas del Romano agora nueuamente impressas y añadidas de muchas pieças e figuras muy necessarias alos officiales que quieren seguir las formaciones delas basas, colunas, capiteles, y otras pieças de los edificios antíguos*. Lisbon: Luis Rodrigues, 1541.

Sagredo, Diego de. *Medidas del Romano: Necessarias alos oficiales que quieren seguir las formaciones delas Basas, Colunas, Capiteles, y otras pieças delos edificios antíguos*. Toledo: Remó de Petras, 1526.

Salvador, Fernando Sanches, and Margarida Grácio Nunes. "A Sinagoga de Tomar e o Museu Luso-Hebraico Abraão Zacuto Projecto de conservação e reabilitação." *Monumentos*, no. 37 (November 2019): 178–187.

Sanchez, Formosinho. *O De Arquitettura de Vitrúvio, numa recolha bibliográfica manuscrita e impressa existente em Portugal*. Lisbon, 1991.

Scamozzi, Vincenzo. *Dell'idea della Architettura Universale*. Venice: Expensis Auctoris, 1615.

Schnapp, Alain. "The Antiquarian Culture of Eighteenth-Century Naples as a Laboratory of New Ideas." Edited by Carol C. Mattusch. In *Rediscovering the Ancient World on the Bay of Naples, 1710–1890*, 13–34. Washington, DC: National Gallery of Art, 2013.

Serlio, Sebastiano. *Il primo e secondo libro d'architettura di Sebastiano Serlio*. Translated by Jean Martin. Paris, 1545.

Serlio, Sebastiano. *Il terzo libro di Sebastiano Serlio bolognese: Nel qual si figurano, e descrivono le antiquita di Roma, e le altre che sono in Italia, e fuori d'Italia*. Venice: Francesco Marcolino da Forli, 1540.

Serlio, Sebastiano. *Regole generali di architetvra sopra le cinqve maniere de gliedifici: Cioe, thoscano, dorico, ionico, ccrinthio, et composito; Con gliessempi dell'antiqvita, che per la magior parte concordano con la dottrina di Vitrvvio*. Venice: F. Marcolini da Forli, 1537.

Serlio, Sebastiano. *Sesto libro d'architettura: Delle habitationi fuori e dentro delle città*. Bayerische Staatsbibliothek, cod. icon. 189. Lyon, 1547–1550. https://www.digitale-sammlungen.de/en/view/bsb00018617?page=1.

Shaw, Paul, and Peter Bain. "Blackletter vs. Roman: Type as Ideological Surrogate." In *Blackletter: Type and National Identity*, 10–15. New York: Princeton Architectural Press, 1998.

Sherman, William H. *Used Books: Marking Readers in Renaissance England*. Philadelphia: University of Pennsylvania Press, 2008.

Silva, Ricardo Jorge Nunes da. "O paradigma da arquitetura em Portugal na Idade Moderna: Entre o tardo-gótico e o Renascimento; João de Castilho 'o mestre que amanhece e anoitece na obra'." PhD diss., Faculdade de Letras da Universidade de Lisboa, 2018.

Simões, J. M. Santos. *Tomar e a sua Judiaria*. Tomar: Museu Luso-Hebraico, 1943.

Smith, Thomas Gordon. *Classical Architecture: Rule and Invention*. Layton, UT: Gibbs M. Smith, 1988.

Soletti, Adriana, and Paolo Belardi. *Dell'architettura civile di Baldassarre Orsini*. Rome: Officina Edizioni, 1997.

Steinmann, Martin, ed. *Tendenzen: Neuere Architektur im Tessin/Tendencies: Recent Architecture in Ticino/Tendenze: architettura recente nel Ticino*. 1st ed. 1977. Zurich: gta Verlag, 2010.

Stephan, Peter. *Das Obere Belvedere in Wien: Architektonisches Konzept und Ikonographie; Das Schloss des Prinzen Eugen als Abbild seines Selbstverständnisses*. Vienna: Böhlau, 2010.

Stroud, Dorothy. *Sir John Soane Architect*. 1st ed. 1984. London: De la Mare, 1996.

Szacka, Léa-Catherine. *Exhibiting the Postmodern: The 1980 Venice Architecture Biennale*. Venice: Marsilio, 2016.

Tafuri, Manfredo. "Cesare Cesariano e gli scritti vitruviani del quattrocento." Edited by Arnaldo Bruschi. In *Scritti rinascimentali di architettura*, 389–437. Milan: Polifilo, 1978.

Tavares, André. *The Anatomy of the Architectural Book*. Zurich: Lars Müller/Canadian Centre for Architecture, 2016.

Tavares, Domingos. *António Rodrigues: Renascimento em Portugal*. Porto: Dafne Editora, 2007.

The Mark J. Millard Architectural Collection. 4 vols. Washington, DC: National Gallery of Art, 1993–2003.

Tuttle, Richard J. "On Vignola's Rule of the Five Orders of Architecture." Edited by Vaughan Hart and Peter Hicks. In *Paper Palaces: The Rise of the Renaissance Architectural Treatise*, 199–218.

New Haven, CT: Yale University Press, 1998.

Uniack, Gérard. *De Vitruve à Le Corbusier: Textes d'architectes*. Paris: Dunod, 1968.

Urrea, Miguel. "Marco Vitrubio *De architectura* dividido en X libros traduzido de latin en lengua castellana." Biblioteca Nacional de Portugal, cod. 5179, 1582. https://purl.pt/24885.

Vagnetti, Luigi, and Laura Marcucci. *2000 anni di Vitruvio*. Serie Studi e documenti di architettura, vol. 8. Florence: Edizione della Cattedra di Composizione Architettonica IA di Firenze, 1978.

Vène, Magali. *Bibliographia Serliana: Catalogue des éditions imprimées des livres du traité d'architecture de Sebastiano Serlio (1537–1681)*. Paris: Picard, 2007.

Viterbo, Sousa. *Dicionário histórico e documental dos arquitectos, engenheiros e construtores portugueses ou a serviço de Portugal*. 1st ed. 1899-1922. 3 vols. Lisbon: Imprensa Nacional Casa da Moeda, 1988.

Vries, Hans Vredeman de. *Variae architectvrae formae: A Ionne Vredemanni Vriesio magno artis hvivs stvdiosorvm commodo, inventae*. Antwerp: Theodorus Galleaeus, 1601.

Wiebenson, Dora. *French Books: Sixteenth through Nineteenth Centuries*. 4 vols. The Mark J. Millard Architectural Collection, vol. 1. Washington, DC: National Gallery of Art, 1993. https://www.nga.gov/content/dam/ngaweb/research/publications/pdfs/mark-j-millard-french-books.pdf.

Wiebenson, Dora. "Guilaume Philander's Annotations to Vitruvius." In *Les traités d'architecture de la Renaissance*. Paris: J. Guillaume, 1988.

Willberg, Hans Peter. "Fraktur and Nationalism." Edited by Peter Bain and Paul Shaw. In *Blackletter: Type and National Identity*, 40–49. New York: Princeton Architectural Press, 1998.

William Wilkins' Grand Tour. https://www.dow.cam.ac.uk/about/downing-college-archive/archives/william-wilkins-grand-tour.

Williams, Kim, trans. *Daniele Barbaro's Vitruvius of 1567*. [Basel]: Birkhäuser, 2019.

Willies, Margaret. "Building a Library: The Books of Sir John Soane." In *Reading Matters: Five Centuries of Discovering Books*, 109–135. New Haven, CT: Yale University Press, 2010.

Xavier, João Pedro. "Geometria e proporção." Edited by Domingos Tavares. In *António Rodrigues: Renascimento em Portugal*, 103–119. Porto: Dafne Editora, 2007.

Xavier, João Pedro. *Sobre as origens da perspectiva em Portugal: O "Livro de Perspectiva" do Códice 3675 da Biblioteca Nacional, um Tratado de Arquitectura do século XVI*. Porto: Faup Publicações, 2006.

Zou, Hui. "China (Sixteenth to Eighteenth Centuries): Renaissance Humanism and Chinese Architecture." Edited by Nicholas Temple, Andrzej Piotorwski, and Juan Manuel Heredia. In *The Routledge Handbook on the Reception of Classical Architecture*. London: Routledge, 2019.

IMAGE CREDITS

1. Fundação Instituto Marques da Silva, Biblioteca Fernando Távora, Porto. FIMS/FT/Monografias-979
2. Photograph by Nuno Cera, courtesy of the Bibliothèque Nationale de France, Paris. RES M-V-48 (1)
3. Photograph by Nuno Cera, courtesy of the Academia Nacional de Belas Artes, Lisbon. L-4-61
4. Photograph by Nuno Cera, courtesy of the Centro Internazionale di Studi di Architettura Andrea Palladio, Vicenza. Inv. 8124 col. CAP a XVI 6
5. Photograph by Nuno Cera, courtesy of the Canadian Centre for Architecture, Montreal. NA44.V848 (6180)
6. Photograph by Nuno Cera, courtesy of the Biblioteca Nacional de Portugal, Lisbon. RES. 6082 P
7. Photograph by Nuno Cera, courtesy of the Bibliothèque Nationale de France, Paris. V-21988
8. Photograph by Simon Javed Baumberger, courtesy of the ETH Library, Rara und Karten, Zurich. RA 488
9. Photograph by Nuno Cera, courtesy of the Bibliothèque Nationale de France, Paris. RES-V-1370
10. Photograph by Nuno Cera, courtesy of the Canadian Centre for Architecture, Montreal. NA44.V848 (W238)
11. Photograph by Nuno Cera, courtesy of the Centro Internazionale di Studi di Architettura Andrea Palladio, Vicenza. Inv. 9744 col F.A. II 9
12. Photograph by Nuno Cera, courtesy of the Academia Nacional de Belas Artes, Lisbon. KK-4-5 / A-5-19
13. Photograph by Nuno Cera, courtesy of the Academia Nacional de Belas Artes, Lisbon. FF-5-8 / A-6-13
14. Photograph by Nuno Cera, courtesy of the Academia Nacional de Belas Artes, Lisbon. L-1-55 / O-2-31
15. Photograph by Nuno Cera, courtesy of the Canadian Centre for Architecture, Montreal. NA44.V848 (W1066)
16. Photograph by Nuno Cera, courtesy of the Bibliothèque Nationale de France, Paris. V-21994
17. Photograph by Nuno Cera, courtesy of the Canadian Centre for Architecture, Montreal. NA44.V848 (147)
18. Photograph by Nuno Cera, courtesy of the Biblioteca Nacional de Portugal, Lisbon. B.A. 31 A
19. Photograph by Nuno Cera, courtesy of the Bibliothèque Nationale de France, Paris. V-1938
20. Photograph by Nuno Cera, courtesy of the Centro Internazionale di Studi di Architettura Andrea Palladio, Vicenza. Inv. 9061 col CAP a XIX 17.1
21. Photograph by Nuno Cera, courtesy of the Academia Nacional de Belas Artes, Lisbon. L-4-64 / O-2-31
22. Photograph by Nuno Cera, courtesy of the Canadian Centre for Architecture, Montreal. NA44.V848 (7204)
23. Photograph by Nuno Cera, courtesy of the Centro Internazionale di Studi di Architettura Andrea Palladio, Vicenza. Inv. 9170 col CAP x XIX 5(1)
24. Photograph by Nuno Cera, courtesy of the Bibliothèque Nationale de France, Paris. V-55155
25. Photograph by Nuno Cera, courtesy of the Canadian Centre for Architecture, Montreal. CORM4 (ID:90-B577)

IMAGE CREDITS

26 Photograph by Nuno Cera, courtesy of the Canadian Centre for Architecture, Montreal. NA44.V848.A62 1926
27 Photograph by Nuno Cera
28 Photograph by Nuno Cera
29 Photograph by Nuno Cera, courtesy of the Centro Internazionale di Studi di Architettura Andrea Palladio, Vicenza. Inv. 10853 col C/2 VITR II 10 9
30 Photograph by Nuno Cera
31 Photograph by Nuno Cera
32 Drawings by André Tavares and Aitor Ochoa Argany
33 Drawings by André Tavares and Aitor Ochoa Argany
34 Photographs by Nuno Cera
35 Scheme by André Tavares and Daniel Duarte Pereira
36 Photographs by Nuno Cera
37 Photographs by Nuno Cera
38 Photographs by Nuno Cera
39 Photographs by Nuno Cera
40 Photograph by Fototecnica, Centro Internazionale di Studi di Architettura Andrea Palladio, Vicenza. F4064
41 Centro Internazionale di Studi di Architettura Andrea Palladio, Vicenza. F2409
42 Photograph by A. Rossi, Centro Internazionale di Studi di Architettura Andrea Palladio, Vicenza. F2265
43 Sir John Soane's Museum, London. SM 13/5/5
44 Louis Pierre Haudebourte, *Le Laurentin maison de campagne de Pline le Jeune: restituée d'après la description de Pline*, Paris, Carilian-Goeury, 1838
45 Photograph by Königlich Preußische Messbild-Anstalt, courtesy of the Architekturmuseum der Technischen Universität Berlin, F 0503
46 Photograph by Ambroise Tézenas, © 2021 Centre des monuments nationaux, France, dist. Scala, Florence. ATW19-0038
47 Photograph by Nuno Cera
48 Photograph by Nelson Kon
49 Photograph by Alan McIntyre Smith
50 Photograph attributed to Charles Gérard, courtesy of the Fondation Le Corbusier, Paris © ProLitteris, 2021
51 August Mau, *Pompeii: Its Life and Art*, New York, The Macmillan Company, 1899, page 28, figure 8
52 Drawings by André Tavares and João Faria
53 Drawings by André Tavares and João Faria
54 Vitruviana cartography, drawings by André Tavares and Daniel Duarte Pereira
55 Vitruviana cartography, drawings by André Tavares and Daniel Duarte Pereira
56 Vitruviana cartography, drawings by André Tavares and Daniel Duarte Pereira
57 Vitruviana cartography, drawings by André Tavares and Daniel Duarte Pereira
58 Vitruviana cartography, drawings by André Tavares and Danie Duarte Pereira
59 Vitruviana cartography, drawings by André Tavares and Daniel Duarte Pereira
60 Vitruviana cartography, drawings by André Tavares and Daniel Duarte Pereira
61 Vitruviana cartography, drawings by André Tavares and Daniel Duarte Pereira

ACKNOWLEDGMENTS

This book is the product of a postdoctoral fellowship from the Institute for the History and Theory of Architecture (gta) of ETH Zurich, where I am grateful to Laurent Stalder and Philip Ursprung for their trust and continuous encouragement. The work grew from my contact with the unique Einsiedeln library, a collection assembled by Professor Werner Oechslin over a lifetime as a passionate bibliophile, and I am grateful to him for allowing me access. My research work would not have been possible without the support of the School of Architecture of Minho University and its Lab2PT, Landscape, Heritage and Territory Laboratory, as well as the Faculty of Architecture of the University of Porto.

ETH Zurich provided a lively and challenging intellectual environment in which I was privileged to have fruitful exchanges with old and new friends. I first shared an office with Irina Davidovici, whose company and insights were key for my work in shaping its initial form. Meanwhile, Maarten Delbeke's Chair was being set up, and his team, especially Erik Wegerhoff and Emma Letizia Jones, provided me with precious methodological insights. Among my colleagues and the PhD students at the gta Institute, I want to thank in particular Samia Heni, Andreas Kalpakci, Nikolaos Magouliotis, Alfredo Thiermann, Markus Lähteenmäki, Helene Romakin, Linda Stagni, Davide Spina, Sarah Nichols, Lukas Imgold, and Daniela Ortiz dos Santos. Beyond the department, Mario Rinke became a close companion on my Vitruvian quest. The librarians at Hönggerberg, Rara Collection, and Einsiedeln—especially Markus Joachim, Meda Diana Hotea, and Christoph Lanthemann—endured my endless requests with great patience, as did Bruno Maurer and Filine Wagner at the gta Archives.

In Zurich I reconnected with old friends and made new ones, and I especially appreciated the company of Ana Laureano Alves, Kai Zipse, Verena Jacob, Manuel Gysel, Lars Müller, Annie Blackadder, Johannes Käferstein, Ivo Barão, Manuel Montenegro, Alberto Alessi, Christoph Schifferli, Rainer Schützeichel, Harald Stühlinger, Christoph Dubler, Mathias Brücke, Ian Wooldridge, Diego Zanghi, and my Neubühl neighbours during a memorable spring stay. My time in Switzerland was enriched by the powerful and engaging relationship between the material qualities of architecture and objects at Sitterwerk, and I would like to thank Katalin Deér, Felix Lehner, and Roland Früh for their hospitality in St Gallen. Throughout my Vitruvian travels Ani Schulze was a patient and close companion.

For help with the Vitruviana section of the book and its iconography, I want to thank Aitor Ochoa Argany for assistance with the tetrastyle drawings and Daniel Duarte Pereira for the layout of the Vitruviana maps. João Faria translated my book measurements into layout diagrams and we discussed the designs of the various editions together. Simon Cowper's attention to minutiae made my clumsy Vitruviana into a plausible bibliography. Early in the research, Nuno Cera began to build an iconography to accompany my argument, taking photographs of various editions of Vitruvius and tetrastyle spaces. These photographs would not have been possible without the support of various libraries, and I am indebted to the ETH Zurich Hönggerberg and Rara libraries, the Canadian Centre for Architecture in Montreal, the National Library of Portugal and the Academia Nacional de Belas-Artes in Lisbon, the Centro Internazionale di Studi di Architettura Andrea Palladio in Vicenza, and the Bibliothèque Nationale de France in Paris.

The text started to be shaped in various lectures, and I am grateful to the crucial invitations to lecture on Vitruvius by Miguel Magalhães at the Gulbenkian Foundation and Eric Lapierre in Marne-la-Valée, both in Paris, the friends from

ACKNOWLEDGMENTS

Bertha's Kitchen in Zurich, Mario Moura in Porto, and Mari Hvattum and Victor Plahte Tschudi in Oslo.

Moritz Gleich from gta Verlag gave the final push I needed to finish the text manuscript, which in turn benefited from the sharp critical insight of Indra McEwen, Maarten Delbeke, and Jacques Gubler, as well as the careful reading of Thomas Skelton-Robinson. Also much appreciated were the suggestions and book smuggling from Christian Gänshirt, Benoît Jacquet, Diego Inglez de Souza, Paulo Pereira, Carolina B. García-Estévez, Selda Bancı, Aktan Acar, Justino Maciel, and from many other colleagues and librarians who took an interest in the work.

Last but not least, I want to express my gratitude to Megan Spriggs for the patience and care she devoted to my writing. She was the first reader of this book and transformed my improvised English into plausible prose. Her constant encouragement and enthusiasm provided the fuel I needed to conclude my Vitruvian adventures.

gta edition is a peer-reviewed series of short monographs that take a fresh and provocative look at seemingly well-known aspects of architectural history, thus engaging in contemporary historiography and the production of theory in architecture.

The infrastructure for this hybrid format, which technically and graphically combines the production of printed books with an online, open-access version, was developed collaboratively between gta Verlag and intercom Verlag.

gta-edition.ch

Series concept
Moritz Gleich, Niki Rhyner, Max Stadler

Graphic concept and design
Reinhard Schmidt, Nadine Wüthrich

Development
Urs Hofer

Content management
Jennifer Bartmess, Vinzenz Meyner

Copyediting
Thomas Skelton-Robinson

Printing
TBS, La Buona Stampa SA, Switzerland

Binding
Legatoria Mosca SA, Switzerland

Cover image
Gustave Boulanger, Répétition du "Joueur de flûte" et de la "Femme de Diomède" chez le prince Napoléon, 1861. © Musée d'Orsay, RMN-Grand Palais / Alexis Brandt

2nd printing
© 2023, gta Verlag, ETH Zurich
Institute for the History and
Theory of Architecture
Department of Architecture
8093 Zurich, Switzerland
www.verlag.gta.arch.ethz.ch
© Texts: by the author
© Illustrations: by the image authors and their legal successors; for copyrights, see image credits

Every reasonable attempt has been made by the author and the publisher to identify owners of copyrights. Should any errors or omissions have occurred, please notify us.

CC BY-NC-ND License

ISBN print: 978-3-85676-422-7
ISBN PDF: 978-3-85676-430-2